BARBARIAN LOST

BARBARIAN LOST

Travels in the New China

ALEXANDRE TRUDEAU

HarperCollins Publishers Ltd

Published by HarperCollins Publishers Ltd

First edition

HarperCollins books may be purchased for educational, business,
or sales promotional use through our Special Markets Department.

HarperCollins Publishers Ltd
2 Bloor Street East, 20th Floor
Toronto, Ontario, Canada
M4W 1A8

www.harpercollins.ca

Library and Archives Canada Cataloguing in Publication
information is available upon request.

ISBN 978-1-44344-140-7

Printed and bound in the United States

RRD 9 8 7 6 5 4 3 2 1

À Zoë

CONTENTS

BARBARIAN LOST

CHAPTER 1

China Calling

Where the potential first arises, / Nothing has yet come to life.
–Shao Yong, "Ode to the Winter Solstice," *River Yi Ground Beating Anthology of Poems*, eleventh century

As a young child, I remember contemplating a book that my father had written on China. How grand and mighty it seemed that he had his name printed in large letters on the cover. I've no memories from that time of any other books he'd written, just the one.

Perhaps I remember it because it had a colourful and odd-looking cover that featured a picture of him, much younger but recognizable, posing with his friend Jacques Hébert, with whom he'd travelled and written the book. The title made little sense to me: *Two Innocents in Red China.*

Who were these innocents anyway?

Canadian children learn about China in the sandbox; it's the place that they will reach if they dig deep enough. They also learn about China when they find out what a billion is. There are over a billion people in China, they're told. A billion people!

My personal mythology linked me to China in another way. The idea of China as a place always accompanied the story of me in my mother's belly: my parents had visited China in October

1

1973 and I was born in December. Quite a thought for a toddler: in the womb in China!

When my brothers and I were quite young, before we had started to travel ourselves, our father went away for a whole month to China and Tibet. It was the longest time that he'd been away since we were born. Before he left, we asked him why he was going, and he replied that he was going because he had never been to Tibet before.

What a mysterious answer that was! Maybe we would go there someday as well, because we certainly hadn't been there either.

Because it was his first long trip away from us, my father's journey fascinated me. We grew ever more excited as his return date approached. And when he returned, he was changed. He looked and smelt slightly different. He had a beard and a tan and a strange energy about him. He radiated a kind of power, seemed more aggressive and alive than usual. As if his eyes still reflected the sights that he had seen. His body was poised to meet them head on.

This was a new father, not the patient and adoring father of before but the free spirit who had wandered the world. The lone traveller. The observer of things. The holder of secret knowledge.

The souvenirs he brought with him also left their mark on me: incense and prayer wheels, scroll paintings of mountains, fantastically illustrated books of the Chinese classic of the Monkey King fighting baby-faced Nezha, dramatic painted papier-mâché masks and painted wooden swords from the Beijing opera.

This was travelling for me: going to places one had never visited but somehow needed to go to, and then returning home with strange and wonderful things, changed, both inside and out. I'd begun to grasp what my father meant when he said that he'd travelled around the world and been to a hundred countries; to sense the transformative power of journeys and to understand why one travels. And, in my mind at least, I'd begun to become a traveller myself.

Knowledge, travel and China were all muddled together for me. Journeys, I obscurely felt, have a mental quality. They happen in the mind. One might be innocent before one travels, I thought, but surely less so afterward. We're filled with desires—needs, even—to go somewhere because untravelled places are dark holes in the mind that draw us toward them. So China lay out there like a gateway. The shapes of my childhood awareness of it, of my father's book, my womb-bound journey there left more mysteries than understanding.

My father, a politician, retired with the goal of spending more time with us, his children. This was shortly after the divorce of my parents. My mother had remarried and started a new life in Ottawa, happily out of the limelight. Meanwhile, my father relocated us to Montreal, his hometown, where he wanted us to go to school. He also intended to show us the world in its varied shapes and colours. Through the late 1980s and early 1990s, we embarked upon a series of trips with him to the "great nations of the world." These were completed over the course of a few summers. My brothers and I were still too young to be out travelling on our own but were old enough to comprehend a little of what we saw.

The time for these journeys was limited. So we decided that our destinations would be constrained by the Cold War definition of the great powers: the permanent members of the United Nations Security Council. In the summer of 1984, we made our first journey through the Soviet Union, six years before the waning empire began to break apart. We meandered south from Moscow to the Caucasus Mountains and as far east as the Amur River, deep in eastern Siberia. In the years that followed, we made trips to France, the United Kingdom and Ireland, the lands of our ancestors. In rented cars, we criss-crossed these old nations, staying at bed and breakfasts and budget inns.

In the winter of 1988–89, we decided that the coming summer's trip would be to China. But that spring, a protest began to brew in Beijing's central and most important public space, Tiananmen Square. After the death of a respected and reform-minded Communist Party leader, Beijing's university students began congregating in the square in ever greater numbers, demanding political change and democracy. They set up tents and camped out for weeks. They were joined by more and more students from the provinces, and by intellectuals and academics. Eventually, even influential Communist Party members came to the square in support of the youth.

Paid less attention to by the Western media but more worrying for the Chinese government, urban workers also began to gather in large numbers, demanding that free-market reforms be stopped, since they were causing inflation and job losses. A volatile combination of opposites was occurring. The dynasty was beginning to crack.

My family followed these events with interest. Only months previous, my father had contacted the Chinese diplomatic mission and requested a visa to visit the country with his boys. I was excited at the thought of travelling to China at a time of change. Even my typically impassive father was more and more stimulated by these events and by what they might mean for that summer's trip.

He'd been to China several times by this point. He'd made his first trip in 1949, just before the Communists finally routed the remainder of Chiang Kai-shek's Nationalist forces, pushing them out of their last stronghold in Shanghai. He'd seen China in the throes of massive change; perhaps he'd now witness yet another dramatic period of its history.

I was fifteen at the time, so my excitement was more than just an eagerness to see history unfolding before my eyes. I was impressed by the charismatic young student leaders who were standing up to the venerable figures of authority in their country. I already felt inclined to stand up to authority myself. I had come to believe, as I still believe, that the world belongs to those who seize it and that every generation has to seize the world anew.

As long as I could remember, my father had entertained us with tales of his worldly adventures. He told us of encounters with pirates and bandits, of his journeys through war zones and across wastelands. China in the middle of a huge nationwide protest— even an uprising, perhaps—would be a good start to the life adventure I hoped for myself.

On June 4, 1989, after weeks of protest and tense negotiations between the student leaders and the government, the tanks of the People's Liberation Army were called in and the protests violently quashed. The world watched in horror.

We knew our China trip was suddenly called into question. Could we still go to China? Would we be received there at this time? Did we even want to go after such a bloody event?

"Who cares about appearances?" I argued.

"It's more than a matter of appearances," my father cautioned. "What state do you think China finds itself in right now?"

"So what? That's what we should go see," I insisted.

5

"I applaud your position," my father said, "but you can embark on such trips when you are a little older and alone. Right now, the Chinese are in no position to entertain visitors."

Our China trip was postponed. I waited until the following spring and then began to insist we start planning it again. Still my father had reservations. "It means travelling to a country with which Canada has broken all ties," he said.

"So what? We're not diplomats. You're a retired politician on a private visit with his family. It doesn't mean anything," I argued.

"The Chinese might not see it that way," he said.

In the end, I won the debate. We'd go to China. My father probably knew deep down that we had to go then or we'd never go, not as a family at least. I was sixteen; my older brother, eighteen. My little brother had already found the Canadian wilderness a far more enticing place for him to journey than faraway lands with his father and brothers. Soon we'd all be out travelling on our own.

Looking back, I realize that the thought of this made my father lonely. He had always encouraged us to set out into the world, to seek its challenges and mysteries. But he'd been caught off guard by how fast we'd grown. Perhaps he felt that he'd have little time left to teach us lessons or to share in our learning. So China it was, a place that had taught him so much. A place to impart something meaningful and lasting to his boys.

Only a year after Tiananmen, the country still had bleak undertones. But I did have my wish: there were practically no other foreigners to be seen there. The tourist hotels were empty. Although the country had already embarked upon the road to economic liberalization and growth, some of the characteristics of earlier Chinese periods, such as stark authoritarian rule and a lack of contact with the outside world, had reappeared following the crackdown at Tiananmen. The China of 1990 was more like the Red China of yore than the economic powerhouse it would soon become. The winds of change were momentarily stilled.

As my father predicted, the Chinese did not let us travel alone in their country. "We wouldn't want you to hurt yourselves," they told us.

So we were hosted by the Chinese on an elaborate private tour. We saw many parts of the country but were guided everywhere. As we moved across China, we were passed along from official to official, keeping at all times a retinue of an officer of the foreign affairs department and a translator. It was a rare if stodgy trip.

Among the things my father most wanted to see were the sacred mountains of China. He also talked of a train trip from the Sichuan plateau to the subtropical Himalayan foothills of Yunnan Province.

I remember not quite getting a handle on the idea of the sacred mountains. In my mind, I pictured the rocky bluffs in the clouds I had seen depicted on the scrolls hanging in our house. I pictured the stone palaces of the Heavenly Emperor where the Monkey King went to steal peaches.

We ended up climbing two of the sacred mountains. Our first stop out of the capital, Beijing, was Taishan—apparently one of the more famous of the set. It rose from the plain such that as we approached we could see it in its entirety like an archetype. From afar, the mountain's numerous temples were tiny white specks on an immense mass of green and blue. It was exciting to think we would reach the summit later that very day.

But arriving at the base of Taishan, we learnt that our Chinese guides had underestimated my father's physicality and arranged for a cable-car ride to the summit. My father protested and a compromise was soon reached: we would drive halfway up the mountain on a service road but climb the final distance on foot.

The ascent was an occasion for my brother and me to burn the excess energy that had been building up during all the formalities of Beijing. At a temple that was almost entirely transformed into a bazaar for Chinese tourists, we were too impatient to pay proper attention to the strange spectacle of an ancient Taoist monk roused from a deep, dark chamber by our handlers. The monk seemed easily a hundred years old and could barely see through his thick cataracts. He was draped in black and blue robes and hunched over. His skin was blemished, and his whiskers, though hardly numerous, were half a metre long. He reeked of urine and strange herbs. For a moment, we were in awe of this old man of the mountain. But our own mission on the mountain beckoned us and soon we were continuing our ascent, hastily scrambling up the stone stairs.

The mountaintop was mostly bare, and it was windy. A few temples were scattered about. Primed and ready for more action as we waited for our father to catch up, Justin and I soon concocted a plan to run down the mountain, meeting the group at the bottom. The initial descent was treacherous, the stone stairs narrow and extremely steep. We proceeded down them sideways in a kind of fast trot. The more we dropped, the more the mountain levelled off and short flights of stairs began to alternate with narrow landings. So we jumped down each flight, covering multiple stairs at once. We sprinted across the landings and leapt out again over the next section. We felt incredible and figured we must be setting some kind of record.

Gallivanting down the sacred mountain, we had no thought of

the toll our antics might take on our bodies. Soon after our arrival back at the hotel a few hours later, it caught up with us. By dinnertime in the hotel restaurant, Justin and I had trouble holding up our heads or even lifting the chopsticks to our mouths. We were both shivering, and our legs had seized up and trembled spasmodically. We retreated to our rooms; I fell asleep immediately.

In the morning, I could barely get out of bed. My legs were stiff as wood and could not be bent. My back had also seized up and resisted straightening. I called on my brother. He was in a similar state but had just come from breakfast with our father, who was not amused and was expecting me in the dining room. So, one tiny step at a time, I walked toward the restaurant. For my own sake and to deflect my father's ire, I decided that it was a humorous predicament and made light of it.

Later that day, as Justin and I hobbled from the car to some tourist site we were visiting, my father pulled us aside and said, "Boys, you must not forget, the Chinese have often perceived westerners as barbarians. Think carefully about those occasions when you might be giving them good reason to do so."

In the years that followed, I became a traveller myself. I journeyed to war zones and uncharted hinterlands. China remained on the horizon, a distant figure whose call I ignored. I heard about the profound metamorphosis it was undergoing but felt I was not yet ready for it. I was ever the barbarian whose travel skills were no match for the Middle Kingdom. The journey would have to wait.

I focused instead on places remote and misunderstood, regions into which I could disappear. Searching for singularities, I journeyed to Yekepa, Liberia; Tessalit, Mali; Maroantsetra, Madagascar; Ngalimila, Tanzania; and Maprik, Papua New Guinea. I took to places where few others cared to go, tried to grow wise to some small places of big drama, where strange things happened on the margins. Meanwhile, China was still distant, wrapped in mystery and doubt, immense, troubled, stiff and austere. Still it called.

In 1998, a news editor asked if I'd consider a full-time job at his network's Beijing office. The idea was truly tempting: to become an early witness of the new China, to learn its language and make my name in a place that mattered. But I would not walk through that gate either. How quickly turns the wheel. Age had finally caught up to my father, and his health was deteriorating fast. No other mission could matter. I would stay close to him, be there for him as he had been for me, see him off on his final journey and return perhaps some of the powerful devotion he had shown us.

In 2005, a Shanghai publisher released a Chinese translation of my late father and Jacques Hébert's book on China and invited Jacques and me to the launch in Shanghai. So, with that funny little book in hand, I was finally back in China.

I barely recognized the place from when I was there in 1990. I decided that this short trip to China would be the first of many over the coming years. I resolved to devote myself to understanding China.

The country's lightning-fast ascent and increasing impact on the world have now become clichés. China is a global superpower. Its appetite for resources and its astounding manufacturing capacity have transformed the planet's economies. China is no longer the mysterious, distant and inaccessible pariah it once was. These days, fortunes are being made in China on a daily basis. The intrepid adventurer has been all but replaced by the mundane business traveller and the pedestrian tourist.

Yet China is still not an easy place to understand. One can meander the country soaking up the sights, as millions now do every year. We walk along the Great Wall, marvel at the Forbidden City and travel down the Yangtze. We fill our lives with things made in China, but still we have a hard time understanding what the place is all about.

China can be frustratingly opaque, a most inwardly directed place. It moves fast and furiously. Hardly stopping for the Chinese, it certainly doesn't stop for foreigners. Although not dangerous, China is still overwhelming.

All foreign lands are puzzles. They reduce the newly arrived traveller to a kind of innocence, a childlike state in which the basics of communication and movement have to be relearnt. In many parts of the world, that alienation is relatively mild; in China, it can be extreme. The sheer size of the place, the frenzy of activity, the deep detachment from Western ways make its puzzles much more difficult to solve, their every clue that much harder to discern.

Language is another hurdle. If I was going to question China and its people deeply, I would need a translator. In the summer of 2006, I contacted an old classmate, Deryk, who had been living in China for years, and asked him to interview a short list of candidates that I had put together through contacts. I told him to look for good spoken English, an outgoing personality, a developed intellect and a sense of humour.

After several interviews, he suggested a young woman who used the English name Vivien. She had studied humanities at China's finest university. She had done some rough travel in remote regions of China and had worked as a translator in several foreign offices. Deryk also said that she had a sense of humour and was above crass commercial interests. After exchanging brief emails with her, my instincts told me that she had some understanding of the Western mind—a must if she was going to deal with the likes of me.

I feared my own disposition. I still felt myself something of a barbarian, a boisterous and judgmental type, the boy who injured himself by moving too fast and lightly through the sacred landscape, never noticing the stone stairs upon which he jumped. Blind to the work that went into them. Deaf to the prayers they were meant to carry.

Would I be in China long enough, experience it deeply enough, for revelations to occur? Would my guide, Vivien, hold up against the onslaught of my quickly formed opinions? Would she tolerate my brash methods? Not demur at my bold ideas but instead provide them with their proper test?

I cringed to think that my mind and manner might still make a mess of things in China. But in loving memory of my father and what he once tried to teach me, I would give the place my best shot.

CHAPTER 2

North Capital

*Always and in everything let there be reverence; the deport-
ment grave as when one is thinking deeply, speech composed
and definite. This will make the people tranquil.*
—Liji (The Book of Rites), last century BC

September 2006. I descend on Beijing in one of the hundreds of daily international flights through which people now pour in and out of China. As my plane taxis across the runway, I get a glimpse of Beijing's international terminal, a gigantic lurching structure. In the smog and dust, it splays out across the horizon like a shimmering celestial palace, there but not quite real.

The terminal is immense and cavernous. In its glassy depths, I join a flowing horde of business people and tourists. The road to China is by now well travelled; few obstacles greet whoever enters the country. I declare myself a tourist and am smoothly ushered into the Middle Kingdom.

At first sight, Vivien, my translator, guide and soon-to-be advocate and interlocutor, comes off as slight, a little shy, yet subtly intense. She's twenty-five years old, with the polished, old-fashioned manners of a conscientious young Chinese woman. As we ride toward the city, I discover that under her quiet surface she's as highly opinionated as I am. She freelances as a print journalist and is ready to defend her opinions in good English.

"In the spring, I'll be applying to graduate programs in the United States," she tells me.

"You know people who've done this?"

"My closest friends are abroad already," she says.

"And after that where will you go?"

She laughs. "I don't know."

"Here?"

"Not sure."

"Have you worked with foreigners before?"

"A few." Then adds, "Also some ABCs, BBCs; even CBCs."

"Sorry?"

"One of our expressions," she explains. "*ABCs* and *BBCs* mean 'American-born, British-born Chinese.'"

"I suppose they're not at all like Chinese nationals?"

"No, very different."

I imagine what lies behind her statements: a curious and adventurous mind, one that evaluates, judges and builds theories, crystal castles that glimmer with meaning, then are ruined and abandoned. There will be so much for her and me to talk about, but for now I am groggy and jet-lagged. Our taxi, a banged-up Chinese-made Volkswagen, glides along the smooth new highway through heavy smog toward the capital. In silence I turn my attention to the sights materializing before my eyes.

Beijing is not China, but it reveals a lot about China nonetheless. These days, the capital is arguably more potent and central to the country than ever before. It stews with its own specific flavours and habits, and somewhere in the mix is also a little bit of everything in China.

When I first came to Beijing, with my father and brother in 1990, it was altogether a stodgier time. I remember seeing a show of various ethnic groups displaying their traditional outfits and singing their folk songs, a kind of Communist variety show. I'd seen similar stuff in the Soviet Union.

As emblems of the radically diverse ways of life to be found within China's immense borders, these displays were forced and phoney. I was generally pretty bored by them. At age sixteen, I had other things on my mind and spent the time scanning the young performers, looking for the curves and faces I liked best.

Distracted as I was, I didn't understand that it was not so much diversity that was on display as unity. What mattered was the connectedness of these diverse peoples who, like the spokes of a wheel, were linked to an axle that commanded all movement forward. The Communists, more prominent and visible then, were claiming to be at the centre of China and that they alone had brought the unity that had eluded China since the early Qing dynasty, three centuries before.

Parading peoples and things from the far reaches of the empire has long been a show of imperial might, proof of a central government's hold on all the regions. Far-fetched energies and passions descending upon the capital are thus made to radiate together as the Chinese people, ancient, diverse and united.

The capital city has been undergoing a great metamorphosis since I was first here. New symbols are on display. Buildings surpassing even the greatest halls of Red China have popped up across the city. The immense National Stadium being built for the Olympics is both beautiful and slightly terrifying, with its countless spidery girders. Beside it, the enormous bubbly and translucent box that will house the swimming pool gives off an otherworldly feel. Across town in the new business district, the national television building will appear as an immense crooked arch—a giant pair of pants, some like to say. In the centre of the city, an immense egg will take shape—the new national opera house. Often cloaked in thickly polluted air, these fantastic creations speak to new and unexplored sources of Chinese reality, to both danger and renewal.

As in times past, legions of workers from the far reaches of the land toil anonymously, constructing a new capital, a new forbidden city radiant with power.

At the heart of Beijing is the Forbidden City proper, the world's biggest empty museum. The structure still stands, but its content and inhabitants have long since disappeared. Amid the throngs of visitors, their ghosts can scarcely even be imagined now.

In its heyday, the Forbidden City was a supremely orderly place, a tool of obedience and worship. The Forbidden City was so powerful precisely because it was closed, the unattainable nucleus at the very heart of the Middle Kingdom, itself the centre of the earth. It was never meant to be open for contemplation. Pedestrian access to the holy sanctuary would have been a fatal breach of its sanctity.

The capital is laid out in concentric rings around the Forbidden City. The First Ring Road is the huge boulevard dissecting the city from east to west, passing beneath Mao's portrait on the Gate of Heavenly Peace, also known as the Tiananmen, which looks out over the square of the same name. Parkways go north from this boulevard to circumscribe the Forbidden City and complete the first ring.

The Second Ring Road follows the old walls of the city; the Ming dynasty capital sits within its confines. It remains as a map still etched into the territory—a great rectangle organized along cardinal lines. The north-south median was the imperial way. Along it, at the intersection with the east-west median, sat the emperor, the son of heaven, lord of the earth, commander of the four directions. From the Forbidden City at the centre, the emperor ruled the earth. Due south of the Forbidden City is Tiananmen Square—the Square of Heavenly Peace—and beyond it the Temple of Heaven, where the emperor communicated with the heavens.

These days, great halls flank Tiananmen Square. They are the people's assembly halls, the seats of modern government. Mao's mausoleum is also in the square, in the centre surrounded by the people's halls and on the old axis between the Forbidden City and the Temple of Heaven, on the south side of the square. The symbols of power may be at the centre, but real power is now elsewhere and mostly invisible. Perhaps real power lies in the ancient *hutong* neighbourhoods, crammed as they are with traditional abodes. In the tiny, tortuous streets beyond the great square, the temples and the empty palaces, China goes about its way.

Residences are hidden behind three-metre-high walls. Behind some of these walls, families—often as many as eight to a compound—dwell in stone or concrete houses set around cluttered central courtyards; behind others, a single general or party leader might live amid tranquil gardens. But in the open lanes, they all mix together. A bicycle squeezes by a black Mercedes and dodges a vegetable cart. Newspaper in hand, grandpa shuffles on his way to the public latrine. Grandma heads to the market; grandson, to school.

Beijing has long exceeded the Second Ring Road. For centuries, various folk from different regions and callings established themselves beyond the old Ming walls to answer the biddings of power. Within this third orbit, soldiers, merchants, foreigners and workers came to dwell, tools of the establishment without being landholders.

When the Communists took control of the capital, they too relied on the service quarters of the third ring and housed their workers and their soldiers there, building factories, schools and laboratories—everything they needed to govern Red China and triumph against its foes.

Increasingly within the third ring, Communism bows to capitalism. Office towers have taken over the area. In them, China's hybrid economy churns. Chinese private businesses, state interests, foreign investors and multinational trading companies interact here daily. The power of the new China resides in its immense economy, partly free, partly planned. And an important part of this economy is managed along the third ring.

The sprawling territory of the fourth ring was long considered more mundane and less significant than that of the others. Primarily residential, it is home to all sorts of people and a place of certain flux. But with the boom of the new China, the territories of both the fourth and fifth rings have undergone tremendous transformations, with shopping malls, residential complexes and sports centres appearing all over.

I'm staying at my friend Deryk's place in the north of the city, on the seventeenth floor of a slick, brand-new apartment tower, one of five arranged around a central gated esplanade. Deryk lives with his English fiancée, and from their crisp new quarters high above the city, they can gaze out over the Fourth Ring Road, a massive highway a dozen lanes wide. The traffic is mind-boggling. Day and night, the apartment faintly resonates with the incessant vibration of a thousand engines. Deryk tells me that on a clear day they can see the jagged mountains of the north from the living-room window, but clear days are infrequent.

After my first night's sleep in China, Vivien meets me at the apartment. We talk about the most banal elements of our respective biographies. She's from a medium-sized coastal town in Shandong Province to the south, a very old region not too far from the hometown of Confucius, the greatest of all Chinese rationalists.

We'd exchanged emails outlining a vague itinerary for a month-long trip. Beijing. Somewhere typical of present-day China, perhaps in her home province. A village. The Yangtze River. Automobile factories in central China. Shanghai. The Pearl River area. Guangzhou. Shenzhen. Hong Kong. And Beijing again.

"I'm here to figure things out," I say. "I want us to see as many things and meet as many people as possible—journalists, intellectuals. But also farmers and workers, as well as activists, artists, prostitutes and business people."

"Last week, I sent Deryk some articles for you to read," she tells me. "There was one about a woman who is fighting for the preservation of *hutongs*. I know her. Would you like to meet her?"

"I read it," I reply, "as well as a lot of other articles and books about China and Beijing, before arriving. The destruction of the *hutongs* is well documented. I'd like to stay away from covering what other journalists have already covered. I'm really looking for new subjects. But since we're just starting to fill our schedule, we can meet your *hutong* preservationist," I arrogantly conclude.

Unfazed, Viv immediately makes more suggestions. "How about a television producer? A constitutional lawyer?"

"Yes to both. What about the Beijing infrastructure? Do you know any city officials? Any public works people? Water? Power? Sewage?"

"Hmm, I don't think so," she says, hesitating. "And I don't think we should meet any officials at the beginning of the trip. They ask a lot of questions, and it takes time to set up meetings with them. But we could go to the city's water reservoir."

"Great."

I had skipped breakfast, so by now, almost noon, I'm starving. We descend from Deryk's apartment into the gated esplanade. At the foot of a sister tower is a commercial area with restaurants. But the place is being renovated, and the only restaurant in operation is a sushi joint.

"Do you eat Japanese food?" I ask Vivien.

"Our first meal together in China and you are suggesting we eat Japanese food?"

"Yeah, a little funny, I guess. Anyhow, do you like it?"

"Yes, I do," she says, a tad sheepishly.

We go in and place an order.

"Are you one to hold a grudge against the Japanese for problems of the past?" I ask.

"Maybe," she says with a smile, knowing that I'm teasing her.

"Tell me about Japan and China," I ask innocently as we wait for our food.

"Come on! You must know a little of the history of the Japanese in China."

"That was a long time ago, Viv."

"In China, sixty years is not a long time."

I tease her, knowing how predictable anti-Japanese sentiments are in China.

"Just leave it be," she says politely but sternly.

Of all the foreign occupations China endured, it's no surprise that the people still have the keenest memory of the last one, by the Japanese. They consider it especially harsh. From the Chinese perspective, Japan was a pupil of China, a child of Confucius and Chinese Buddhism. Many significant parts of Japan's culture, including its formal script, came from China. Thus, for Japan to turn around and make China a vassal was a cruel deed for the Chinese. Reminders of the occupation also remain a useful tool in China for stirring up nationalist sentiment and deflecting bad energies from the centre outward. So anger against the Japanese is still widely encouraged in the schools.

After lunch, on the way to meet Viv's friend, the *hutong* preservationist, we take the Second Ring Road around the old quarter of the city. After the Shanghai book launch in 2005, I briefly visited Beijing and stopped in a *hutong* neighbourhood just off the ring road to get the bicycle I was using repaired at an old blacksmith's shop. The *hutong* jutted right up onto the ring road and was sooty and cramped—quite the display when compared with the modern highway.

As we glide along the Second Ring Road now, I realize that the blacksmith's *hutong* neighbourhood is gone. An area two arteries deep into the old city—hundreds of shops and houses, laneways and ancient trees—has been wiped off the face of the earth. In its place, a pleasant park has been installed. It just appeared out of nowhere: big old trees, lawns and flower beds, park benches and mood lighting, even sections of old stone walls that provide pleasant little obstacles for the walkways to wind around. The illusion of permanence is so great that I get Viv to ask the cab driver if the park is in fact new or if my memory is playing tricks on me.

"It's new," the cabbie says with a knowing smile, perhaps even proud of what his government can do.

Gone. Gone are the blacksmith and his shop, I start to imagine. Gone is the poultry seller. The old widow and her minuscule home behind the barber shop. Gone, all gone. Gone and forgotten. I turn to Viv and admit that the destruction of *hutongs* is an important subject.

"Yes, and I won't need to translate. Madame Hua speaks good French," she tells me.

"Really? How come?"

"Her grandfather was the first Chinese man to study in Paris. He studied civil engineering and married a Polish woman. They lived in China. But their son went on to complete his architecture studies in Paris. There he married a French woman. They returned to China to raise their daughter, whom you'll meet."

"But how Chinese is she?" I wonder aloud.

"She has said that sometimes people question how Chinese she is to undermine her. She considers herself Chinese."

Catherine Hua meets us at a café in the diplomatic quarter. She's in her fifties and has a motherly look about her. She has Asian-shaped eyes that are blue and grey-tinged hair that was once light brown. We exchange a few niceties and then she gets straight to the point.

"Do you know who owns the land in Beijing?" she asks in proper if slightly rusty French.

"I assume the state does. That is, the people."

"No," she quietly corrects me, "that's a mistake that most people make about China. The Communist government only went about systematic land reform in the countryside. It did not collectivize the land in big cities."

"So people—I mean, individuals—still own their residences in the *hutongs*?"

"Yes, many of them," she says in a matter-of-fact tone. "Until recently, I owned my house in the *hutongs*. It was the house of my grandfather and of my father. I grew up there, playing in the gardens."

"What happened?"

"Well, the state demolished my home. I guess I can still claim to own the land under the demolished house, but it has built a giant shopping mall on the site. It demolished a whole neighbourhood."

"You couldn't stop it?"

"We tried. But we failed. In this instance."

"Was it an expropriation?" I query.

"Here's how it works," Madame Hua says. "The city is already divided up into exploitation areas. The top developers have designs on everything. They cut a deal with the city and state officials to share some of the immense profits to be generated by the sale of condos, offices and commercial space in the new structures. We're talking hundreds of millions of dollars. Then the state issues an expropriation notice for a given area and imposes a strict time limit for evacuation. It relocates the inhabitants to apartment blocks on the outskirts of the city and pays out tiny sums for the lost property. You must leave your home, your gardens, your neighbours, everything. If you don't leave, you're arrested. Then your home is demolished."

"What can you do?"

"Luckily, things tend not to be done very carefully," she says. "The developers hold land titles and building permits that predate the expropriation acts. They mostly concentrate just on taking the land, not on the legal procedure for doing so. Which means the state's paperwork is full of inconsistencies. I'm fighting the state in court. But the courts often refuse to hear the cases. So I talk to the media. I make a fuss. I go to friends in high places. I show up at cocktail parties and belittle the developers. They're criminals. It should be known."

She pauses, thinking about her loss, then says, "I could not save my own home. But I may be able to save some of the *hutongs*. Come, I'll show you," she says, urging us to go to her house nearby.

Catherine Hua lives in a modern apartment building just around the corner from the café. The interior confirms that she is a woman of culture. The space is simple and graceful, the walls decorated with old paintings and silk screens. I imagine her personal history. She's from an old family, and her grandfather must have been an exceptional man. If he studied in Paris in the earliest years of the twentieth century, he must have been born into the Chinese elite. A famous builder in old Peking, he was surely quite the gentleman. His son was raised in the best of Chinese and Western traditions, trained in the old arts and then educated like his father at the best Parisian architecture school. In Madame Hua's family, one was clearly expected to respect art. I ask her about the Cultural Revolution, that brutal time when such people of culture were targeted and purged.

"Ah, that was an interesting time," she begins with a smile. "Before then, we had a big house with a big garden around it. As a child, I used to pretend that I was in the jungle in that garden. During the Cultural Revolution, the Red Guards forced a lot of families from the countryside into our big house. My family retreated to the servant house at the back of the compound. It could have been a lot worse: my father had been a quiet servant of the revolution—the original one, that is—so we were luckily not subjected to any further measures."

She retrieves a large photo album, places it on the coffee table and begins to guide me through it. There are photos of old stone houses, of courtyards, trees, delicately carved wooden eaves, stone dragons and intricately cobbled walkways. These are glimpses of the treasures of the *hutongs*, the precious private spaces where great poems were composed and passionate love affairs conducted, where people were taught how to think, how to honour their ancestors properly and how to be good scions of a great culture.

"This house," Catherine tells me as she points to a series of photos, "once belonged to a famous general. He was also a master calligrapher. The house had the most amazing garden walkway, with incredible arches. Look at this photo; you can see them."

"What happened to it?" I ask.

"It's gone. They didn't even salvage the stonework." She turns the page.

"Look at the gate to this house," she says, directing my focus to a stone gateway in the photo that has an elaborate wooden roof over it. "It too is gone, crushed by a bulldozer. I was there to see it happen."

"Who lived in these houses?"

"Many families. Normal people," she continues. "They call me for help. Or at the very least, they tell me to come and take pictures of their treasured homes. 'Come quick,' they say, 'the bulldozers are here!'"

There are pages and pages of photos. Catherine occasionally points out a house and tells me that she managed to save it. But the vast majority of the photos are of ghosts: homes, ways of life, banished into nothing. I nod my head sympathetically as I flip through the album.

"I guess the developers, the state officials, have no sense of history," I comment.

"No," she says, "they are without sense, without culture. They are motivated by one thing alone. Greed."

Catherine Hua feels the need to say one final thing: "Earlier in the revolution, great changes were made. Things were turned upside down, yes. But I feel that we are now going somewhere totally new and even more radical—yes, even compared with the Cultural Revolution. Then at least, when temples and historical houses were destroyed, they were destroyed for a reason. There was an ideology. Now Chinese history is simply being eradicated without thought. This is barbaric, nihilistic even."

Welcome to modernity, I think.

Over the next days, Viv and I criss-cross the capital preparing for our trip, getting plane tickets, doing research. Beijing is a sprawling megalopolis; we are stuck in traffic a lot, sometimes for hours. This gives us time to throw ideas around and get to know each other more. Vivien doesn't make it difficult for me to assess her opinions about the government. She loathes and distrusts the Communist Party and tells me so point-blank.

"I'm not the ideological type and certainly not a Communist," I tell Viv, "but then again, nor is China anymore. I just don't want to try draw conclusions too quickly about this place."

"I assure you that if you stay a while and see how things work here, you couldn't support the party," she says somewhat fiercely.

"Well, one thing I'm fairly certain of is that China cannot simply copy the political system of some other place."

"So how do you feel about Tiananmen?" she asks pointedly.

"I would like to think that if I were Chinese, I would have been on the square, facing down the tanks for my freedom. But at the same time, I'm not blind to the benefits that stability has brought China since Tiananmen."

"Sacha, trust me, I've lived here my whole life. I'm familiar with this government and its ways," she says with conviction. "I don't see any good coming from corruption and injustice."

"But look around," I argue. "I see tremendous wealth creation. The economy is getting freer, and China is getting more and more rich and powerful."

"It's not all like this," she says with a small smile. "Anyhow, you know that Confucius had nothing but contempt for the pursuit of wealth?"

"I didn't know that. I always thought Confucius told us to seek harmony. Prosperity is a kind of harmony, I thought."

"No. Confucius taught that harmony comes only from virtue."

We head to a seafood restaurant called Ten Thousand Dragon Continent. Passing through the ornate entrance, we enter a big room filled with aquariums. A selection of exotic creatures squirms in the open tanks: fish of all sizes and colours, squid, octopuses, eight types of crab, four kinds of lobster, half a dozen varieties of shrimp, every kind of mollusc imaginable, a healthy selection of insects: bee pupae, silk larvae and dangerous-looking scorpions. The aquariums take the place of a menu; to order, you point at a tank and specify a quantity and cooking style: poached, steamed or fried, with black bean, imperial sauce, or garlic and ginger. The waitress then nets your selection and sends the live seafood to the kitchen.

For the Chinese, it seems there's no greater joy in life than sitting down to a rare feast with friends and family. Even given

Vivien's discreet manner, it's clear she loves food as well. Over tender razor clams with shallots and ginger and spiced baby octopus, I ask Vivien about her father.

"He was a mathematics professor. And later a high-school principal."

"What did his father do?"

"He was a peasant. A farmer."

"I could say my father's father was born on a farm as well. But he died in 1934. So I hardly consider myself a farmer. You?"

"Not really," she says, laughing. "I'm a city girl. But I did spend a lot of time with my grandparents on the farm when I was a child. So country life is not at all foreign to me."

"Are your grandparents still alive?"

"Oh yes, all of them."

"I'm curious what it was like for your family during the Cultural Revolution."

"Well, for my grandparents nothing much changed. They were classified as 'low to middle' farmers. So they were spared any attacks. As for my father, since he was of peasant stock, at the university he was one of the few people who benefited from the Cultural Revolution. While the so-called intellectuals were being chased from the universities, my father did his doctorate."

"Can I meet him?"

"Certainly not!" Viv says unequivocally. "I haven't talked to him in several years and am not planning to. In fact, he's not a topic of conversation that I enjoy."

After lunch, we head back to Deryk's apartment to book more flights for our journey. We ride the elevator to the seventeenth floor. I comment that it's actually the fourteenth floor, since the fourth, thirteenth and fourteenth floors are missing.

"It makes sense that Deryk lives on this floor and it's partly empty. Anyone Chinese would hesitate to live on the fourteenth flour, even though it's listed as the seventeenth flour. Four and fourteen are very bad numbers. The words in Mandarin sound like death."

"That strikes me as rather foolish. Not you?"

"Oh, come on! It's tradition. We Chinese are raised to be superstitious."

"But you seem so rational." I say teasingly.

"You don't get it. I choose to be superstitious," she counters. "It's a way to honour one's ancestors by carrying forth their beliefs. Superstition is an act of awe. Ancestors should be held in awe," she says, a little unsure of her footing in English.

"*Awe*? Are you sure you intend to use that word?"

"It means fear and respect, right?"

"Yes. And that's how you would describe your feelings toward these beliefs?"

"Yes," she says firmly.

Vivien certainly has no awe for the Chinese Communist Party. She has even cultivated a group of friends who have distinguished themselves through their opposition to the central government. Many of her contacts in activist and intellectual circles are from her days at Peking University. She was clearly a dedicated student and has maintained ties to many of her professors.

She sets up a meeting for us with her former professor, Hé Weifang, at a place called Thinker's Café, a hangout for students of the humanities. As we approach, Viv explains the café's real name: "*Xing Ke* means sober guest, probably after one of the greatest of

Chinese poets, Qu Yuan, who was persecuted and committed suicide twenty-three hundred years ago. He wrote: 'I was banished because everyone is drunk while I'm the only one sober.'"

The café's front door is discreet; it leads to a dirty staircase, at the bottom of which sits a bald-headed old man smiling a toothless grin.

"I love this place," Viv tells me as we climb the stairs.

Landing on the second floor, I notice that the atmosphere has changed: the walls are painted black. The café is on one side; the All Sages Bookstore, the other. We turn toward the café. We pass a few display cabinets and I see Chinese titles for Jared Diamond, Milton Friedman and Edward Said.

The café is stylish and moody. It's obviously popular with young intellectuals. We head to a table by the window to wait for Professor Hé. Viv is excited to see him again and briefs me on his biography. Hé specializes in constitutional law. He has been particularly involved in cases of discrimination arising from China's dual residency system, known as the *hukou* system. He has become a critic of the government and was one of a few legal academics to write an open letter criticizing the central government.

"There was a famous case a few years ago of a student dying in police custody," Viv explains. "This student was out one night without his papers. If you are from the countryside, you must have written authorization to live in the city. If you don't, you can be fined by the local authorities. If you can't pay the fine immediately, they can force you to work. The authorities farm out this indentured labour to local contractors. In this case, the student was unable to prove on the spot that he was in fact a student. The police took him in as a potential labourer. Some people say that the student was lippy with the police when they interrogated him.

He died in police custody twenty-four hours later. Professor Hé came out against the measure that led to this unnecessary death."

Hé arrives. He's in his mid- to late fifties. He's at once professorial, weathered and elegant. After preliminaries and several cigarettes, he begins to tell me about the Chinese constitution.

"I'm devoted to the constitution, but my government isn't. The fundamental political philosophy of the Communist Party is Marxism. Marx advocated no laws. As such, constitutionalism was never of much interest or relevance to the party. A constitution sets out to define a certain number of rights and rules. But regardless of the constitution, the party always presents all rights and rules as it sees fit at any given moment."

Hé then explains that, in practical terms, this means there is no legitimate avenue for social activism and no acceptable way to implement new models of society, whether democracy, freedom of speech, human rights or even trade unions.

Hé has staked out an interesting stand for himself. He believes in rule-making and the law. It's important, he thinks, to create laws that represent the best interests of present and future society and that society can follow without too much difficulty. The constitution thus has to both frame existing laws and enshrine a law-making process that gently leads society forward.

Hé is strategically opposed to his government. He's not arguing against the Chinese government's laws. Quite the contrary: he is arguing that the government must respect the rules and laws that it gives itself, whatever they might be. He's thus not making a moral argument against his government but a practical one in support of it. He's arguing for consistency, not righteousness. In this sense, one can argue that Professor Hé is helping the government follow its own logic.

Hé believes that law can transform society. China may no longer be commanded from the Forbidden City. But the model of government it represents continues. Power remains opaque and inaccessible. This must change. By forcing the empire to bow its head to the law, power will be returned to a place where it can be witnessed, participated in and transformed.

The professor then takes me through the *hukou* system. He explains that at the beginning of the People's Republic, in its first constitution of 1954, freedom of movement was guaranteed to the people. But that constitution was never properly implemented. And from the beginning, the People's Republic of China was involved in managing and restraining the rural population. It needed that population for defence, and for food and industrial production.

This increased after the failed industrial policies of Mao's Great Leap Forward, when millions of peasants were forced out of the fields and into haphazard industrial production. Having abandoned their crops, the peasants began to starve. Many left the countryside and the famines worsened. The free flow of people had to be restricted.

The later constitutions eventually reflected the need to restrain the movement of rural populations. Over the last thirty years, the trend has been moving the other way. The growth of the manufacturing sector in the cities requires a constant influx of labour from the countryside. The limits on free movement have been lifted to allow the cities to attract this workforce. But this workforce is highly volatile and has to be managed carefully. Not everybody can be allowed to settle in the cities. The movement of people is tolerated, but legal status is not easily granted. So the workforce remains transient and cheap.

"The best friends of the party are now capitalist entrepreneurs who profit from the cheap labour," the professor explains. "This alliance makes for little interest in the bargaining power of the workers."

"But this alliance has also helped China secure its position in the world economy," I point out.

"Yes, it's the reason China has become the world's factory. But without any proper legal environment, there's no real stability in the long run. The next twenty years are crucial," he concludes with a sigh.

"Do you think China can implement a liberal democracy any time soon?" I ask.

"Well, one thing is sure: we need change. We need something different while there is still latitude for change. Even for our economy, we need judicial independence."

"Did an old party leader not say that good things take time?"

"Well, I say to that old leader, no good things can come through institutions that don't answer to the people. I see no other alternative for us than democracy. Western-style democracy."

"So many people participating in so great a project?"

"I cannot say it'll be easy," he says with a gentle smile.

"Has it started?"

"It has for some."

Another of Vivien's teachers, Professor Wang Yue, taught her documentary filmmaking and is now a television producer for CCTV, China's national television network, which broadcasts on dozens of channels. Wang produces a show on channel 10, the state documentary channel, called *Great Masters*. Vivien tells me it is one of the best shows on Chinese state television and that she likes to watch it. It airs at 10 p.m. every weeknight.

Viv and I arrange to meet in front of the CCTV buildings, in the eastern part of town. She tells me to wait at the front gate near Professor Wang's office building. "You'll see soldiers guarding it," she adds.

Indeed, the CCTV offices are guarded by the People's Liberation Army. I imagine the CBC offices being on a Canadian military base.

Viv's stuck in traffic, so Wang comes out to meet me at the gate and usher me through the military checkpoint. He apologizes for the nature of his workplace. "Television stations are not like this in your country," he says as we climb a grimy staircase in an old concrete office building. He is fairly young and fit.

"Actually, CCTV has a huge new fortress for all its channels," he continues, "a modern and expensive building that I'm sure you have seen. But I keep an office in this less assuming setting."

Wang's office is cramped—and empty except for his brand-new computer. I'm not quite sure what to talk about, so I begin throwing him technical questions about his channel, his program and the individual documentaries.

I learn that his program produces portrait documentaries. He has only recently become its producer. He's in charge of half a dozen directors and a dozen post-production personnel. He was a director on the show before being promoted.

"Who are your documentaries about?" I ask.

"Famous people—movie stars, filmmakers, artists, some business people."

"Politicians?"

"Yes, sometimes."

"Your show's powerful."

"It can be," he happily acknowledges.

"Who tells you what to do?"

"No one tells me what to do. They only tell me what not to do."

"Who are *they*?" I inquire.

"The CCTV 10 producers," he says. "I produce *Great Masters*. They are in charge of the whole channel's programming." Then he adds curiously, "My job is very hard," and waits for me to probe.

"Why's that?"

"Because a lot of people think they know whom I should make documentaries about. Sometimes people come to me with gifts."

"I see."

He nods, grinning, then continues: "I refuse them, of course. But managing this is not easy."

Wang's show is broadcast throughout China. Virtually every television set in the country gets the signal. Canadian producers are proud when a million people watch their documentaries. Wang's show gets tens of millions of viewers every night. A main vein, one might say. From his bare office on the third floor of building E, Wang has a say over the Chinese people's values, a say over celebrity in China, the new cult of personality.

"Movie stars are always a safe bet," he says. "Very popular."

Wang explains that this is because they can be worshipped without consequence. Business people are easy as well, he admits, because their agenda is clear and simple: they want to sell stuff. Artists and musicians are typically more difficult—it can be more difficult to control the message. Politicians are more sensitive still. Political power is a delicate affair in China. Wang tells me that he walks a thin line when dealing with certain types of people.

"What makes a good documentary filmmaker, Professor?" Viv asks, once she arrives.

35

"I look for people who have lived a lot," Wang says. "People who have suffered. People who have had many crazy love affairs, who have been divorced, who have been flat broke and have moved around a lot. People who have known upsets and instability. They always have the most empathy and understanding for human nature."

Beijing is built on a great plain surrounded on all sides by mountains. To the north of the city is the Great Wall, charting its way across an extremely rugged stretch of mountains. A visit to the wall or to those mountains will reveal how arid the territory is. Beijing is a city at the edge of a desert. Beyond the mountains toward the west is a vast wasteland of dusty, rocky landscapes and shifting sands. When the wind kicks up in the west, the capital of China is engulfed in dust.

Like Los Angeles or Mexico City, the Chinese capital is in a valley, trapped by the surrounding mountains. When no wind blows, a pocket of air forms above the valley that fills up with the fumes of automobiles and the acrid smoke of industry. In Beijing, eyes are constantly irritated and bloodshot. Respiratory troubles are rife among children. The city's air can sometimes be a serious assault on the body. With hundreds if not thousands of new cars out on the road every day, the air quality is not likely to improve.

But the capital has even more serious concerns than its air quality: water. The provinces around the capital have been experiencing an unprecedented drought over the past decade. There's simply less water in the region; meanwhile, the city needs more and more.

In the old neighbourhoods within the second ring, many of the *hutong* dwellings were without flush toilets. Several dozen families shared a single public latrine. But with so many of these old lodgings now demolished to make room for modern buildings, and the new high-rises equipped with all the modern amenities, including flush toilets, water mains into the city are multiplying.

The city's water comes from reservoirs in the same dry mountains where the dust clouds originate. Sometimes when the dust gets unbearable, public works brigades shoot rockets into the sky to release silver iodide crystals into the atmosphere. These crystals soak up the moisture and release it upon the capital in the form of rain, dampening the dust. But this bizarre method comes at a cost: wicked from the atmosphere, less moisture reaches the mountains and the western barrens, further drying them and thus taxing Beijing water sources and exasperating the erosion and dust problems.

Where this cycle is leading is anybody's guess. One thing is for sure: bigger water and air problems are ahead for the capital. Vivien and I are keen to make a trip to one of the city's main reservoirs, so we charter a car and head north.

Viv has repeatedly told me about how reluctant average people might be to talk to us. "Your average Chinese person is guarded around foreigners," she says.

I have never been good at making first contact. Viv's pessimistic outlook doesn't make it any less daunting for me. I emphasize that she needs to be the one to make contact with people. I tell her I will act like I'm completely out of it—bored, distracted or simple-minded. "Like I'm hardly even present," I say. "Like a tourist inadvertently following you around on some detailed tour of China."

"Hard to imagine, really," she counters, "but we'll try."

The city sprawls almost to the mountains. Smog makes them invisible until we are very close. At their foot, the urban areas give way to the countryside, sprinkled with a few apple and peach orchards. The Ming emperors are buried in these foothills. Their tombs remain an attraction for tourists on their way to the Great Wall.

Tombs are important to the Chinese. They are stone reminders of our fleeting presence on earth. Chinese civilization was built on the memory of ancestors; its continuity cemented by ancestor rituals. Imperial tombs are that much more important. They're relics of an era. But our journey leads us to other ghosts.

We turn toward the northeast, following civilization along the mountains, and reach an area of intense construction. Through great clouds of dust churned up by huge machines making new roads and housing developments, we see our first old village across the plain. Beijing stops here.

Earlier that morning, we drank a lot of tea. We decide to head into the village to find a place to pee. The road through the village was once paved. But it hasn't got any attention in decades. Traffic and trucks have ground wide potholes into the road. There are now more potholes than road.

I have seen this kind of road in many places in the Third World. These places aren't developing. They are falling apart, torn up by disease, war and poverty. But this village is not simply ignored by powerless corrupt cliques like those in the other places I have seen, not simply forgotten and bereft of any economic activity or state structures. This village is not neglected. It's doomed.

At least the trucks don't pass through the village anymore, not since the government started building the big road. In fact, the feeling I get driving through the village is that no cars come here anymore at all, save the delivery guy once a week.

The street is filled with people. Old people. They obligingly clear the road for our car. They are coldly curious as to why we have come to their village. I laughingly say to Viv to announce to them that we have come to piss in their village. Vulgarity aside, she thinks that it would be a reasonable thing to do. "It's why we're here, isn't it?" she says.

"Damn right," I concur.

We stop the car and proceed on foot.

The garb of the village is dusty black; the style, pyjama, unisex. But these are not just clothes, they are uniforms, long ago issued by the government. They even come with matching caps. For all the poverty of their surroundings, these elderly people are in fact extremely dignified, filled with silent purpose.

Respectfully, Viv asks an old woman where the public washroom is. She points us down an earth road just off the main street. The washroom is a single-unit brick outhouse built into the side of a building. Qing dynasty, by the looks of it. I let Viv have the privilege and head to an empty field down the road. She tells me to take as long a time as possible.

I loiter, looking at the clay-brick constructions bordering the field. On my return, I find the old woman and Viv chatting. I decide not to interrupt and so go look for something to drink. Not a chance in this village, I quickly see. I remember that we have bottled tea in the car. As I fetch it, a group of old men catch my eye. There are seven of them in a row on the front stoop of a post office–like building. Some squatting, some standing, some sitting on minuscule folding stools. A few of the men wear not black but grey uniforms. They're all dapper. Clearly the old guard, I tell myself.

Viv approaches and tells me that the old woman is a widow and a grandmother. Her grandchildren are in school nearby. Her daughter is in the city working. Her son is also working but far away. He came back once a few years ago. He stayed for a while, then left again. She misses him terribly but doesn't know if she'll ever see him again. All the grown children have now gone away to work as well.

Viv asked her about the water situation, but the old woman couldn't understand the question and didn't give a coherent answer.

"One more thing," Viv says. "They're Manchu people."

"How do you know?"

"Their appearance, her accent. And look at the school," she says, pointing up the street. Its walls are covered with small Manchu flags. They flutter in the wind, brandishing colours and symbols. They look like children's cut-outs strung up on a line. We concentrate a little and then our ears perk up. The sound of children chanting in Mandarin faintly echoes through the village.

"Ask these men behind me where the reservoir is," I urge Viv.

A couple of them point in its direction, but they tell her that we can't get to it that way. Go back the way you came, they say. Then they ask her who I am and why I look so serious.

"He's a tourist. That's just the way he looks," she says.

So much for my distracted imbecile routine.

Viv asks a few things about the village, then inquires about their banner tribes. The men offer only shrugs and smiles, then wish us a happy journey. We respectfully withdraw.

"The Manchu came here as an army," Viv explains as we drive out of the village. "Every man was part of a regiment or clan. We call these groups 'banners' for the flags they carried. Those are what the flags on the school represented."

The sly looks the men gave Viv suddenly make more sense. "Yes, you're right, we are men of the Manchu clan," their loaded silence conveyed. The statement is as much a warning as an apology; it means that Viv's question was pointless—that, sadly, the clans' time in these parts has passed and they, men of the Manchu, are now as irrelevant as her question about their banners.

The Manchu were the people of the last dynasty in China. Their great armies descended from the north upon the decaying Ming Empire. As with the Mongols before the Ming, the Manchu rule, called the Qing dynasty, was at first seen by the Han Chinese majority as a kind of foreign occupation.

The early Qing emperors kept control of China through a network of Manchu clansmen or bannermen, as they were called, placed throughout all Chinese institutions. The Qing emperors backed up this soft power with hard power: their own Manchu armies were always ready and never stood down.

The Qing armies were like no modern army. They were more like tribes. When the Manchu aristocracies set themselves up as sovereigns over all of China, their tribesmen followed them into China by the hundreds of thousands. Bannermen and their dependents were given land around strategic cities throughout China; their camps would have been military villages.

The villages north of Beijing, around the Ming tombs, are probably a residue of the Manchu forces established there several centuries ago. For a while, they kept the peace in China. The people of these villages, living so close to both the old capital and the mountains beyond which lies Manchuria proper, might even have been of the Qing emperor's reserve. With a moment's notice, the emperor in the Forbidden City could call on these men to mobilize and seek marching orders. The early Qing military would have been impressive; the soldiers would have fought as one force, one will. They would have been fierce, organized and loyal. For a while, they would have been what China needed. But alas they were not masters of the sea in an age when maritime supremacy became paramount.

So, in time, even the flag of the hard and military Manchu order grew tattered. Exposed to China, soaking up Chinese ways, the Qing too gave into the cycle of all things and grew weak. In China, the cycle of the yin and the yang has ruled since time immemorial. What is black will be white, what is hot, cold. Man, woman, strong, weak.

We leave the village and head back toward the construction at the edge of Beijing. It isn't hard to see what fate awaits the village. It will be swept away by machines, devoured by the new capital of the new Middle Kingdom, and in its place, a new kind of life will begin, the like of which China has never seen before.

Soon the stoop, the latrine, the post office–like building, the old people themselves will be gone. The children will go to a new, big school. Perhaps this is why they fly the flags at their current school—to say, Children, whatever happens, remember that you carry the banners. Whatever is said, hold your heads up, for you are of the Manchu clan, which once brought peace and prosperity to China.

Finally, we're heading in the right direction. A broad valley between two ridges opens up to us. It's sunny and fertile and without villages. The great dam is visible. It's an immense concrete wall connecting one hilltop to the next. We follow a narrow road that winds its way up one of the hills, passing a multitude of pagodas and tourist-trap restaurants as our car climbs toward the reservoir.

As we reach a crest, the vista opens up to the reservoir. It's vast, and picturesque with its surrounding mountains. The road circumscribes the man-made lake. It leads us to the back of the valley, where the reservoir is fed by a creek flowing from the mountains. This September, the creek looks dry. We find a small village and decide to stop.

The village is a series of earth-brick houses tightly grouped around central courtyards. Between the courtyards tight alleyways chart their way. I can make out, over a wall, two crops: corn—unmistakable with its high, plumed ears—and gourds, on vines. We turn into an alley that makes its way deep into the dense village and come upon an old man in a straw hat.

"Please excuse my bothering you, respected elder," Viv appropriately starts, "but I would like to know about this village. Is this an old village?"

"Oh yes," the old man keenly answers. "It has been around for a time."

"And how old are you?"

"Over eighty."

"Wow, you're in great health for someone over eighty," Viv comments.

"Yes, this mountain living's good for the health," the old man cheerfully says, "not like in the cities. Every morning I climb into the mountains to check on my nut trees. It's all the exercise that I need."

He pulls from his pocket walnuts, which he proudly shows us. Then he looks squarely at me and laughs. "Oh, I can tell right away that he is a foreigner. There's no mistaking that."

43

"Yes," Viv continues, "we have come from the city to see the reservoir. Is the water level usually this low?"

"Not usually. It has been a hot summer. A drought even. But the creek is flowing now."

"How long have you been here?" Viv asks.

"All my life. Since before the reservoir was built. But when I was young I was a soldier of the People's Liberation Army. I fought under Lin Biao."

Lin Biao was one of the greatest of the Communist generals. His armies defeated huge Nationalist formations in a series of battles across Manchuria. Those were the boldest hours of the revolution. The victories in Manchuria, with hundreds of thousands of northerners switching sides during battle, resulted in the flight of Chiang Kai-shek to Taiwan and overwhelming Communist victory in China.

By winning in the north, the Communists won over the Manchu clan and Mao had succeeded: a man from Hunan had convinced all of China, even the northerners, that the heavens had opened to him and through him would bless China with a new order. Mao never could have done this without Lin Biao and countless others. But nonetheless, the East was Red.

A bizarre culmination of events led to a tragic end for Lin Biao. In the late 1960s, the general rose to become Mao's designated successor and one of the leaders of the Cultural Revolution. But in the maddening events of the revolution, Mao grew tired of his champion and turned on him. Sensing the walls closing in on him, Lin made a break for it and attempted to flee China for the Soviet Union. His plane reportedly crashed in the mountains of Mongolia.

History will probably lose track of the spiralling of events that led to Lin Biao's disgrace, flight and death. Such is already the fate of the Cultural Revolution—those at the top responsible for the madness are all dead; those who took part in it, like those who suffered it, do not want or need to remember it, and now even they grow old.

Chinese historians gloss over the Cultural Revolution as if it barely existed. Foreign historians mostly characterize it as something sinister, grotesque, infantile and bizarre. No one can fully explain it. But here in the Manchu fringe of the old capital, Lin Biao is proudly remembered by this old man as a warrior chief whose banner you definitely wanted to fight under.

Two elderly woman show up carrying baskets of vegetables. They gently chide the old man for shooting his mouth off to strangers. They're friendly but direct with us.

"Who are you?"

"A tourist and his guide," Viv says.

"What are you looking for?"

"A place to eat."

After a lengthy deliberation, they finally agree on one household near the entrance of the village that might serve food. By now, the women are positively chatty. Viv gets them to talk about water.

They have running water in the morning, they say without the faintest intimation that such a thing wouldn't be perfectly usual and obvious. Perhaps they remember having to fetch water from a well, so a tap into the house that gives water a few hours every day must seem luxurious.

"Beijing gets its water right here," Viv tells me. "It flows all day in Beijing, but see how it is rationed here? Further afield, it's scarce. I remember reading several articles saying that people on the fringes of Beijing don't always have enough water for their crops."

We head toward the house that was recommended to us. It turns out to be right next to where we parked the car. We fetch the driver and ask him to join us for lunch. After an exchange of questions, the woman of the house understands her opportunity. She leads us through a building and into a courtyard surrounded by a few brick houses. Our hostess is in her mid-thirties and is assisted by an older woman. Her young son is also present, just back from school.

They are peasants, weathered, pragmatic and tough. On this sunny, warm autumn day, it's lovely in the courtyard. Half the space is brick-floored; the other half, planted earth. The fall harvest is near. The corn is ripe and golden. The vines climb on a trellis, providing dappled shade to a good part of the floored courtyard. Gourds hang down, fat and rich. Stools are pulled out of a wooden kitchen hut that has been built against the back wall of the courtyard; they are placed around a table beneath the vines. We're brought hot water to drink and invited to sit down.

I study the outdoor stove. A brick base cradles an immense steel wok. Our hostess fires it up by throwing dried corn husks and chaff into hot embers beneath it. Moments later, she's frying a handful of fresh herbs and garlic. The woman notices me hovering about and laughs at my interest, which I can scarcely hide.

Our meal consists of shrimp from the reservoir, fried in their shells with salt and spice, big flat beans fried with garlic and herbs, and a thick soup of meat and vegetables.

The young boy has been shy but intrigued, pretending to do his homework to the side but instead watching us intently. He has a shaved head and roughed-up knees and face—the kind of sturdy child with whom I might have run wild as a boy.

Viv asks him if he's learning his characters. He answers in the affirmative in a gruff but friendly manner. His mother then tells him that we are people of the wide world and he should talk to us to see what we're like. She tells us he's learning English and urges him to speak to us. The boy indulges her: "One, two, three," he says with great concentration.

The conversation continues between us all with few words but much laughter. The hostess is curious to know where Viv and the driver come from. It turns out that they are both from Shandong Province. We all share an unabashed chuckle about this happy coincidence and toast Shandong. The meal costs us twenty dollars altogether.

"Tell me about Shandong," I ask Viv on the way back to Beijing.

"Well, my people, Shandong people, are everywhere," she says.

"Why?"

"Shandong has always been populous. The floods and the droughts and the poverty have long made people emigrate from the place. But it is also the province of Chinese religion, where both Confucius and Mencius originated, so it's always on our minds."

"I'm glad we're going there next. A place to think about the Chinese soul," I say.

"Are you religious?"

"Let's just say I believe in ghosts," I answer with a smile.

"Ghosts! Weren't you laughing at me for being superstitious?" she says. "I figured you were the scientific, rationalist type."

"I was just prodding your beliefs."

"Well, I think it makes sense to remain vigilant toward religion," Vivien says, then adds, "Lao-tzu says, 'It was when intelligence and knowledge appeared that the Great Artifice began.' He meant for us to be wary of any organized system of belief."

"To me, all organized systems of belief are beautiful. And fragile."

"I have to admit that I have also always been curious about all matters spiritual," she says. "Who taught you about religion?"

"My father."

"Mine too."

CHAPTER 3

The Old East

The head pillowed on a spear, waiting for the day to break.
—biography of Liu Kun, *Book of Jin*, seventh century

We are headed toward Shandong Province in our chartered car. Our first objective is Jinan, an industrial city on the banks of the Yellow River. It's a six-hour drive south from Beijing. The highway passes through a melancholy landscape of intensive farming. The area is oppressively flat and entirely pressed into food production. Grain, cabbage, soy and corn are interspersed with the occasional grove of poplar, planted as windbreaks. From the highway, the territory seems almost empty of human inhabitation. The planners who built the highway charted its path to avoid the congestion of human settlements that can only occasionally be spotted on the horizon.

Just before Jinan, the landscape becomes more watery. The Yellow River has been tapped for irrigation for millennia and still is. Dikes and waterways are everywhere. Finally, the river proper appears. It's spanned by many low-lying bridges. As we cross one, the vista opens up a little. Jinan splays out along the river. Its numerous concrete high-rises and smokestacks contrast with a backdrop of hazy blue hills. To complete the industrial picture, there's a train crossing the river and another train working its way along tracks on the distant shore.

A major hub, Jinan is where the main north-south axis from Beijing to Shanghai and the old east-west axis of the Yellow River converge. Although big and active, the city still doesn't have much to attract outsiders.

We're stopping in industrial Jinan to meet with a young man who's a proponent of the New Confucianism movement. Discovered on the Internet, Wu Fei's personal website features patterns for the ancient robes worn by disciples of the master. Apparently, Wu makes his own clothing using them.

As we approach, numerous phone calls are made to determine his precise whereabouts within the rambling, nondescript city. Wu isn't altogether comfortable with our visit. He passes on several cautionary messages: he lives with his parents in a modest flat; he hardly speaks English; he may or may not be wearing his robes to greet us. These caveats only make us more curious about this unusual individual.

We finally locate his building. It's deep in the city, one among many indistinct apartment buildings. To maximize space in these cramped living quarters, the balconies are often enclosed in glass or plastic and used as storage lockers, laundry rooms, kitchens or greenhouses. So the buildings' facades resemble stacks of glass boxes packed with stuff and plants.

From the street, we proceed through an opening into an inner courtyard. The display there is even more chaotic. Part of the courtyard serves as a parking lot, but the vehicles strewn about are in mid-repair. There is the space allotted to a thick clutter of bicycles. An area for children to play. A few rows of vegetable beds, plus a multitude of gourd vines climbing all over the place. More ramshackle and cluttered balconies rise high above us. Several brick huts have also been erected in the courtyard. Wu's place is on the ground floor at the back.

The flat's a dank cell made of a succession of jam-packed rooms. The first two serve as living and sleeping rooms. The back room is a kitchen. A tiny wooden locker encloses the toilet. The few windows open onto walls or windows of adjoining buildings. The place is filthy.

Wu's appearance contrasts with that of his earthly abode. He has elected to wear his robes and appears to us in a full gown of bright white. His long hair is worn in a topknot. He's young and sports the wispiest of beards. He greets us in the traditional manner: with a bow, his hands clenched together in a fist at chest level.

He tells us that New Confucianism is mostly a grassroots movement. He then carefully explains its doctrine to us: "Some might say that when our country regained prosperity, there was a desire to restore our cultural identity, to return to the roots of the nation. Others might say it sprang from the heart of every Chinese person who hopes to discover where we came from and who we are. Whatever the case, people came to the movement from all levels of society. For example, many young people, younger even than me, started wearing traditional Han clothing. There are also people ten or twenty years older than me who spend their time in the study of the old texts. Others are utopian practitioners. My friends and I have mostly picked the scholarly path.

"Whatever our divergences, all New Confucianists are outside the system. We all want to take responsibility as Chinese men and women to pass on our culture to the next generation. Of course, we have our worries, but we are optimists."

"How did you get involved?" I ask.

"When I began my studies," he tells me, "I was interested in Western ways of thinking. Existentialism especially. I was interested in notions of freedom and equality, and the idea of individual participation in social change. But at the same time, at school, I found the atmosphere for learning oppressive and obstructive. I was miserable. I needed a way out. I started reading the classics. To my surprise, they weren't at all like what we had been taught. I was stunned by Confucius's positive attitude in the face of terrific hardships. I was inspired. And I began to adjust my own emotions. I became optimistic."

He admits not imagining at first that he would become a Confucian scholar, but he describes growing more interested in Chinese history: "I began to imagine what the ancient times were like, what the people looked like, how they behaved and what they believed. Then, some years ago, I met a great master online. He'd made a traditional robe for himself, like the one I'm wearing. I realized that the lives of the ancient people and their poise were not just faraway dreams. They were things that I could embrace now. All I needed was to just do it."

"Did your decision to live like this encounter any resistance?"

"My parents always gave me a lot of freedom, as long as I can remember. If my desire was reasonable, they would not interfere. I guess my wearing of Chinese ceremonial clothes and researching the classics seems reasonable enough to them. Some distant relatives may think that I'm weird, but there wasn't any serious disapproval. As for my friends, they're all supportive, though they sometimes shy away from me when I wear these kinds of clothes in the street," he admits with a smile.

Wu's room is the middle one in the apartment and is the path from the front room and his parents' bedroom to the kitchen. The passage is almost totally obstructed by storage boxes. His bed is against the wall, beneath an opaque glass window with several cracked panes. It's stacked with clothing. A diminutive desk is covered with old books and papers. He barely has room for his computer.

He shows me some of the online publications he's authored. They're technical drawings of ceremonial robes, with instructions on how to fabricate them by hand. "Gowns for ancestor worship," he says.

"Do you worship your ancestors?"

"Sort of. I try to find out who they were and learn from them."

As we exit the courtyard and return to our car, ready to move on from Jinan, I joke, "Well, the ghost of Master Kong is certainly present in unit 7 on the ground floor of block C."

To the east of Jinan, on the coast, Qingdao is Shandong's biggest city and a place well known in the West for its beer. Viv once lived there and knows of two people whose profiles touch upon things for which I'd expressed an interest: middle-class entrepreneurship and export production. She even suggests a third person whose profile involves a totally different yet fascinating aspect of China: a medical professor who publishes China's biggest gay magazine.

We fly to Qingdao. Once a symbol of the Communist Revolution, the passenger railroad is giving way to other forms of travel. Like the multiplication of personal automobiles on Chinese roads, the proliferation of air travel is a sign of the burgeoning freedom of the middle class. Until recently, the means to fly around the country were beyond the vast majority of Chinese citizens. Air travel was the sparse realm of the upper echelons of the Communist Party. But on our evening flight, there are students, officials, entrepreneurs and even a few old workers and peasants.

Qingdao airport is clean and new, built to handle an even greater volume of passenger traffic. China's current leaders are also great believers in the power of optimism. Sustained growth tends to do this. In any case, the belief has driven bold investment in infrastructure. Hundreds of grand new airports and highways have been built across China over the last couple of decades.

Qingdao is a hilly city. We speed along the brightly lit elevated highway that winds its way from the airport to the coast where the old city lies. Viv explains that though she grew up in a city a hundred kilometres down the coast, Qingdao is where she started her adult life.

She chats with the taxi driver. Through the pitch and rhythm of her words, she adopts a respectful, girlish approach with the gruff older man, made all the more sympathetic by her oblique flattery and seemingly naive curiosity. This approach would coax even the roughest type into calmly sharing his experiences.

"No, I don't own this cab," he tells her. "Some cabbies acquired their vehicles over the past years, but more recently, big conglomerates have made it difficult for independents to get their licences."

We've chosen to stay at a youth hostel. It's ridiculously cheap: seven bucks a night each. It occupies an old hall of some sort, perhaps a former regimental mess or men's club. Qingdao was once a bustling German colonial town. German builders or adept Chinese imitators erected the old building the hostel occupies, along with many others in the central areas of the city. They're all cream-coloured stucco, three or four storeys high, with steeply peaked red-tiled roofs in the style of Bremen. Many old cobbled streets also remain.

At the hostel, the modern Western presence manifests itself differently. The usual drifters are loitering around the lobby; an American girl is gabbing loudly on the house phone. A goateed hipster is surfing the Web at the bar. We climb sturdy wooden stairs to a long, sonorous corridor leading to rooms under the gables.

My room's bare; the walls, scuffed. All it contains is a hospital-like metal bed, a sink, and a wooden chair and table that look as if they have been painted a dozen times. The gabled window is cut into the steep roof. Dropping my bag, I open it to let in some air, then head out to meet Viv in the lounge.

She's not yet there. An aging Californian with a perma-tan, dyed hair and multiple piercings is chatting up two Australian girls. He looks slightly manic and is on the edge of losing their attention. I bury my face in an old magazine to avoid becoming his next target. Viv finally shows up.

"From here on, let's avoid hostels," I say as we exit the building.

"They're the cheapest accommodation."

"I don't care. Let's just stay where the Chinese stay."

We descend the hill toward the bustle, hoping to find food. We don't have to look far, even at this late hour. We come to a street still full of noise and action. On this balmy night, people are eating and drinking at tables right in the middle of the dirty street. Trash and empty kegs are piled up along the sidewalks.

Amid the chaos, we choose the establishment that seems the least degenerate. Fat Sister, by name. Its keeper is a mighty matron who greets us energetically. After authoritative commands, a table is quickly cleaned. We are seated and attended to immediately. Fat Sister herself takes our order, making emphatic suggestions that we are wise to follow.

The main course consists of a large plate of steamed clams served with a dipping sauce of light vinegar and ginger. The clams are sweet and nicely firm.

"My kind of food," Viv gushes.

A delegation of petty officials turns up and Fat Sister swings into action. Tables are cleaned and pushed together. Pints of beer are quickly brought out. Some of the officials are already inebriated and begin cheerfully toasting the group and Fat Sister.

"They're party officials from Sichuan Province," Viv tells us. "I can tell by their accent. And their rough manners."

Although boisterous, they're obviously good-humoured. Fat Sister is proud to minister to their needs. Viv, however, is disdainful. "You see how Chinese officials behave with public money."

"Do you think they're corrupt?" I ask.

"Well, they obviously benefit from a corrupt system. And I can assure you that in a thousand small ways, they are using their power to create advantage for themselves."

"Do you think petty officials are worse now than in other eras?" I ask. "Or worse here than in other places?"

"All I know is that the average party cadre in China is without morals or scruples," she says.

Watching the men enjoy easy company, fresh seafood and cold beer, I have trouble picturing these petty bureaucrats through Viv's highly critical prism. They're forces of conformity, behaving just as they are told. But then I have trouble feeling, as Viv might, how such officials might threaten my precious freedom, how their hypocritical ministrations might attempt to govern my whole world, suffocating me beneath their self-important mediocrity.

"At the end of high school, I was sent to the party school," Viv suddenly confesses. "I did my time, learnt Marx and Mao, and then moved on. I declined party membership."

We return to the hostel. The coarse clamour of drunken Aussies stumbling back to their rooms serenades me to sleep.

The next morning, we make a quick escape from the hostel. We have but a day to spend in Qingdao, as a flight will carry us on in the evening. Our first stop is the Tsingtao brewery.

Tsingtao beer is one of the only remaining legacies of German China. It's a crisp Germanic lager, brewed according to an old recipe. For many years, Tsingtao beer was one of the few recognizable exports out of China. The company claims itself to be at the vanguard of the new Chinese economy.

In the late nineteenth century, the great powers were racing to keep up with the vast British maritime empire. Unified Germany had become a formidable terrestrial power, but it realized that its place of prominence at the table of nations required it to maintain colonies and a worldwide trade network. So Germany too barged its way into China and set up operations at the tip of the Shandong Peninsula. Qingdao was a useful port for the Germans. Its occupation by Germany marked the Kaiserreich's greatest expansion. Steamers from Hamburg and Königsberg might make their final stop at the wharfs of Qingdao before beginning the long return journey to the fatherland. At Qingdao, ships could be restocked with coal, water and grain. Steel hulls could be repaired. Lutheran missionaries and their families would disembark. Local entrepreneurs would load the ships with cheap textile or meat products or beer, for sale in far-off metropoles.

In Qingdao, beer is the only commercial activity remaining from this era. With its sharply peaked roofs and cobbled courtyard, the old Tsingtao brewery is an emblem of this bygone age of brick, iron, oak and coal.

When Japan was granted Shandong at Versailles, it exploited the area much in the same way the Germans had. Its excellent port, fertile land and sizable population base made the area a natural industrial hub to bolster further imperial expansion. During this time, the brewery began to grow, exporting beer up and down the Chinese coast and to neighbouring inland provinces.

During war or peace, beer is usually available. Tsingtao kept churning out the beverage through the Second World War, supplying soldiers on fronts across Asia with the beer they craved. Production did not cease with the Communist Revolution. The Communists could not afford to shut down such an essential industry. Through shortages, a huge decrease in foreign trade and various radical reorganizations of the economy, the Tsingtao brewery kept making the good stuff. Beer, like coal, was a necessity of industry.

Deng Xiaoping finally redirected Chinese society toward wealth creation in the late 1970s. He abandoned Mao's impossible obsession with self-sufficiency and embraced foreign trade once more. The brewery was once again poised to thrive. The very factors that had allowed it to survive all these years—good water, good soil, a good port and a good recipe—would make it a competitive export product. In the 1980s, Tsingtao beer may well have been one of the first Chinese industrial products to break its way back into Western markets. Cheap, crisp and clean, it was the natural beverage to accompany the familiar egg rolls, hot-and-sour soup, sweet-and-sour pork and General Tao's chicken.

In Qingdao, electronics, hardware and textiles have now surpassed the first exports of beer, tea, canned bamboo shoots and mushrooms, disposable razor blades and the like. The city has become yet another Chinese hub feeding the globalized market's hunger for manufactured products.

Viv has set up a meeting with a man who works for a large export company. The firm deals in home-improvement tools, one of the markets that has exploded over the past decades. "I should let you know, he's my ex-boyfriend," Viv says. "We dated when we were studying in Beijing."

"What did he study?"

"Engineering."

"What kind?"

"You will have to ask him the particulars. But I think it was some kind of mechanical engineering."

"You're on good terms, I assume?"

"Yes, of course. He has a new girlfriend now, and I've met her."

We meet Gan in a city square in front of some kind of *Rathaus*, typically German, with a prominent clock tower. Gan is a polite and friendly bespectacled young man. In the Chinese way, his quiet studiousness glitters with an inner intensity. We head to a nearby restaurant for lunch. Little is said along the way. At one point, he even tells Viv with a smile that I can ask him anything that I would like.

"I understand that you are in import-export."

"I'm in export alone. I'm a manager in the sales and expedition department."

"The company is state owned?" I ask.

"It has various owners, including the different levels of government."

After further exchanges about the company structure, I gather Gan's employer is the prototypical Chinese business entity. It's a government enterprise formed from both local and central government elements but with ill-defined yet growing private participation.

Gan studied mechanical engineering at Tsinghua University. He did his doctoral work on high-precision velocity sensors. But he got frustrated and left before finishing his dissertation. "Too much focus on reverse engineering in the department," he explains. "It wasn't interesting to me. Frankly, there's little room for real science in China."

"Why?"

"Because of politics," Gan says. "How can you have a legitimate pursuit of science when the leaders of the university are first and foremost politicians, not scientists? Even the professors are ranked according to their political power, not the quality of their work. Students are judged for whatever advantage or prestige the professors can personally extract from their work. I witnessed professors selling their students' research projects as their own. I got disgusted."

Viv interjects to say that Gan is perhaps being overly critical. "That sounds too harsh. Tsinghua University still has the reputation of being the finest technical university in China. We call it the MIT of China," she tells me. "So it's hard to imagine what he's describing being so widespread at Tsinghua."

Gan calmly counters that stories of intellectual fraud among students and professors commonly appear in the news all the time. Vivien acquiesces.

"So you left and got a sales job?" I ask him. "I would have thought that sales work would be odious to a scientist."

"There's nothing to it, really," he says. "My company has huge manufacturing deals with Western retailers. I'm hardly selling them anything. They come to us for a whole series of products that we get from Chinese manufacturers. I am really only engaging the clients on the details of their orders: which quantities of which specific products. It's an easy and predictable job."

He tells me that he doesn't even have to negotiate prices. They're set according to purchase quantities. The tools he sells are also usually branded after the purchase is made: foreign clients have their own brand names added to various tools. Often, the same factory produces virtually identical products sold under different brand names.

"You like your job?" I ask.

"It's all right. Boring but steady. No surprises."

"Don't you miss research?"

"A bit, but as I said, China's still a long way from doing real research. Values will have to change before deep scientific progress can happen."

"Are you optimistic?"

"Not really."

"What needs to happen?" I venture.

Gan pauses, then says with a dash of fire in his eyes, "War is always a good source of innovation. Maybe China needs one to put things in perspective."

"That's a bold thought. Wars tend to make a mess of things."

"Well, something has to change radically, because it isn't happening naturally. Politics are still involved in everything here. They're exerting an irrational influence on things. This has to stop if China wants to be a serious country, scientifically and technically."

We accompany Gan back to his office in a building down by the water. He serves us tea and shows me catalogues of the product lines he sells. They comprise a vast selection of tools and hardware at incredibly low prices. I can't imagine any country in the world being able to compete with these prices. Gan doesn't even have to push the product. He merely takes the orders.

His bare office has a view of the grey ocean. Hunched over the thick catalogues, Gan seems perplexed, perhaps by his own destiny. His mild manners don't completely cover his deep, latent frustration. Surely he worked extremely hard to get to the top of his academic field? Surely he made many sacrifices? Maybe he entertained terrific thoughts about China's capacities to out-think and outperform all other nations.

Once at the top, Gan found his country unworthy of his efforts. He found only petty greed and a narrow sense of advantage hiding behind ideological dogma. Now he blandly clocks hours as a tiny cog in the global economy.

China throws it together. Gan gets it to us. We accumulate it. All the while he dreams of war.

Our next appointment is with Doctor Zhang Beichuan, professor of medicine and public health and publisher of a prominent gay magazine. He has an office on the campus of Qingdao University. Locating his office turns out to be complicated: his address doesn't correspond with any of the buildings on the street. The guards we consult at several of the buildings claim no knowledge of Zhang's office. Finally, an old groundskeeper points us in the right direction. Between two main buildings on the university campus, both of them Germanic and imposing, are two rows of brick hovels. The doctor's office is in a hut at the back. The alley leading to it is a mini-*hutong*, cluttered with bicycles, water basins and clotheslines. Along the way, we pass a rough-looking elderly woman cooking something on a brick stove. Viv and I exchange perplexed looks. Some place for a university office.

The good doctor must be about sixty. He's thin and hunched over and has unruly white hair and thick eyeglasses. He wears a white button-down shirt and a worn pair of polyester slacks. Zhang greets us with muted warmth.

His office barely has space for us to sit. It's one long room filled with several tables and cabinets, all covered with huge piles of paper and books. Amid this disarray, the doctor publishes a monthly magazine devoted to homosexual living in China. The doctor's assistant, a round little woman, exits the office to make space for us.

"Forgive me for starting with some facts about myself," the doctor tells me through Vivien. "I'm a doctor of medicine and a professor at this university. By specialization, I'm a nephrologist. But over time my practice has become less involved in case treatment and more and more involved with issues of public health."

"So the magazine has a public health focus?" I venture.

"The magazine's content has a broad focus, but the magazine itself is a public health instrument. We public health workers often say that disease thrives in the dark. So we endeavour to shed light on things, to remove the stigma that favours disease propagation. This was certainly the case with HIV/AIDS in China for many years. In fact, it was one of the reasons this magazine was started. To educate the people and professionals about something that was being ignored while becoming more prevalent."

The doctor then explains how the magazine began addressing

homosexuality: "The stigma toward homosexuality has characteristics similar to the one toward HIV/AIDS. There was a concern that homosexuality too was subject to institutional and individual denial. This facilitated the propagation of HIV, but it also had broad health consequences. In medical terms, denial causes suffering."

"So the magazine is a way of shedding light on an issue and fighting denial?"

"Yes."

"How is homosexuality perceived in China?" I ask.

"There are traditional models in China for understanding homosexuality. It has been tolerated at various times. In modern times, homosexuality is not characterized as some kind of pathological deviancy, as is common in Western culture. Instead, great positive emphasis is put on the Confucian idea of filial duty— which means that to get married and have children is seen as necessary. This again is a factor that encourages denial."

"So denial is inherently unhealthy?"

"Yes. Whatever causes human suffering is unhealthy, both physically and psychologically."

"Who reads the magazine?"

"The magazine is circulated throughout China to individuals and to institutions and NGOs. We distribute four or five thousand copies a month. But we also encourage people to make copies."

"What about Internet publication?"

"No," the doctor says with a humble smile, as though to profess an unfamiliarity with the Web.

The material surroundings of the doctor point to financial challenges also. Internet publication would surely bring greater political obstacles. And perhaps paper lends itself to more intimate reading than the Internet.

Doctor Zhang hands me a copy of the most recent issue. *Magazine* is too strong a word to describe the publication—it's more of a newsletter or brochure. It consists of a half-dozen short articles printed on white paper. I'm unable to understand any of the article titles, but I'm struck by the images: a series of schematic drawings graphically depict various sexual positions. The drawings are clinical, frank and informative. Viv points out an article on oral sex. Another article is about the prevention of sexually transmitted diseases.

I warmly thank the doctor for his time. I am intrigued by this bookish doctor in his obscure cubbyhole of an office.

"Westerners are such prudes," I admit to Viv as we leave. "They make simple things so complicated sometimes."

"I *thought* you might find him interesting."

"He's probably right—acceptance of reality makes for much healthier living for everyone. You know what else I found fascinating about him? I couldn't say whether he himself was gay. I would've thought it relevant."

"Yes, before I met him the first time, I wondered myself."

Our next appointment is with Wei Fang, a businessman Vivien knows. We head toward the water.

"He's of the middle class?" I ask as we walk.

"In China, it isn't always clear who the middle class really is. I'm not always sure how universal such characterizations are," Viv tells me, "but Wei owns a computer and network service business. He has several employees. He has a car and money."

"Well, he sounds like your typical small businessman," I say. "What do you think his politics are? For or against the Communist Party?"

"Businessmen are all the same here," Viv says. "They don't care. As long as they can make money, they work with whoever has the power."

Wei picks us up on the breakwater along the bay. He's a tall and well-groomed man in his mid-thirties. He wears the casual but neat golf attire that entrepreneurs worldwide favour. He drives a new car, a Chinese copy of a Korean sedan. He's confident and generous in his ways. Hardly soft-spoken, he turns to me with a big smile as he speaks. He knows some English but unfortunately not enough to engage in easy conversation.

"I'm always hoping to learn more English," he says, looking pensively at the traffic, "but when?"

We're driving north.

"I'm taking you to the most beautiful and famous part of Qingdao," he says.

With its pleasant hills, large protected bay and mellow maritime climate, Qingdao was once favoured as a retreat by foreigners and later by the Chinese elite. They built Italian-style villas, surrounded by lush gardens and manicured woodlands. These now antiquated domains sprawl up the coast from the harbour. After the flight of the denizens of these neighbourhoods, the Communists took control of the quarter. They enjoyed the luxurious abodes or turned them into guesthouses with which to woo foreign visitors. Recently, many of these mansions have been finding their way back into private hands.

Most prominent among these estates on the water is the stone palace that once belonged to a Russian aristocrat. The villa was later used by Chiang Kai-shek. The ample grounds have now been converted into a public park. We leave the car and set off on foot to meander through the neo-rococo gardens toward the sea.

Although it is a Monday afternoon, the park is filled with people. Couples and families leisurely stroll the grounds. Vendors have set up stalls along the wooded footpaths leading down to the beaches. As we reach the seaside, I am struck by the sight of scores of wedding parties scattered across the rugged and rocky coast. In the afternoon sun, the irregular coastline is indeed quite pretty: the reddish rocky outcroppings strike dramatic poses against the white sand beaches and the blue-green sea. The wooded hills are dotted with cream-coloured Romanesque villas. Photographers scramble about taking pictures of brides and grooms, all identically dressed in flowing white gowns and white tuxedos. It's a happy scene, rife with shrieks and laughter as grooms help their begowned and high-heeled brides over the rocks to choice portrait settings.

"The Mid-Autumn Festival starts soon," Wei says. "It's a very romantic time."

Viv stops to admire some jewellery at one of the beach vendors. Wei magnanimously buys her a pendant.

As we walk the coast, I count over thirty wedding couples, and there's a constant turnover, with new pairs arriving as others depart. Almost every element of the scene is borrowed from the West—the romantic, Europeanized landscape, the white gowns and suits. Still, I find the joyous conformism strikingly Chinese. The same wedding portraits are repeated over and over again by newly arriving couples, dressed identically. The idea is right, so it must be obeyed.

A popular interpretation of Confucius is that, to be happy and respected, we need to all behave in harmonious accord. All dress in the same way, in acknowledgement of our service to common ideals. All make the same oaths. This is a logical consequence of extreme demographic pressures. A billion people packed together require a strong notion of collective harmony. Already long ago, the large populations of the Yellow River basin made for constant friction. A highly developed sense of station and custom provides some relief.

As we continue walking, Wei tells me that his computer business gets contracts to install and maintain networks of computers in offices. He buys the hardware from wholesalers or straight from manufacturers. Most of the gear is Chinese-made, but for the more sophisticated networking gear—server equipment and switches—he occasionally uses foreign-made.

He employs a handful of permanent employees, using outside contractors for most jobs. He explains to me that his business finalizes a new contract perhaps every week. But most work is for large existing clients who are expanding, moving or upgrading.

Wei describes a rather loose tax system in China. In principle, his company must pay a tax on profit, but really it is more like a small flat fee, and his company's reporting requirements are slim. He adds that many of his clients are government entities.

"How do you find clients?" I ask.

"Through contacts."

"Do you advertise? Or do you approach companies with proposals of services?"

Wei grins. "No, it's not like that here. I get contracts from people who know me. You can't get contracts for work here without some kind of relationship."

"You mean, you won't get the job because you have the lowest prices or provide better services?"

Wei grins again, then nods his head in the negative.

"So you pay to get work?" I ask.

"Of course. Anyone involved in getting you work at their company expects something in return."

As for getting paid, Wei explains that all his prices are nego-tiated, often after the work is provided. He admits that it's often hard to get paid. Even when a price is determined beforehand, clients often pay only a portion of it. When I ask him if he some-times needs to use lawyers to ensure that he is paid, he blandly says, "I never have. No, really, I can't imagine it. Also, the gov-ernment clients are the worst at paying. I have still not been paid for work I did last year for some government clients. But I can't exactly start threatening them with lawyers."

"So how do you collect?"

"I use persuasion."

"Sounds hard to do business here," I say sincerely.

"Yes, I work hard. But I enjoy my work," he counters with good humour.

It seems that Wei doesn't find this way of doing business as alarming or as challenging as I do. Perhaps he even accepts these practices as part of the game. And perhaps eager to demonstrate that he plays it with some skill and has prospered, he insists on treating us to an early dinner before our flight onward.

We drive up the coast. I'm amazed that instead of the city dwindling as we get further from the port and old centre, a whole new city erupts before our eyes. This recently built business quar-ter has little to do with the old city. Slick new skyscrapers line up along the wide boulevards. We pull up to a restaurant at the base of a residential tower.

"It's a chain restaurant, but a good one," Viv tells me.

As is often the case in Chinese restaurants, the establishment displays a wide variety of ingredients and prepared dishes, covered by transparent plastic, on tables near the entrance. To order, cus-tomers need only point to those they desire. Within minutes, freshly prepared versions are brought from the kitchen. Good-humoured as ever, Wei is intent that I help him order. Among other things, we order tofu with fish eggs, garlic-stewed eggplant and sea intestine, a kind of marine worm popular in Qingdao, with peppers.

As we eat, I can't help but notice the profusion of soft words that Wei's directing at Viv. She's mostly silent and blushing. As I happily chew on leathery sea intestine, there is no mistaking what is happening: Wei is declaring his romantic feelings for Vivien. Viv's natural coyness soon turns to rigidity and discomfort. Lucky for her, a flight awaits us and we soon have reason to take our leave.

After a pleasant but awkward goodbye, Viv and I climb into a taxi. Viv lets out a big sigh. "Wei's a nice man," she says. "But he's not my type, and he just doesn't want to give up. I don't think that I can see him again."

"Wow, Viv! Shandong is brimming with ex-boyfriends and unwanted suitors."

"He was really starting to get on my nerves. He was listing off all his good qualities! Can you think of anything less appealing?"

"Viv, maybe you should settle down to a comfortable life of marital bliss with a stable businessman husband?"

"Come on!"

"Doesn't Confucius advocate getting married? A simple happy life of devotion?"

"Stop it," she says firmly, turning her head to look out of the window before finally saying, "I don't think I could make a life here. Every time I come back here, it's a little weirder for me. This time seemed especially weird because I'm here working with you and we stayed at a hotel. It's like I'm no longer really connected to this place. It's already far behind me."

CHAPTER 4

The Village

He kept beasts for sacrificial purposes in his kitchen and so was called Kitchen Victims.
—Sima Qian, *Records of the Grand Historian*, first century BC

From a distance, it is easy to gaze upon the dirty farms and rice paddies of China. From the window of a speeding car or train, one can see the occasional man or woman up to their knees in mud, tools in hand. One can only imagine what life might be like in the squalor of these villages where the age-old agricultural practices of China's heartlands are in use.

Country people are crossed in every city and town. In certain places, a good many of the brave folk one encounters were born in the countryside—people who left everything behind to find employment. They are sucked up into city life, with little thought for the landscapes of their childhoods.

At first, Viv cautions me about staying in villages. She doubts that I am "up to it." Wincing, she tells me that they don't have running water there, that they eat strange things and that their homes aren't clean.

I only laugh. Those inconveniences won't bother me.

Then she admits that there's a reason other than comfort for being skeptical about the feasibility of such an enterprise. "Villagers will not be very open to us," she says. "The local authorities will ask us to leave. From their perspective, we have no good reason to visit them."

"How about we stage a car breakdown? We find ourselves suddenly stuck in a village while our vehicle is being repaired."

Viv laughs. "The villagers would organize transportation before offering their homes for us to sleep in."

Behind our humour is some darkness. Vivien is describing villagers inherently suspicious of outsiders, and sure to wonder what hidden agenda or danger might lurk behind our arrival in their hamlet.

But to be fair to them, isn't the idea of going somewhere perfectly mundane and average not questionable? Why would anyone want to travel to somewhere dirty and poor? Where no great person was ever born? Where nothing important ever transpired? What blessing could one possibly seek in such a place?

Viv and I can't simply explain that by sleeping in their village, we hope to learn about the plight of the Chinese peasant class. We would come off as deeply offensive, dishonest or crazy.

"Let's just keep thinking about it, Viv," I say. "There's a lot of countryside in China. Eventually we'll find a way there."

Ironically, the door is opened to us in Chongqing, a huge city. The Chinese call it the biggest municipality in China. But Chongqing is more of a province than a city. It was carved out of Sichuan Province and given "special" status in the mid-nineties. Its territory encompasses a large swath of farmland and numerous towns and villages quite distinct from Chongqing proper, yet the entire thirty million denizens of this territory are considered residents of the city of Chongqing and can move freely within the territory.

Chongqing is deep within China. During the Second World War, Chiang Kai-shek's Kuomintang government retreated here to escape the Japanese occupation along the coast. As Japanese control extended all the way to Burma, the American air force flew supplies into the city from India, over the Himalayas.

Chongqing is the riverine gateway to mythic and enigmatic western China. It is both unique and highly representative. Unique because it is huge and politically autonomous. Representative because it exemplifies the Chinese megalopolis: both ancient and brand spanking new. Chongqing grows at a tremendous rate, sucking in incredible amounts of resources from the countryside. An example of the rapid growth made possible by rapid urbanization, it's a place of much hope and some despair.

We arrive in Chongqing late at night, the airport bright, new and relatively empty. The taxi, clean and also new, speeds us silently along a sleek highway toward the city. Crisp illuminated billboards line the road. The windows of the taxi are rolled down, and a balmy, moist breeze floods in. Hints of jungle are in the air.

In the thick, dark night, the city core where we'll be staying is like a fortress, perched on steep cliffs above great rivers. Access to it is through a network of bridges, elevated highways and tunnels that wind their way over river and through mountain up to the city's high redoubt.

Our hotel's neighbourhood looks shut down for the night. Tree-lined avenues snake through dense rows of skyscrapers. But human life is absent. A Chinese Gotham, ever so slightly sinister. Shops hide behind metal shutters.

Our taxi driver is not quite sure where we're going. He drops us in front of a building that looks closed and dark. Viv tells him to wait. We bang on the glass doors of the supposed hotel, peering in at a wide, dark and dusty lobby, then return to the car, laughing anxiously.

When we finally find our hotel, we beat a quick retreat to our rooms to sleep. I'm filled with the mystery of the disturbingly quiet, urban landscape outside my window. I pay heed to every sound, then remind myself that I'm in China, not Beirut or Baghdad, and that no violence lurks in the silence.

By morning, the anxiety is forgotten. Chongqing is now completely different. It's hot, noisy and busy. It makes me think of what Pittsburgh might have been in its heyday. A rambling, hilly place above its rivers—the mighty Yangtze and the still respectable Jialing. But its proportions are unprecedented. Its clusters of high-rises multiply across the hills, a true urban jungle, still quite organic with tufts of thicket and bamboo growing wherever it's too steep to build. A marvellous chaos.

Travel in Chongqing can be done in two ways: by automobile through tortuous and traffic-choked streets, or on foot along an intricate network of stone staircases that connect the upper city on the hills to the lower city along the river. Occasionally, one discovers patches of old Chongqing neighbourhoods accessible only by foot, too treacherous and wild to be properly controlled. Once places of gambling and vice, fire and magic, the few remaining are now clearly doomed.

The traditional guardians of these quarters were porters. Chongqing once used manpower to carry goods between the Yangtze and the city above. Some of these men remain. They are an ancient and disappearing caste; a cog, a prototypical migrant worker, hewn from the hardiest peasant stock and armed with rope and a bamboo pole.

These men are not only old school—carrying two bundles hanging off either end of their shoulder-slung poles—they are old for such hard work. Most of them seem to be in their fifties or older. A dying breed. Too old to find work in the factories, these are men who have been displaced, who lost their land or were somehow unable to make it work as farmers or in the new economy. I can only imagine where they live.

Still, silent and dedicated, the porters seem to take pride in their work as human beasts of burden. Old Chongqing may almost be gone, but wherever the porters still carry goods up from the muddy flux, the old order faintly endures.

Our journey leads us to a more modern type of migrant worker. Through a colleague of hers, Vivien established contact with a Chongqing lawyer who acts for injured migrant workers. Although the lawyer is now based in Shenzhen, a southern manu-facturing city, his brother runs an office for him in Chongqing and agreed to introduce us to some migrant workers.

Li Gang is presented to us in the gloomy halls on the seven-teenth floor of a partially completed office tower. He's ripping out plaster with a hammer. As we follow him down a few flights of stairs, I am momentarily confused about what we are doing. A hint of war-zone anxiety kicks in and I suddenly feel uneasy about following someone I don't know to an unknown location through a darkened stairwell. It doesn't take me long to buck out of it and remind myself that I'm in China, not some dangerous place.

Li Gang leads us to a dishevelled sitting room where we can talk more comfortably. Light floods through the windows and I take a better look at him. He's short and slight, with long and bony features. He sports a wispy moustache and goatee. His right fore-arm is missing.

He tells us his arm was smashed in a faulty industrial press in Guangzhou some years ago. Li Gang was born to a very poor peasant family in a village about sixty kilometres up the Yangtze from Chongqing. The elementary school, which he attended, was a good hour's walk from his home. The high school was at least a four-hour walk away. To study there he would have had to find boarding near the school, and his parents didn't have the money for that.

With few other options, Li Gang hit the road. In 1994, at age fourteen, he headed to the south coast of China, where the first free-market boom occurred. He quickly found that no fac-tories would employ someone as young as him. He gravitated to construction sites and eventually got the only kind of work an unskilled kid could get: portering. It was hard, crude work and kept him just barely fed for a couple of years.

When he was sixteen, he managed to land work at a television manufacturer, where he was assigned to a giant plastics press that churned out casings for the televisions. His pay was four hundred yuan a month—less than two dollars a day—and he worked seven days a week. The machines at the factory were all quite old. Li Gang tells us that from the start he was slightly afraid of the one he operated. The plastic press was a huge metal beast: old, angry and noisy. After the plastic had been heated and pressed into the appropriate shape, Li would reach into the monster's jaws and pry out the casing.

For months he complained that the safety lock on the press's jaws was not functioning properly. His superiors only chided him for his repeated complaints. Then one day it happened. As he was reaching into the beast, its enormous jaws closed. It got his arm. From just below Li's elbow right down to his hand, his forearm was pulp.

Vivien squirms in her seat.

"What did it feel like?" she nervously inquires. Li Gang is perfectly calm. He has told the story a thousand times.

"Nothing," he says. "I didn't feel anything. Actually, only small pains hurt. Big pains like mine don't hurt at all. That's what makes them even scarier. My mangled arm looked and felt like it was not even a part of me."

The manufacturer initially offered him the yuan equivalent of three thousand dollars as compensation. He felt that he had no choice but to accept it. But later he heard about a lawyer who specialized in workplace accidents; he was told that this lawyer could argue for more appropriate compensation. He contacted the lawyer, who agreed to take his case. After a lengthy trial at which numerous witnesses were called, the lawyer managed to prove that the company had indeed been negligent, that it hadn't maintained its machinery properly and that this had led to Li's injury. The court ordered the company to pay Li the equivalent of about twenty-two thousand dollars, which the company never fully paid out.

Li eventually returned to his village. He used the money to buy stock for a little grocery store he opened in his home. But he soon found that the store and attending to his mother's tiny parcel of land didn't generate much of an income, so he returned to Chongqing to find odd jobs at construction sites, leaving the store for his mother and wife to look after. He has become proficient at handling tools with the stump where his arm was amputated.

Li Gang may be a dirt-poor migrant worker, but he has a

strangely peaceful energy about him. He has a certain poise, and radiates a calm and wisdom. I long to know more about his origins. We talk more about his village and his life there.

Li has two children. He explains that peasants were partially exempt from China's recently abolished one-child policy: some were allowed to have a second child. Li's first child, a son, lives with his wife's parents in a village fifty kilometres north of Chongqing. He explains that his wife's parents never liked him and insisted on taking the boy from their daughter. Because Li needed to make his living in the city and was away from home for weeks on end, he was unable to resist his parents-in-law. He sees his son perhaps once a year.

Li's situation with his son, whereby his in-laws virtually kidnapped his first-born, is not unique in China. Beyond the particular dynamics of Li's family, children are precious but until recently also forbidden in any numbers. So they are stashed away in unlikely ways.

And behind all this, the Confucian way still dominates. For the Chinese, children are the only obvious way toward immortality. We're immortal only insofar as we live on through our children's children—a belief that's hard to argue with.

The cornerstone of Confucian morality is filial duty, and the respect that children must have for their parents. It's not simply enough to have children; they have to make a real contribution to the common good, beginning with their family. This ensures a family of a name, a place and perhaps a legacy.

Through the ages, Confucius has been regularly discredited as elitist—or worse, a friend of tyranny and oppression. But the sage's teachings still have huge resonance in China and need to be understood if Chinese society is to be understood.

In Confucian thought, the individual is regarded as the builder of the nation. But all nation building starts with the family. One builds by making sacrifices for one's family and assuming more and more responsibility, making more and more sacrifices for higher purposes. One is not judged by what one has achieved for oneself, but by what one has achieved for one's family, one's town and one's country. What indeed is wealth, or success, if it is not a blessing on one's kin through the ages?

At bottom, Confucianism is a responsibility of memory. Parents teach their children to one day assume responsibility for themselves and others. They teach them to become good parents and good citizens, to accept, obey and respect. At a deeper level, parents teach their children and grandchildren to remember, and teach them that an individual is no individual at all, standing alone and for oneself, but that every man, woman, father, mother, son and daughter is a piece of a bridge. With both past and future resting heavy on their shoulders, something grand is being passed on through the ages.

Li Gang, his injury, his family life and his village are a window deep into China. Sensing my curiosity, Li offers to take us to his village. Viv and I immediately realize that this is our opening.

Li suggests that we rent a four-by-four, to make the journey there and back in a single day. Too expensive and not interesting, I decide. I ask Viv to find out if we can sleep in the village and use local transportation to get there and back.

Li feels the need to explain the obvious: we would be welcome to spend the night, but his village and his family are extremely poor. We cannot expect to find the comforts of the city there.

Once more, Viv cautions me about the nature of country living, but I'm grinning from cheek to cheek and Li himself cuts her off. "This one," he says to Viv, referring to me, "seems like the type of guy who seeks out hardships and enjoys them."

With the lawyer's assistance, Li makes the arrangements to take two days off work. A taxi brings us to a suburb of Chongqing. From there, we need to find a bus that will take us deep into the countryside. At the station, Li goes off to look for the right bus. He comes back and reports that one is leaving right away, but it's not a new bus and he again wonders whether we are up to a rough journey. This time both Viv and I laugh off his doubts as we head to the ticket booth. Li nods to us amiably, as if to say, "I know, I know, country living is no problem for you, but don't blame me for the formality of being considerate."

The bus has seen long years of action. Inside it has been stripped down to the barest necessities of service and is packed with the largest possible number of rough metal seats. When we climb onto it, it's already half-filled with a colourful assortment of peasants: the old and toothless are amused by the sight of me; the young and hardy, too self-absorbed to bother caring. I grab a seat near the back and am charmed to see that, although I'm by no means a tall man, the space between the backrest of my seat and the seat in front of me will not fit my thighs from hip to knee. To accommodate them, I have to swivel my legs diagonally toward the seat beside me.

Just after we leave the station, the bus stops to pick up a middle-aged woman with big baskets filled with groceries. Immediately after that, the bus is waved to a halt by some cops. A bizarre scene ensues. A policeman climbs onto the bus, armed with a video camera. Listing off their faults, he films the bus driver and the woman passenger. He then proceeds to record their personal details and recites the offence of boarding the bus at an unregistered stop.

Viv tells me that this is a common occurrence in China. By boarding outside the station, the middle-aged woman could ride without a ticket, for a lesser fee. By the driver accepting this unofficial passenger, the operator can avoid giving the state its robust portion of the ticket price. Li adds that the bus actually belongs to his second cousin, but he'll soon be selling it.

The costs to operate the buses have been increasing, and police crackdowns are making it more difficult for bus operators to collect under-the-table fees. One company is purchasing all the licences in this area. This might mean new buses but higher ticket prices, Li muses.

"You can bet that someone bribed some official to be able to take control of all the routes," Viv says. "With traps like this, the police are helping pressure the independents out of business."

As we wait for the police to finish with the formalities, a mini-van drives by making a huge racket. It's one of those old-school "town crier" vehicles, with huge multidirectional loudspeakers mounted on its roof.

"Someone wants to get elected?" I wonder aloud.

"No," Viv says, giggling, "they're announcing that strippers are now putting on a show at some venue on the outskirts of town."

The bus leaves town and proceeds deeper and deeper into the countryside. After an hour or so, we get off at a crossroads in a newly built part of a little town. Although it's in the middle of nowhere, the place hardly even feels like it's still in the country-side. It's strangely built up. The street has not even been prop-erly paved yet, yet it's lined with more than a dozen three- and four-storey concrete-block apartment buildings, freshly erected, mostly uninhabited.

"Buildings for people displaced by the flooded Yangtze River," Li explains.

As we walk toward the centre of the village, Li conceals his missing forearm by putting the end of the stump in his jacket pocket. He leads us to eat at the village's finest restaurant. Viv and I raise our eyebrows when we see that the only other diners for lunch are the town's police chief and some town officials.

"Make sure that the foreigner registers with us as soon as possible," one of them barks at us as he leaves the restaurant.

"He's just visiting and won't be staying," Li responds politely. Before he finishes his sentence, the official is already walking out the door.

Li takes us to find another bus that will take us closer to his home village. Another dishevelled vehicle packed with locals stops to pick us up. It embarks into the hilly countryside on an ancient, unpaved road.

"Look how dry the countryside is," Viv points out. "I even heard about it in the news: this region is experiencing the worst drought in living memory."

In the afternoon sun, the colours of the blighted landscape are enchanting. The exposed and parched earth is a beautiful chocolate brown. The fields are pockmarked with well-defined cracks and crevices. The dried stalks of rice and corn remain, golden and shiny. Here and there, bamboo groves bring a fresh green tint to the vista.

The road is rough and rugged. We pass innumerable farms. Their red-brick walls and dark grey roofs add yet more hues to the portrait. Viv notices that we drive past someone walking his bicycle, two baskets hanging off either side. In each basket is a pig.

"Pig baskets!" she exclaims. "Until now, I didn't quite know what one was. We are told that in old times, adulterous women were put in them and then thrown in a pond. Not a nice thing!"

Finally, we arrive in yet another village. It's not our final destination, I'm told, but we're close. We cross the street toward some shops. An elderly farmer passing by looks at me with complete surprise and happily pipes up, "Aieee! *Yang Da Ren.*"

Viv can hardly hide her amusement. "I have never heard a more antiquated title: Your Highness Foreigner!"

Viv and I are left to wait in a shop that sells pig feed. We take a seat on the big bags of it. Li goes to arrange transportation to his village. He returns with three men on mopeds.

"Sorry for the wait," he says, "but I wanted to find really good moped drivers. They're more expensive, perhaps, but are less likely to wipe out on the trail."

The trail is indeed a little treacherous. Making its way through the hilly terrain, it climbs along the sides of steep banks. With patches of exposed stones, the trail is at times extremely bumpy. We clench our moped seats as the two-wheeled vehicles toss about on the rugged trail. Finally, after six or seven kilometres, we come to a halt amid a dozen or so brick and stone huts: Li's village.

Li's home is a hovel. It's an ancient one-room, thatched-roof habitation built of stone. It seems the poorest hut in the village and is packed with stuff. The family's bed takes up the back third of the room. To one side, a wooden couch makes for a sitting area. At the front of the hut, beside its only window—which is glassless—is Li's tiny grocery store. He sells dried noodles, a few canned goods, batteries and a limited selection of sweets. Li's wife is very young and sweet-faced. In the tiny dark room, she quietly tends to the couple's one-year-old daughter.

The people in the village can hardly be deemed friendly; they make no effort to come say hello to us. For the briefest of moments they study us from a distance without expression, then go back to their business.

Within minutes of arriving, I notice two mah-jong games going on nearby. These villagers play the game seriously, quickly and energetically. They don't speak a lot while playing. They play immediately when it's their turn. And they slap their tiles down on the table with force. It would seem that the goal is to make a crisp, snapping sound with the tiles as they hit the surface.

I can see why they play mah-jong: What else is there to do in the village, when there is nothing to plant or harvest? Amused by the lack of activity, I turn to Viv with a smile. "What do you think?"

"Actually, not a whole lot different from my grandparents' village. I was there for months as a child. Sure, the landscape's not the same. They plant different things. They build differently. But the village feels very similar."

Suddenly and without warning, right in front of us in the middle of the village, a boisterous argument breaks out between a middle-aged farmer and a slightly younger, rough-looking man with a bicycle. They shout and shout, sputtering a daunting successions of syllables at each other. It's like machine-gun fire, and totally incomprehensible to me. Sometimes they shoot their invective in bursts, sometimes in long sequences; sometimes they take turns shouting at each other. But most often, they simultaneously let it rip at each other at high volume. Amazingly, they argue for over half an hour. This boggles my mind. I have never seen this before, two people just standing there, furiously yelling at each other for such a long time.

The farmer wears ragged cut-off pyjamas and sandals. He carries a three-metre-long paddy hoe. He's short and wiry. The other man is heavier-set and looks tough in his black pants and black shirt. Yet neither of them looks like he will resort to physical violence. The farmer eventually begins to walk out to the dried-up rice paddies, yet doesn't relent in his verbal attacks. The other man continues down the road. For the last ten minutes of the argument, the two men are yelling at each other over quite a distance. Stranger still, I seem to be the only person in the village paying attention to them.

Worn out by our rough journey, Viv is dozing on Li's couch. At the first sign of consciousness, I rouse her so that she can explain to me what is happening. She has trouble making out the dialect but determines that they keep repeating "one hundred and thirty-five yuan." It seems they're arguing over twenty dollars.

Perhaps they are just putting their feud on public record. Now, whether they like it or not, everyone in the village knows their respective grievances. Perhaps so begins a slow process of justice by which people will be held responsible for their wrongs and subtly sanctioned. Or most likely, they are just in a grumpy mood like everyone else because of the drought that ended the season early and is eating into already meagre incomes.

Li takes us out into the fields. He shows us his mother's dried-up paddies. The ground is really parched.

"Where do you get your drinking water?" I ask him.

"The county government brings it in with a water truck."

Beyond the paddies, the plateau unexpectedly recedes and a big gorge opens up in the landscape. We descend into it, and Li shows us a small temple built into the cliff.

"The village shrine," he explains.

A man is working in the shrine, sculpting statuettes out of clay.

"Some of the old figures were damaged, so the village has hired this artist to make new ones," Li says.

No clear faith is represented in the shrine. Distant ancestors. Buddhism mixed with local lore, with some Taoism for good measure, a modicum of protection and benevolence from beyond in a time of need.

When we return to the village, I realize that the village is completely devoid of young people. It's inhabited by toddlers, babies, the middle-aged and the elderly. Apart from Li Gang and his wife, I cannot spot a single soul older than five years or younger than forty.

In the late afternoon, one missing demographic group finally makes an appearance. The school-age children return, having walked the seven kilometres back from their elementary school, and are greeted with joy by their grandparents.

I learn that the teenagers are either boarding in the closest town or are out in the wide world, working odd jobs as Li once did. The parents of the children, people in their twenties and thirties, are mostly in the cities, working in the factories. The children are often raised by grandparents.

As the magic hour approaches when the shadows are long and for a few precious minutes the sunrays run almost parallel to the land, I decide to take a walk out of the village. To get a good look at the surrounding countryside, I climb a nearby hill. From the top, I can see up to several kilometres away.

Across the rolling hills, as far as I can see, are farms and fields. I count a dozen groupings of houses like Li's village. Each one only a few hundred metres apart. Not a centimetre of this vast land left to its own devices. Every parcel of soil put to use. Every contour of the terrain terraced and planted. Each plot of land a tiny parcel only a few hundred square metres in area.

I focus on the sounds of the landscape: the barking of dogs, the clucking of chickens, the crying of children, the banging, the brushing. As each sound becomes distinct, the land comes alive with activity. I get an eerie sense of just how many people inhabit this countryside and conclude that I'm looking upon the most densely populated farmland I have ever seen, and that this territory has been full of people for several millennia.

I then picture the countryside unfolding for tens of kilometres in all directions, all of it densely filled with little farms and villages. Then I stretch my mind out further to include a few small cities like the ones we passed through on our way here, each inhabited by tens of thousands of people, each surrounded by dense countryside. Then I envision a city like Chongqing: a cluster of people living one on top of the other, by the millions. I think of the territory I flew over to get to Chongqing from Qingdao, the thousand or so kilometres of terrain, the central heartland of China, filled for the near entirety of the distance with countryside much like this one: village upon village, clustered around big and small towns and around immense cities. I smile as I realize that, after so many years, I finally have a good image of the measure of more than a billion people.

When I return to the village, I notice how my walk made people uncomfortable, another proof of their foul mood. When in plain sight and accounted for, my presence is slightly discomforting to them, but when I am out wandering the countryside on my own, unaccounted for, I must be downright nerve-racking.

In this dense landscape of people held together in a delicate balance, everything must be measured carefully, right down to the twenty dollars that the butcher may owe the farmer if he is to be charged this year's price of feed corn for last year's corn delivered but still not entirely paid for. New variables that might upset the equilibrium are greeted with apprehension. The persistent lack of rain this year is a source of constant worry. It could upset everything. But the lone westerner may also bring chaos into the fine balance. He may attract unwanted attention from the authorities or disturb something while he passes through.

This is not to say that this countryside is unchanging. Li's hut has a telephone in it. When I return from my walk, he asks whether I have a laptop computer with me. When I tell him that I didn't bring it, he tells me that I could have connected it to the Internet through his phone line. I also notice that my cell phone is getting a signal.

This village is nowhere, really, but it's connected to the rest of China in a whole variety of ways, both wired and wireless. It is home to people a thousand kilometres away, living in dormitories and toiling away in factories, or camping out in makeshift shacks and working on huge construction sites. In its own way, this village is an active part of the whole. It cannot be ignored or neglected. It's important. Called on to provide food and labour to the full extent of its capacities, one child at a time. In turn, China must bring blessings upon this village and its people.

China's accumulation of people has not been a smooth process, a mellow slope of gradual increase through the ages. Historical population numbers are never easy to measure, but those featured in historical records show the population in China as mostly stable for long periods. The living merely replace the dead. Occasionally, in times of disease, upheaval and famine, the population was in decline and the dead steadily outnumbered new arrivals to life. And sometimes, the living grew legion and the population was in such rapid expansion as to send the counter forward by huge leaps.

But on such a scale, growth can also conceal disastrous singularities. Whole villages can be obliterated by starvation or war while elsewhere in the country children multiply. Family after family can emerge into lives of permanent hardship yet survive long enough to, like those who came before them, procreate profusely. Immense demographic gains can be achieved with five of every ten children perishing of violence, hunger and disease.

In the late Qing dynasty, just over a hundred years ago, much of the Chinese countryside was owned by large landholders who relied on masses of impoverished peasants to farm the land. These peasants' annual salary was little more than a bag of rice and rent on a hut. The peasants who actually owned land were also dismally poor, and whatever meagre surplus they could generate was often entirely owed in taxes. The utterly destitute roamed the land and insecurity was rife. Births were numerous but so were deaths.

Born of a rich peasant father in a territory of abuse and misery, Mao Zedong was acutely sensitive to the pulse of rural China. Unlike the city-born sons of privilege, he was viscerally aware of the rage and endurance of the peasant. His arguments for a peasant revolution were made forcefully in the early meetings of the burgeoning Communist Party of China, but he was chided or ignored by the movement's elite, whose views espoused the Marxist doctrine of a workers' revolution that would first harness the power of the nation and take control of industrial production. For the urbane Communist intellectuals, the fraternity of enlightened factory workers must have seemed far more solid a foundation for a new society than the depravity of peasants.

But Mao was stubborn. Despite being sidelined through the 1920s, he never relinquished his idea of a peasant revolution. He remained convinced that only the peasant's wretchedness, borne of immense suffering, had the potency to turn the poor and parasite-ridden earth of China and allow a new nation to bloom. He instinctively understood that the revolution had to start in the countryside.

From 1928 to 1933—dark and difficult times for the Communist Party of China—Mao formed a small band of adepts and roamed the hills of the border region of southern Jiangxi, eastern Hunan and western Fujian. In these remote corners of China, he perfected his understanding of rural society and experimented with peasant violence.

Wherever he went it was easy to find malcontents—plenty of people were barely surviving and receiving nothing from the powers above them, treated not as humans but as commodities to be consumed and traded. From among them, men and women could be recruited. Mobs could be assembled rapidly, especially if first allowed to bring violence upon the most immediate sources of injustice: the greedy local trader, the corrupt magistrate or the venal landlord family. Mao would promise the malcontents a new China and a new world, and would encourage them to be bold and decisive, to become a force of justice—a new people's army— and to purge China of her scourges.

He played with the forces of chaos and order. Coming upon communities, he sought to decant their frustrations and unleash waves of violence on what was a semblance of order. Yet at the same time, he attempted to galvanize and unify into a single harmonious force the people's guilt and will to survive and prosper. Once atrocities were committed, the peasants could hardly turn back; they were fully invested in the revolution.

As he fostered this principle across village after village, commune after commune, Mao began to wield an incredible weapon. Although it remained unclear what society might emerge from the destruction, it became more and more certain that Mao and the peasants could destroy all things before them and might well vanquish the Kuomintang and gain control of China.

Peasant violence had its advantages but also its disadvantages. It was crude and messy. Peasants were not skilled soldiers. They were unpredictable. And pulling them from their already-poor farms to be sent into costly battles often resulted in further shortages and an increase of suffering. The violence could also be induced by competing factions and turned on itself in destructive rampages. In the wilderness, rival camps within the Communist Party wielding peasant mobs repeatedly waged vicious purges and campaigns against each other.

Mao was a careful witness to all of this. He began to conclude that discord among the peasants mirrored the larger discord within China itself. Once unified, the nation would be free of contradictions and find balance.

Mao had great faith in the land itself. He believed that if rid of its scourges of greed and decadence, China would provide for its people. If the forces of food production were rationalized and rid of parasitical elements, the people would prosper, food would be plentiful and more sophisticated types of production could be implemented.

Mao's vision was hardly novel: the virtuous society, free of all vices, had long promised a rich bounty. But Mao was as much conqueror as philosopher, and like Alexander, Genghis or Napoleon, he embraced and admired catastrophic violence. New orders, he felt, could be forged only in battle, through great destruction and upheavals. But the bold would be rewarded.

In conquest, it's a natural and logical step to embrace the idea of ambitious population growth. A movement finds its ultimate expression of success in a new world full of healthy children, children who grow up to be strong and selfless servants of a harmonious new order. So Mao adamantly encouraged childbirth, and China's population experienced immense growth in the early years of the revolution.

During the Great Leap Forward, starting in the late 1950s, Mao concluded that peasant force alone would not safeguard China from its enemies. He decided that China should be in a position to satisfy on its own the entirety of its various appetites. He thus enacted a series of reforms aimed primarily at the countryside. Mao dreamt that the countryside would become the new centre of industry in China, a diffuse and inexhaustible source of essential products. Farmers were told to build iron smelters.

The Great Leap Forward was born of the sense of urgency to match Western and even Soviet achievements in the nuclear age. But the Leap also had as its foundation Mao's ideal that Communism could not help but bring about vast material improvements and innovations. It was only a question of virtue. And this merely had to be taught to the people.

Mao, however, had grown far from the people. His ideas were increasingly abstract and philosophical. If implemented, they would bring about damaging absurdities. More often, they were never fully implemented. Whole societies chanted them aloud and pretended they were real, but they were not, nor could they be.

Slogans multiplied, and villages across the country were integrated into a national campaign for rapid self-sufficiency and slapped with impossible production quotas. Not only did the rural population fail to produce anything close to the quantity and quality of goods that were necessary for China to assure its position as a modern industrial power but, distracted from their farms, the peasants who fed China began to experience massive food shortages. The Great Leap Forward caused a great famine.

To this day, the party has made it impossible to properly fathom how many people died in the famines caused by the policies of Mao's Great Leap Forward. But the Chinese population still grew under Chairman Mao. Even in error and calamity, he achieved his billionaire kingdom.

But China's ancient measure of success was always much more than a demographic milestone reached by the masses, or a matter of mere numbers. There was something more subtle and grandiose to which Mao and his party needed to answer.

It is said that the emperors of China governed the land by virtue of a heavenly mandate. As such, their authority was sacrosanct. But the mandate also meant that, through the emperor, the people had to be the benefactors of heaven's blessings. The emperor was beyond reproach but only so long as his rule was by and large beneficial. Of course, no single person could decide that the emperor's rule was not a happy one; only China as a whole could conclude that it was not blessed by the heavens under the rule of such and such emperor. This could only mean that the dynasty had lost the heavenly mandate and the emperor had lost his legitimacy. So ended many dynasties in China.

In the few decades immediately after the revolution, the Communist Party was largely embraced by China because it was perceived to hold the heavenly mandate by which great blessings would be meted out to a long-suffering people. It delivered a wholly Chinese government to China for the first time in centuries. It united China for the first time in a long time and offered a new hope to the poorest class of China: the landless peasants, hundreds of millions strong. It also commanded violence so convincingly that no one dared oppose it.

But by the time of Mao's death in the mid-1970s, too many great experiments had gone desperately wrong. Popular belief in the Communist Party was mostly bankrupt. Although more numerous than ever, the people were tired, unhappy and afraid. They began to sense that the heavenly mandate might be withdrawing.

Still, the dynasty had its quiet protectors. With Mao's increasing withdrawal into senility, Mao's right-hand man, the venerable and wise Zhou Enlai, allowed a reformist movement to survive in the face of fierce opposition within the party. Some even say that Zhou was himself a reformist at heart. But his own life force was waning. He himself would not play an active role in bringing about change but would use his power to protect future champions of change. One such champion was Deng Xiaoping, a diminutive and clever early member of the party.

At the time of Mao's death, an extremist clique known as the Gang of Four (which included the chairman's monstrous widow, former actress Jiang Qing) was poised to take over. But in a quick and unexpected succession of events, the Gang of Four was summarily purged by discreet military leaders still part of the remaining old guard, and Deng Xiaoping was summoned back from the abyss and propelled to the fore. Without Mao above him, Deng would ensure that his pragmatic vision for China would succeed. He became the Communist Party's dominant figure after Mao Zedong, a second emperor of the Communist dynasty.

Deng was not a man of forceful slogans. His most famous mantras show a flexibility never exhibited by Mao. "Who cares if the cat is black or white as long as it catches mice?" was Deng's cry for the triumph of pragmatism in party policy above and beyond rigid ideology. Deng also famously said of Mao that he made mistakes but was right seven-tenths of the time. A strange endorsement considering the sizable divergences of vision between the two and the calamities Deng suffered during the Cultural Revolution. In truth, Deng knew that his own authority and the political stability he needed for reform required the dynastic legitimacy of Mao. So Deng carefully ensured that Mao's party, the Communist Party of China, and Mao's image if not his ideas would oversee the next phase of China's transformation. To this day, Mao's iconic mug graces the Chinese currency and lords over Tiananmen Square.

Deng's most telling saying—"To get rich is glorious"—heralded the advent of a new logic, the pursuit of prosperity. Prosperity has perhaps even eclipsed all other virtues of Communist power in China. For many, prosperity has become the only benchmark for legitimacy. As the memory of wars, diseases and famines grows faint, what else could better motivate the people?

Communist Party rule will be tolerated only so long as it creates widespread wealth in China. So, according to Deng's plan, over the last four decades, the Chinese central government has made itself relevant to the people not by making huge ideological demands on them or even requiring huge leaps in their production capacity but by methodically investing in the infrastructure and means of production while gradually allowing the principles of free trade to return to Chinese society.

In the new configuration, Li's village, for instance, is not an unknown speck left to its own devices, as it was a century ago, nor is it expected to produce new and improved kinds of humans, as Mao perhaps might have hoped. The different layers of Chinese government have brought electricity and telecommunications wires to Li's village. They broadcast television and mobile phone signals to it. They truck in drinking water for the people in times of need. Eventually, the Chinese will build a proper road to the village, to make it easier to deliver water and simpler to extract the fruits of the land. Increasingly guided by an invisible hand, China reaches into its bosom, both taking and giving, becoming more united than ever before.

Deng also relinquished Mao's obsession with self-sufficiency. Deng reasoned that China does not need to answer every one of its many needs; it can focus on what it does best and trade for the rest. Such a trade economy became plausible when relations were normalized with the West in the early 1970s. With proper management, Deng calculated, China's immense labour pool could form the basis of a manufacturing economy aimed at the export market.

Four decades into Deng's gambit, he has been proven right: those things that China is lacking, like food, raw materials and energy, are largely made up for by the manufactured products it sells on the world market.

Although Deng started liberalizing the economy in the villages by allowing farmers to trade their surplus produce, the massive wealth in the new China stems more from urban industry than agricultural labour. China has perhaps not turned its back on its age-old agricultural sector, but in most places it now almost seems as though farming is an outlet for surplus labour not used in the factories—like in Li's village, where only the middle-aged and elderly remain to tend to the crops, while the young and able toil in the manufacturing centres.

Yet because much of the manufacturing labour is derived from the villages, wealth is not trapped in the cities but trickles down to the villages. Li and his hundred million brethren send a portion of their income back to their dependents in the villages.

This distribution of wealth is further enforced by the dual residency system. The situation in Chongqing is unique in that, technically, the peasants of Li's village are inhabitants of the municipality of Chongqing and are allowed to work and reside in the city. But in most of China, village dwellers are not allowed to reside in the cities. They cannot legally pay rent or make real estate purchases there and are thus denied a major outlet for their income. If they want to save or invest their earnings, migrant workers are forced to do so in their villages.

That evening, Viv and I are to be Li's guests. He has gone all out for dinner. His tiny table surely hasn't seen a spread like this in a long time: roast duck with scallions, candied pork meat, vegetable broth, mushrooms with ginger, two types of sautéed greens and rice. Wisely, Li has invited the local party secretary and his wife to dine with us.

A more surprising guest also shows up at the feast: the rough chap from the afternoon's dramatic argument, who turns out to be the village butcher and holds a station of some prominence. The heated disagreement with the farmer seems to have had little impact on him. He now cuts a rather merry figure. Li explains that the butcher will be hosting me that night, while Viv will spend the night with Li's mother in the house next to his. I look to the butcher and he is beaming, enthused by the chance to show hospitality to a stranger from halfway across the planet.

The party secretary is eager to know more about Viv and me. Viv answers most of the questions. She explains that I'm a tourist on vacation and that I've hired her to be my guide and translator. The whole story sounds outlandish to me. But somehow Viv manages to explain it to him in a satisfactory way. Still, the party secretary wants to hear me speak.

"What do you do in your home country?" he asks.

As she translates Viv cautions me to make something up. But she catches me off guard and I draw a blank. I finally just blurt out that I'm a television producer. Not exactly a lie, and not exactly helpful either. I should have seized the opportunity to finally become an architect à la George Costanza. Viv makes sure to add that I produce a show on art and culture in my country, something as remote as possible from news and journalism.

"Is this your first time in China?" the secretary asks.

"Say yes," Viv urges. I do.

"Where else have you been in the world?" the man then inquires.

"Oh, I have been to many places, in Europe, Asia and Africa," I tell him, unwilling to continue lying. "I've travelled a lot."

"And what do you think of China?"

"It's simply immense," I say, quite sincerely. "I could travel in China for the rest of my life and not see the half of it."

The party secretary seems to appreciate my somewhat empty answer, which combines both awe and humility. Having won his favour, I try my luck at a flattering line of inquiry. "Has this village produced many university students?"

"Oh yes, nearly a dozen. Our own son is currently studying at a university."

"Congratulations," I say. "I see a good future for this village."

The meal ends pleasantly. The party secretary and his wife take their leave, uttering good wishes to Viv and me. The butcher also heads home. We sit around with Li, drinking tea. Out of the blue, Li says, "I know I'm poor and will probably not achieve much in my life, but I look at the things I have, my wife and my daughter, and you know what? I'm happy. I do not want anything else. I already have all that I'll ever need."

Viv and I look at each other in amazement. This Li Gang really is a unique individual. A free man, perhaps? We are almost envious of him.

My sleepover at the butcher's house turns out to be amusing. The butcher is really a jolly fellow. He's also a better example of village prosperity than Li is. His home serves as a meeting spot for the village, or bar, or mah-jong parlour. The house is relatively big, two storeys high and built out of cement blocks. A large room on the ground floor opens to the street, similar to a garage or mechanic's bay. It's filled with tables and chairs.

When I arrive, the last of the day's mah-jong players are just exiting. A huge television is at the back of the room. The butcher proudly shows me that it's connected to a satellite dish. He flips through the channels, beaming a huge toothless grin at me. Ten channels from India, four from Pakistan, eleven from Arabia, twenty from Europe, and so on. He hands me the remote, and I settle on francophone TV5 and learn of ever more deaths in Iraq.

I notice how incredibly filthy the butcher's parlour is. Impressively filthy, really. Dried earth and spittle are caked on the cement floor, which is littered with cigarette butts and chicken bones, speckled with bloodstains and tea leaves. As I soak it all up, two immense flying cockroaches dive-bomb into the room and hit the floor near my feet.

The butcher rouses me from this poignant spectacle and urges me to follow him. He takes me to the back of the house, where he keeps the pigs. Although the smell of swine dung permeates the building, the concentration of it in the kitchen and in the swine's room just off the kitchen is a showstopper. Three pigs are rummaging away in the darkness. Through a series of gestures, the butcher manages to explain to me that he will slaughter the pigs at four-thirty in the morning. He invites me to watch him. I have seen the slaughter of pigs before; it's quite a spectacle. The pig is one of those animals that somehow has a sense of its impending death. It squeals bloody murder. With a bow and upstretched palms, I indicate to him that I'll pass. Waking up before dawn to witness the last wretched moments of a few pigs is an experience that I can do without.

The butcher then leads me to my bedroom. The room is not actually connected to the other rooms of the house; we access it from outside. Crowded into the room are a huge roofed bed and and an immense basket of unhusked rice. The basket must be a metre and a half across by a metre high. It's overflowing with grain.

The bed is without mattress or sheets. It is just wood slats covered with a straw mat. In Beijing, Viv and I had decided to leave our sleeping bags behind. "Even in the villages," she inaccurately predicted, "there'll be bedding for us." For warmth, I roll myself up in the straw mat like a burrito. The pillow is a cylindrical coil of hard plastic slats to be placed under the crook of the neck.

Sure enough, in the dead of night, I'm woken by the blood-curdling screams of about-to-be murdered swine. Then, through the wee hours, I drift in and out of consciousness, my struggle to sleep exacerbated by the rambunctious activities of a couple of rats. Not far from my head, somewhere on top of the pile of rice, they're chomping away. They sound like someone noisily eating popcorn at the movies. I don't bother taking a look. I silently enter a pact of mutual non-aggression with them and try to stick to the mantra that, while travelling, any night not spent fearing for one's life or nursing a troubled bowel or an infectious fever is a blessing.

In the morning I drop in on the butcher, who is happily hacking away at the pig carcasses splayed on the tables of the mah-jong parlour. I give him a smile and a bow, then head toward Li's house.

Viv is already awake, drinking tea on the doorstep. She tells me that Li's mother was talkative. "Remember yesterday when the children came back from school and a young boy sat on Li Gang's stoop doing his homework? Well, last night before going to bed, Li's mother explained to me that the boy was her youngest brother's son and Li's cousin. The old woman's brother had abducted a wife from Yunnan Province, to the south. But soon after giving birth, the young woman fled back to her people. The boy's father then went to work in some distant city to make money to support the boy and pay for his education. So Li Gang and his mother's family took responsibility for the care of this home-alone boy."

"That's pretty amazing!"

"It's actually fairly common in the Chinese countryside. Because the country people want sons to look after them in their old age, they have been getting rid of female babies by abortion or even sometimes after birth. As a result, there are not enough women to go around. So it's not unheard of that women are abducted or purchased from poor places all over the country."

The night before, Li had proposed that we return to Chongqing a different way than we had come. It was unclear what he had in mind, but I made out that the journey involved a boat. I enthusiastically agreed.

After a quick breakfast, we set out toward the gorge. We descend deep into it. As we climb down the steep path through the morning mist, I make out what looks like a lake at the bottom. Li tells me that it's a reservoir. The night before he had called the boatman on his cell phone and told him to meet us at our end of the reservoir at 8 a.m. I see neither boat nor boatman on the shore. We skip stones as we wait. Li says that the reservoir was hand-hewn in the 1950s. "It took a thousand men a few years, but they managed," he says. It's hard to imagine. The vegetation on the banks also indicates that the reservoir hasn't been at its maximum level in years.

Finally, Li phones the boatman. The boatman is still in bed, badly hungover, but his wife is on her way. Sure enough, before long I make out the flutter of her oars in the distance. She rows fast, standing up, facing backwards, making huge sweeping motions with the oars. Soon the woman has reached the shore.

It takes us a good half-hour to cross the reservoir. We emerge from the gorge into a larger basin. Along the shore, I make out fish and duck farms. The boatwoman tells us her story. The central government has a reforestation program. Her farm was designated as an area to be replanted with trees and expropriated. The government pays her a meagre allowance of the equivalent of sixty dollars a year in compensation. To survive she needs to supplement her income with what she and her husband make by running the skiff across the lake.

Our destination is a town built alongside the reservoir's dam. As the boat glides along, I can see that the water is clearly low:

the base is just nine metres down from the surface of the water. It isn't obvious what purpose the man-made lake serves. With all the livestock around its banks, it's hard to imagine it a source of drinking water. Nor can I see any irrigation works drawing water from it for agricultural use. Perched way up above the reservoir, Li's village surely could not depend on it for water. In fact, the surrounding countryside is far too vast and dry to be properly watered by the reservoir. I conclude that it was probably some kind of make-work project and really only serves as an emergency reserve that waters the immediate vegetable gardens around its banks and provides a supply of fish. Perhaps there is a small electrical plant as well, hidden on the other side of the dam.

It's market day in the town. Dozens of pigs are on the banks of the reservoir, waiting to be purchased. We climb up to the main street, which is packed with vendors. Li takes off to charter a local car.

We first travel south toward the mighty Yangtze and then stop to visit an ancient Buddhist temple built into the cliffs high above the great river's banks. Sheltered within the temple's ancient wooden roofs is a gigantic Buddha carved into the stone. We pay our respects, ponder possible ways toward enlightenment, then grab a bus to continue onward.

Back in Chongqing, the bus drops us at a big station along the river. To get to the upper city, Li guides us toward an interesting feature of this immense and bizarre metropolis: the world's longest escalator. The moving staircase proceeds from the lower city right up onto a high ridge running through the upper city. Once at the top of the ridge, it's time for Viv and me to take our leave from our wise friend Li Gang.

I prepare a hundred dollars' worth of local currency to give to Li for all his troubles. But with a bow, Li swiftly takes his leave without even considering the payment. I have to stop him and make him accept the money, which he does with great reluctance.

"What a rare individual!" Viv says.

"That's probably more peace than we'll ever see," I blurt out, thinking of our hungry and agitated souls.

"The Taoists urge us to be like a rock in a river. The rock doesn't move even as all the water of the world passes overtop," Viv muses.

CHAPTER 5

The River

All the monkeys said to each other:
Wonder where that water comes from.
Got nothing else to do,
why not follow it up to its source?
—Wu Cheng'en, *Journey to the West*, 1592

The riverboats are docked way below the city. As I approach the cruise terminal from the city street, high up on the edge of the cliff, the terminal seems more suited to zeppelins than ships. The banks of the river are so high and steep that a funicular actually brings passengers down from the terminal to the docks.

"Who takes these cruises?" I ask Vivien.

"Tourists, I presume. Chinese tourists, that is. The Yangtze landscapes are famous in China. Everyone wants to see them at least once."

"Maybe the building of the dam on the Yangtze means that people want to see the gorges before they are altered by the rising waters."

"This was surely true a couple of years ago before they started rising," she says, "but the dam's nearly complete, and I think the waters have already risen over a hundred metres. So maybe the opposite is now true. Maybe they're less interested in the flooded landscape. We'll see."

The glassed-in car slides down a near-vertical track to the docks. The slow descent offers a terrific view of the confluence of the Jialing and the Yangtze at Chongqing. Our trip will take us down the Yangtze, but our moorage is on the Jialing. From above, one can see that the two big rivers are quite distinctly coloured: the Jialing is dark blue; the Yangtze is brown with silt. Where they meet, the clear Jialing disappears into the muddy Yangtze, as if it never existed at all.

Viv and I are heading down the Yangtze as far as the great dam. The cruise will take four days. We too are curious to see the river, the landscape and the Three Gorges Dam.

"It'll be like a lesson in Chinese geography," I say to Viv, listing off not only elements of physical geography but human ones as well, for the Yangtze impacts inhabitation, agriculture, transportation and energy.

"Don't forget the arts," Viv adds. "All the beautiful poems and paintings about the Yangtze."

"Yes, never forget the arts."

"Frankly, I'm worried that this journey might prove a sad one," she says. "The destruction of a natural wonder."

At the river's edge, the funicular opens onto a network of floating elevated docks. A huge wall of brown earth looms at our backs, extending way up to the now mysterious city above. As we walk along the gangway to our ship, I look down and back toward the shoreline. It almost isn't there, as if the landscape isn't quite finished. It's just a line where dark water hits vertical earth. The opposite shore is a distant greenish-grey blur. All around us: big water, big mountain, big city. It's enough to make one's heart beat faster.

Some seventy-five metres long and four storeys high, our riverboat floats before us—a flat-bottomed barge-like construction with low gunwales, painted black along the bottom and white everywhere else. The bottom floor, at water level, is fourth class: two large collective cabins with a few wooden benches. The engine room and crew quarters are also down there. But this is all beneath us, since the gangway leads us across to the second floor and into the main lobby, an open area at the centre of the ship where the front desk and a convenience store are located. Hallways lead both forward and aft to third-class dorm rooms, each containing a dozen or so stacked berths. Rough enough travel.

Dressed in white-and-navy polyester uniforms with neckerchiefs and caps, two young women greet us in the lobby, take our tickets and usher us up the main staircase in the usual birdsong Mandarin of hostesses. Second class, one floor up, still feels rudimentary. I peek through open doors at hostel-style berths, maybe six to a room. Finally, the top deck's forward section is first class. Simple, somewhat clean twin rooms with the smallest of private bathrooms—a shower stall, tiny sink and a squat toilet instead of a drain.

"By the looks of it, I would say that this boat isn't just for tourists," Viv comments. "I don't think the third- or fourth-class passengers are on this boat for fun. It must be a cheap way to get somewhere if you have the time."

"Even first class is good value for three nights' accommodation and several hundred kilometres worth of transportation."

"And we can use the front and back observation decks," she says. "The best places on the boat, I'm sure."

Before long, we've taken position on the exclusive if tiny front deck, eager to see our big boat push off. For a few minutes, there is a flurry of activity on the dock and on the lower decks as moorings are released, then engines roar and the ship powers into the flow. It quickly cuts across the Jialing to come into the Yangtze parallel to the current, leaving the city peninsula and docks fast behind.

Softened by a white haze, Chongqing goes on busily for a good while above us, but down on the Yangtze, it's an increasing abstraction. The inscrutable river, milky and brown, becomes our reality. Ripples and bulges, like glimpses of serpents and dragons' backs concealed beneath a film, undulate to remind us that the river is in constant movement.

Rivers are strange to look at for what they are. Raindrops or snowflakes, of course. And before them, clouds, drifting into mountains. And before that, oceans in the sun. All these things so diffuse and multiple, all coming together as a solid, single thing—a river. Looking at the undulating surface, at the drifting yet stable mass, is it a moment that we see? An instant of each of those things, all moving one step downhill together? No, we gaze at a continuous motion in a circuit, underfoot and overhead. A happening in both the heavens and on earth. Something beginning and ending over and over again. Something timeless and complete.

The aft area of the top deck is roofed over but open. It has a number of booths and tables. A counter displays beverages and snacks on offer. Two floors down, the ship's restaurant proper is a windowed-in space at the back of third class. Shabby but splendid, with traditional Chinese round tables bearing dirty tablecloths and, luckily, never full. Most passengers seem to have brought their own food, to eat in their rooms. As for us, we'd return to the restaurant three times a day for its cold beer by the big bottle and salty, oily but reasonably diverse food for small money.

After dinner I wander down to the bottom deck. Unlike the decks above, where cabins with windows line the sides of the boat, the lower deck has open walkways wrapping around the whole ship. The engine room and passenger cabins are closed chambers at the centre of the ship; the place is gloomy and empty. A swift breeze washes down the corridor, but the noise of the motor and the smell of diesel are still strong. The dark water now so close washes by. Downward into the night we go.

China is a country of mountains, an uphill country. From the shores of the Pacific in the east, it rises progressively as one moves westward. Along its southwest border is Earth's highest mountain, Mount Everest, at 8,848 metres. A single high point among a sea of high peaks, it is but a small part of one of planet Earth's most important topographical features: the Himalayan range and the Tibetan Plateau.

I get a strange look when I tell Viv that India is perhaps the key to understanding China. I let her scratch her head a little—perhaps she's thinking about Buddhism. Then I tell her that it is a geographical fact, not a historical or cultural one. India is a tectonic plate, and some fifty million years ago it smashed into the south flank of the Eurasian plate, causing the land to buckle up high over a vast area. The consequences of this are far-ranging. The Yangtze River is but one small consequence of this giant topographical event.

Not just the Yangtze but all the great rivers of the Far East are in fact born of these mountains—the Indus, the Ganges and Brahmaputra, the Irrawaddy, the Salween, the Mekong, the Pearl, the Yellow and even perhaps the Amur. Each draws its water from precipitation from clouds pushed up and against the rising terrain of the India-China orogeny, the mountain-making event.

Mountains are a climatic force. Push clouds up against them and they will drop their water. So the higher one goes, the drier the air is. Above the clouds, the Himalayas and the Tibetan Plateau are vast, high, cold deserts, more akin to the Arctic than the subtropics of northern India and eastern China that they border. Great civilizations sprang up at the feet of these mountains because on their shoulders oceans of evaporated water fall and from their bellies great rivers come forth and nourish many fertile plains.

In human time, this bulging landmass has been a permanent feature, even a mythic barrier. From an Afrocentric view, China is at the far end of the mountains. Around or through them, it's a long arduous journey to get there. This hasn't meant that humans didn't get to China repeatedly. We need only imagine *Homo erectus* working their way around the mountains to go die in the Choukoutien Caves as the Peking Man and his kin three-quarters of a million years ago. Or hundreds of thousands of years later, *Homo sapiens* pushing through India on the way east, then down toward Southeast Asia or up along the Pacific Rim.

The mountains did not stop humans from getting to China. But they meant that movements back and forth around and through them were curtailed. China was at the end of the road, and its approaches protected. It evolved in relative isolation— relative compared with the territory between the Indus and the Ganges, the Nile valley, and the Mesopotamian or Danube plains, through which successive waves of humans rolled, repeatedly bringing great changes to genetics, culture and language.

. . . .

I awake to find our ship moored against another riverboat. I draw the window curtain and see another curtained window. I hear a couple arguing, unseen in the cabin beyond. Before long, the ship is off again. The river remains fathomless, its bottom masked by the silty liquid it carries.

The morning air is hot, and although we are moving, it feels somewhat still. Again a white haze softens the landscape. By mid-morning it's not a pleasant effect, more a dulling one. The thick air blurs the contours of sky, mountain and river and stamps out the colours.

"When do we hit the flood zone?" I ask Viv.

"I think we already have."

"That would mean we are now on a lake. Or a reservoir."

"Yes, I guess," she answers.

"Amazing. We only just left. We have three more days of water ahead. By the looks of it, the reservoir will reach Chongqing as it continues to rise."

"Somewhere around here is a famous stone carving of a fish; it used to show where the river's lowest water level was. Now the whole thing's deep underwater."

"Yeah, a great drowning," I say.

"All the riverside communities for several hundred kilometres are now also gone. It's sad," Viv says.

"I read that in the gorges, cargo ships were once pulled up the current by humans with huge ropes."

"That's true."

"Must have been a fairly miserable existence."

"Of course. The worst," Viv admits.

"And now container ships power their way from the Pacific to Chongqing. And in an apartment building somewhere, the rope pullers' great-grandchildren live lives devoid of all their forefathers' physical suffering. Maybe they work in a factory that produces goods that will be sold into Western markets. Possibly they are now consumers of products manufactured far away and delivered to them by water. An improvement, no?"

"I'm not nostalgic for the old days, Sacha. But one can feel the loss of riverside life without endorsing the old hardships."

"But aren't we all a bit nostalgic? Wasn't beauty an easier thing when humans were still only bit players?"

"Yes. Like the ancient landscape paintings: idealized depictions of harmony in nature without human presence."

"Now we must seek beauty in giant skyscrapers and huge dams," I say with a smile.

"I'll take reeds gently swaying in the current over square concrete and steel," she counters.

"Yes, but at what cost? Filth and darkness for your peers?"

Chinese history is one of geographic transformation. As far back as the semi-mythic Xia dynasty around the second millennium before Christ, China struggled to tame the Yellow River, on whose banks and tributaries disparate tribes had long been collecting. Massive as they are, both the Yellow and the Yangtze Rivers flow from deep within vast and high mountain ranges. They preserve something of spring torrents, but on a formidable scale. With the rivers' upper reaches all in steep mountain valleys and no lazy plains or wetlands to absorb and moderate the runoff, the water comes gushing forth onto the territory that proved so bountiful to early Chinese tribes.

The deposits of silt that made for such reliable agriculture owed their existence to the very same mechanism that brought danger: fast-flowing rivers grinding away at mountains, then bursting out onto flatter ground, laying down their mineral wealth over a wide area and periodically altering course as the water broke through the banks and new channels emerged. As perennial as they were—and necessary for building the rich soils—the floods routinely devastated the farming communities set up along the banks of the rivers.

The annals tell of how the Yu family dedicated itself to trying to control the floods at the behest of an early Yellow River potentate. The father built walls against the current, but the levees ceded to the water pressure and actually worsened the floods. For his failures, father Yu was put to death. Tasked to succeed where his father had failed, Yu the younger channelled the current where it would seek to overflow. It worked. For this feat, he earned the title of Yu the Great, was made the chosen successor of the king and founded the legendary Xia dynasty at the beginning of Chinese history, forever connecting water management with political power in China.

By the end of our first full day on the water, Viv and I have exhausted the various permutations of positioning on the ship and find ourselves rotating pointlessly between front and back deck, restaurant and cabin. Even with the mountains on either side, the landscape seems flat against the broad cloudy expanse of water around us and the white hazy sky above. I can only look at the views with interest for short periods before becoming thoroughly bored.

Vivien and I have long hours to throw ideas around.

"Am I correct in thinking that mountains and gods are connected etymologically in Chinese?" I ask her.

"The Chinese script's pictographic. Character origin and word origin are blurred. We use a few different characters for the English word *god*. We mostly use the word *shen*."

"Does it have the *mountain* character in it?" I ask.

"No, it uses the radical for *spirit*. You mean *xiān*, meaning immortal. Yes, the *mountain* character is there. Perhaps because the Taoists associate gods with mountains."

"So do you feel gods in mountains? Or see mountains when you think of gods?" I ask.

"The nuances are historical. If we are saying *xiān*—immortal—we aren't really thinking about gods in the mountains. We are thinking of their immortality."

"So godliness and mountains don't feel right together for you?"

"What are you trying to get at?"

"I don't know," I say, hesitating before explaining my desire to understand how mountains fit into Chinese cosmology. "Have you ever heard of phenomenology?" I eventually ask.

"Yes, I've heard of the concept. But I must admit not knowing what it means."

"It means to paint the shape of a concept in all its lived experiences. How we experience something directly but also in words, or in images like the paintings we were talking about. Even in dreams. Wherever and however consciousness is."

"And what does phenomenology tell you?"

"Many good stories. A phenomenology tells you what you know about a subject before you even begin thinking about it. Some say that phenomenologies even tell the story of how reality is made."

"And you?"

"Yes, I believe this. Reality is made, and we can deconstruct its fabrication."

"So what do you conclude about gods and mountains?"

"They must be connected deep in Chinese thought. China

is a farming civilization, and water management has long been a feature of the civilization. Rivers have always been important. Especially their seasonal rises and falls, as well as their unexpected bursts that cause floods. The causalities of water flow had to receive special attention from the start. So the source of rivers, the impenetrable, inhospitable mountains that trapped the clouds, took on godly proportions."

"One of the greatest of Chinese classics, *Journey to the West*, is about a journey into the mountains," Viv says. "It's the story of a physical ascension but also implies a Buddhist spiritual ascension toward enlightenment. But the connections there now seem quaint—literary and historical."

"Behind today's ideas," I warn Viv, "there are always other ideas, older ones, long buried. Like hidden mountains with gods in them."

After lunch, the weather takes a turn for the worse and grey storm clouds threaten to bring rain to the Yangtze. Our ship stops at a river town and we are urged to go ashore. Cheap umbrellas are handed to us by the crew. Stone steps lead from the river's edge to a series of temples up the hill. The steps have become slippery in the rain. Viv and I make our way up to a first temple compound about halfway up the hill only to find most of the complex closing because of the weather. Under the eaves of the buildings, vendors huddle, selling tourist trinkets. I find a food stand and stock up on snacks: tofu skins, shrimp chips and soy-soaked eggs. The rain falls harder.

"I often prefer gardens to temples. Especially when there are old trees," I say, looking about for ancient vegetation.

"Well, there doesn't seem to be much of that here. I suspect that this whole area was recently rebuilt for tourists. Maybe there's nothing old or authentic about it at all."

It's now pouring, so we agree to head back to the boat.

Back on board, our fellow passengers grow familiar to us. We seem to share the restaurant with a revolving cast of characters, but one group is always present: a band of middle-aged men. They're third-class passengers and are having a merry old time on the cruise.

From mid-morning to late evening, they occupy one of the big central tables in the restaurant. They drink ample beer, chain-smoke cigarettes and engage in much revelry. The most boisterous of the lot is a rotund bronze-skinned chap with a shaved head and an eager toothless grin. He has the habit of rolling up his shirt to expose his bare nipples and big belly, a sure sign of relaxation in China.

Every time we return to the restaurant, the bald jovialist seems a stronger presence, lording over his comrades, laughing louder, slapping the table, heartily picking his teeth or nose. I imagine him as the foreman of a meat-packing facility or a heavy-equipment operator on a road crew. Whatever he does back on shore, I am sure it's relentless, dirty, hard work. So with no responsibilities here and nothing but empty time to fill with beer and banter with his buddies, he's in a great mood.

Boat life casts a different spell over me. The confinement gets to me. The outside world grows distant and the journey stands in for life itself. As we move monotonously forward, the metaphor becomes real and the passage takes on a feeling of philosophical inevitability. Because I'm no captain of the ship and play no part in piloting us down the river, because I'm but a passive subject of the passage, a slight existential panic sets in: That life's not just fleeting but empty. That I'm wasting it away, steadily proceeding toward death.

My energy begins to falter, and long conversations with Vivien become more strained. I'm loath to burden her with my creeping funk and find it more and more difficult to simply move from deck to deck on the ship. The pointlessness of it freezes me. The scenery, the light, begin to feel oppressive. Even the presence of other people grows uncomfortable.

I retreat to the cabin and set up my computer at the desk, intending to write. But in my gloom, inspiration is mostly absent and I turn to watching pirated DVDs, momentarily escaping my sorrowful existence with illusions. Occasionally, I look out the window. Across the room, through partially closed curtains, the harsh tones of the white sky are muted. With this frame, the vista is somewhat more bearable. Sometimes, with its mountains, bridges and myriad moving vessels, the view of the river is even beautiful. But I can't look for long and quickly seek to harness my attention with still another bit of entertainment.

Almost like a nurse, Viv checks in on me from time to time, sensing something weird about my predicament. "I'm meeting our fellow first-class passengers," she tells me. "Across the hall is a family from Inner Mongolia. Three generations. The grandfather is a retired soldier. He's a funny old guy, asking a lot of questions about you, wondering what you're doing in here all day."

"Just tell him I'm writing," I say.

"He doesn't understand why you would be writing here on the Yangtze. He spends his time quietly sitting on the front deck watching the scenery and eating peanuts."

"I have all the scenery I need through the window."

"You probably also noticed that the front cabins are suites. They have their own big windows facing forward. There's a couple in one of them. The man has all the airs of a corrupt official. The woman is much younger than him—probably his mistress. They don't come out of their cabin very much either."

"He irritates you, doesn't he?" I can't help but asking.

"I know it's none of my business," she admits, "but still they get to me. He reminds me of my father. Once he became principal of his school and got power, he turned his back on my mother and found a much younger wife. This, after years of incessant preaching to me about virtuous conduct."

"Now I understand!" I exclaim, then add, "But people are the same everywhere. We're monkeys, remember."

"Still, I hope for more. It seems to me that we can do better."

"That's a good hope to have."

"I also spent time on the lowest deck," she tells me. "There are a few very poor old men down there, sleeping on the wooden benches. They don't have any luggage, or anything. I don't think they paid to be on this ship, which is why they never leave the bottom deck. They're probably homeless migrants, moving around looking for work wherever they can, begging for rice as they go. What saddens me is how old they are. They're at the end of their lives, with nothing. You would think they would have families to look after them or something."

As I listen to her impassively, she suddenly changes the subject. "Hey, don't you want to get out of this cabin?"

"No, thanks. I'm good here," I say.

"Don't you find it depressing to stay in here all the time?"

"I am depressed. This boat, this river, are giving me the blues. But don't worry, I'll be fine. I'll see you for dinner."

"Okay, then. See you later," she says.

I put sad music on in an effort to restore romance to the journey, to make my pathetic predicament feel more like a grand tragedy. Gazing out the window, I notice the repeated use of markers to indicate the water level. These are like giant rulers up against the steep riverbanks. At one spot, I can see that the mark indicates that the water level is at just below 130 metres; the measure goes up to 175 metres. I'm not sure if the marks started at zero, but the ruler disappearing into the waters alludes to great depths beneath.

Apparently, much of the flooded landscape was bulldozed and dynamited before the waters began to rise. I imagine homes and structures down there beneath the opaque café-au-lait waters. Beyond the markers, there is no indication of a transition between submerged areas and the areas above. No roads descending into the river. No partially submerged structures. Nothing to remind one of a world that has ceased to exist.

I think of my experiences clearing forest. The moment you bring the trees down, the light and openness created are a little shocking, even disturbing. But if all the fallen trees are quickly sawed up and removed, it's not long before you cannot draw a mental picture of the forest that once stood there; it's as if it never existed. The cool, moist darkness it brought cannot be imagined and thus can scarcely be missed.

That night I find myself sleepless. The boat is again stopped and moored. They are really dragging this cruise out. I decide to wander around the boat while everything is quiet and almost everyone is asleep. Maybe I'll bump into some ghosts.

I quickly realize that access to both the front and back decks is barred by locked doors, so I head downstairs. A slumbering hostess gives me a disapproving look as I pass the lobby, but apart from lifting her head from the counter, she doesn't budge. I keep going down. With the motors silenced, the bottom deck is much quieter. I smell cigarette smoke and hear crewmen chatting on the moored side of the boat. I slip to the other side to look out at the river—or rather, at the reservoir. In the distance, a few lights indicate the passage of ships.

The lights are permanently on in the fourth-class passenger cabins. One of Viv's frail old men is there, splayed out asleep on a hard wooden bench. His short pant legs are hiked up, revealing bony ankles and feet bare except for worn-out flip-flops. Instead of rejoicing that I'm far better off than him, that my life is not as pointless as his, my mood flattens everything and I fail to see the difference between me and him. What says I will enjoy any more comforts or purpose than him when I reach his age? And what will the comforts of life matter when we both reach our final destination?

I lumber back up to my cabin and bed, if not to sleep then to lie there in the darkness, hoping to fight off any visions that might come.

The next morning our ship is moving again. Over breakfast, Viv tells me that later that day the ship will again be moored and there will be an expedition on smaller boats up a tributary of the Yangtze that offers beautiful scenery.

"They're called the Little Three Gorges," she explains, "and, apparently, they're like the Yangtze was before the floods."

"You go. I'll stay here," I quickly say.

"Come on. It'll do you good," she says.

"How do you know what will do me good?" I almost snap.

"Okay, don't come then."

While Vivien is off on the expedition, I lie down to catch up on the missed sleep of the night before. But the muggy weather, the bright light and the unmoving ship make for sickly slumbers and feverish dreams, uncomfortably close to reality.

The same boat, the same cabin, the same shouting of crewmen accompany me as I float through the dream space. Then I find myself struggling up the gravel embankment of a giant construction site, as vast as an open mine. As I climb, the unstable ground impedes my progress and I seem to be sliding down more than moving up—much to my dismay, as some vague threat awaits me at the bottom.

Is it the noisy construction machinery that I fear below or simply that I shouldn't be in this zone? I can't tell. Then I find myself on the wrong side of an imposing security fence. Vivien is on the other side, telling me that I shouldn't be there. I am responding angrily that I know and that I want to get to the other side but can't. I make an attempt to scale the fence and find the razor wire on top tearing at my clothes, making it impossible for me to snake through. Agitated Chinese guards arrive to shout at me. There's suddenly the notion that the fence is electric and that I'm snagged only inches from the live wire.

Enough of this! I force myself awake to find myself drenched in sweat. The rest of the afternoon, I lie in bed with my eyes open.

Vivien returns from her expedition in a splendid mood. "I needed that," she tells me when she pops into my cabin. "The Little Three Gorges were absolutely beautiful. Pristine. Like there is hope!"

"Yeah, I can see why they are so keen on conducting tours there."

"The mountains were so steep on either side. The air in the canyon was pleasant and cool. I hate to say it, but you probably should've come. It might have helped your mood."

"Probably. Instead, I stayed in bed to be tormented by unpleasant dreams. We need to get off this boat upon the River Styx."

"Styx?"

"A river from Greek mythology. It flows between the kingdom of the living and the dead," I explain.

"We'll be finished with it tomorrow morning."

In the final leg of its journey, our boat breaks through the mountains onto what appears to be a wide lake. The lake ends at the Three Gorges Dam, but there's no sign of it across the waters. Instead, the ship turns toward the shore and docks at a large modern terminal where several similar boats are already moored. We are ushered toward tour buses that will bring us first to the dam and then Yichang, a large city on the other side. As we approach the dam it's still veiled by the blasted white haze so common in China, which denies us a complete view of the structure. Its massive size is enhanced as it fades into white.

We're brought to a lookout on a hillock above the structure. We can barely make out the full span of concrete crossing the river or the deep man-made canyon of locks leading up through the dam. Then we're brought to a riverside walkway beneath the giant wall holding back the river. From this vantage, the haze isn't quite so bad and we can view the whole dam.

"Intense," I can't help but say.

"Successive Chinese leaders dreamt of this project," Viv explains. "Sun Zhongshan, whom you probably know as Sun Yat-sen, wrote about damming the Yangtze. The Americans and the Japanese contemplated a dam as well. Mao wrote a poem about it. The project has seemed unavoidable for decades. Then it was finally commenced under Li Peng, the most stodgy and repressive of our recent leaders. You could say it just couldn't be stopped."

"Such a huge project would hardly be possible in any inhabited part of my country," I tell her. "It would freak people out."

"Well, there has been significant opposition to the project," Viv says, "even at party levels. But this hasn't stopped it from going forward. Li Peng, remember, was one of the hard-liners, advocating that the Tiananmen protests be crushed with tanks."

"I guess the need for electricity in China is just too great to ignore."

"Even this is controversial," Viv explains. "Critics point to the failed hydroelectric projects on the Yellow River. Apparently, all the silt of these great rivers gets in the turbines and causes them to fail. The proponents say the design here is better and the situation on the river is different. But who really knows? We'll have to see in a few years."

"Perhaps electricity from the dam is better than burning dirty coal."

"Well, there's another problem," she continues. "The numbers don't add up. The total capacity of the dam will be something like twenty thousand megawatts. Apparently, China uses about a million megawatts of electricity. So all this, everything you see, all this flooding and destruction only answers 2 percent of the country's current needs. China's needs are growing faster than that 2 percent. This means more coal plants."

"I see your point."

"I don't think the dam is about electricity, really," she concludes. "It's about an obsession with building. It's for the prestige of the leaders who get to marshal all these resources, funnel boatloads of money into so many pockets and, at the end, have a monument to show their power off to the world."

"But think also of the massive strategic liability that the dam is for China," I say. "Think of what a nuclear hit could do to it and the hundreds of millions who live downstream."

"Surely not a possibility?" Viv asks with worry.

"We do live in a violent world full of sinister forces. And China has just given itself one hell of an Achilles heel."

"China will just have to learn to be a force of peace in the world," she counters.

"Yeah, good luck with that," I say, laughing.

One final horror awaits me on our Yangtze journey. Before dropping us off in Yichang, our tour bus makes a stop at a local museum. From the outside, it looks like a rundown research institute, bereft of any decoration that might make it attractive to happy holidayers. The location is impressive enough, though, snuggled as it is up against a steep embankment looking out over the river.

The museum is as drab inside as it is on the outside. Only one dusty and quite small room with half a dozen or so glass cabinets. A few documents and maps, a diorama. A section on Yangtze ecology catches my eye. There's a preserved Yangtze River dolphin, the baiji, in a coffin-like cabinet. Its wrinkled skin makes it look decrepit and miserable.

"Poor thing," Viv says. "It's believed to be extinct, you know."

"Yes, gone, banished from existence," I say.

Its minuscule eye slot confirms the creature was nearly blind, adapted to the silt-laden waters. Its sophisticated sonar allowed it to use the murky waters to its advantage, sneaking up on fish and snatching them with its long, slender snout.

"I read a report by a marine biologist who conducted surveys along the Yangtze with people who might have last seen the dolphins. He was looking for recent witnesses, attempting to verify the baiji's extinction. One Yangtze fisherman he interviewed told him that the baiji was a 'girl fish,' because it was as shy as a girl at a party and would swim away rapidly if anyone called out to it. Well, the girls are gone and the party's over," I joke.

"Depressing," Vivien says, then adds, "Now *there* is a bleak subject for your phenomenology: extinction."

"Yeah, right, let's see . . . a dolphin's experience of its own annihilation: I see fishnets, motorboat propellers, pollution, disease, great loneliness, starvation and then the flood. Its last thoughts: *Oh monkey, what have you done?*"

"Terrible," Viv says, shaking her head at me.

Looking at the shrivelled creature and its squinty closed eyes, we grow silent and can't help but feel sympathy for this strange but intelligent animal, now disappeared.

"We should be saying a prayer for it," Viv says.

"Yes, we should."

As if the dolphin were some kind of messenger from the gods in the mountains. We should be praying that we haven't forgotten them. But in truth we have. The world has moved on. We don't even know how to pray. And along with their envoy, the baiji, the immortals too are now dead.

CHAPTER 6

Shanghai

Knowledge and action are together. Contrast this with a person who has eyes to see but no legs to walk. Or legs to walk but no eyes to see.

—Zhu Xi, Song dynasty Confucian scholar

It's Thursday, and Viv and I are heading from the interior to Shanghai. Making the bus connections from up the Yangtze entails a bit of a roundabout journey. We spend long hours on a variety of buses.

Although it's part of the all-important central region of China, Shanghai was never a capital. Shanghai is not a figure of unity. It does not represent any great locus of tradition to which the Chinese owe part of themselves. It stands alone, and it's new; anything that happened in Shanghai happened in the last two centuries. Yet the last two centuries have been important and transformative ones for the world and for China.

"Viv, we're going to a wedding in Shanghai," I tell her.

"Who's getting married?"

"An Englishman. He's a close friend of Deryk's. He's marrying a Chinese girl."

"Uh-oh!" she says, laughing. "Girls from Shanghai are famous for being demanding and spoiled wives."

"Well, I think the bride actually spent her teenage years in Kashgar."

"Oh, then I'm sure she's different. Kashgar's the opposite of Shanghai."

Kashgar is China's most westerly major city, a high, hot, dusty town of central Asia, the traditional territory of Turkic tribes. In the new China, it's a rambling boomtown.

"I've noticed the Chinese giving Shanghai and its people a hard time. Is it out of jealousy for being such a rich and successful place?"

"Yes, maybe," Viv concedes. "But also the native people of Shanghai have the reputation for being arrogant, materialistic and superficial."

We laugh and agree that we should make an effort to put prejudices aside. With some twenty-four million inhabitants, Shanghai is one of the world's most populated urban centres and has the planet's greatest port. Only fools would approach it lightly.

As we pass through Nanjing, a city worthy of much reflection, we don't stop; Shanghai is already commanding our attention. On the radio, important news is being conveyed: Shanghai's Communist Party leader, its highest official, has been charged with corruption and dishonourable behaviour toward his party and toward his nation and its people. He's now under arrest.

"That's notable," Viv remarks, "though hardly unprecedented. You must imagine what power this man had mere hours ago."

"And now?"

"Well . . . he'll probably never be heard from again," she says. "Officially, it'll be like he never existed."

"Will he be killed?"

"He might be executed. More likely, he'll be put where they put all the disgraced party leaders."

"Will there be a trial?"

"A trial!? Here, when you are charged, you're already deemed guilty. There'll be a hearing, but the results are predetermined."

"So the public won't know exactly what he did?"

"Nothing beyond the most distant facts. In a way, everyone's expected to already know how guilty he is."

"What kind of corruption might he have engaged in?"

"The same kind of behaviour all party leaders have shown in all big cities in China." Viv goes on to explain that in Shanghai, the temptations and rewards are bigger than anywhere else. She describes how the party leader has the final say on everything that happens there.

"Nothing big's built, no great fortunes are made, without his approval," she tells me. "The central body of the party constantly has to do this in the centres of wealth. The local leaders get too powerful. They stop listening to orders; they constitute a threat to unity. His fate is a warning to other powerful regional leaders."

Of course, his arrest would change nothing for the people. There would be no public reaction. Beyond his initial smile, our driver, for instance, seemed hardly to care. Nothing would be learnt from this event. Corruption would not cease. The cards will only have been shuffled and the venal grip momentarily loosened. This was just part of a cycle that goes on and on, almost harmoniously. That which is big and strong is made small and weak.

It's a well-known pattern in China: Shanghai, at the centre, grows too strong and Beijing must strike to re-exert its dominion. In so many ways, Beijing is the outlier. The capital and its northern reaches can seem distant and irrelevant in the luxuriant Yangtze delta. The north is cold, dry and coarse. It's also vulnerable. Traditionally, it was China's flank, open to the steppe and beyond to vast untamed forests. The north, the realm of horses and great armies, was prone to vigorous change.

In the centre, rice growing reigned supreme. Through ever more advanced water-management techniques, the production of rice sustained China's greatest growth. By the resplendent Tang dynasty, late in the first millennium, the Grand Canal and an intricate network of waterways allowed grain to be moved throughout the land to feed subjects and soldiers, to control, colonize and conquer. The Yangtze and Yellow river cultures formed one unified people.

In its day, Tang China had it all: art and technology. It cast its armies and fleets wide and brought into its orbit, and its knowledge, distant lands. The Tang traded and communicated with the Indians and the Arabs. Grand new ideas were pondered at court and soon found resonance all across China. It was an age of power and of light.

In Tang China, water management meant food management, and this meant power. A civilization that learns to move food around in quantity soon also develops a sophisticated commodity economy. But harmony is as perennial as the seasons, and all orders eventually break. During the Tang dynasty, the world had also grown smaller. Mountains no longer provided the protection they had before. Chinese wealth was talked about in barbarian courts. Covetous thoughts would soon tempt China's neighbours to test China's strength, and it would be found increasingly lacking. In this dynamic, the centre offered refuge. The sheer numbers of Chinese and the enormous bounty of grain they produced in the Yangtze basin made assimilation unlikely.

The Song dynasty emerged from the brief period of chaos that followed the collapse of the House of Tang. The Song claim on the heavenly mandate was not so much founded on such base things as military supremacy but on cultural refinement. Although it carried forth the Tang dedication to technology, manufacture and invention, the Song period was one of inevitable contraction. The centre was losing control of the northern reaches as its forces struggled against foreign powers that roamed there.

The Song Chinese would occasionally muster their armies and send them out to meet the enemy, who invariably came in on horses, but this was always a risky tactic. Faster than the Chinese armies, the hostile cavalries could merely retreat to a battlefield of their choosing and then counterattack. The Chinese lines would be forced to mount a quick defence on unfavourable terrain. The armoured riders would harass the foot soldiers with their arrows, hoping to force them to break rank and open the field. Then the horsemen could run through the great armies, sowing disarray, felling them piece by piece.

The Song mostly chose to retreat behind city walls. A valiant commander who had maintained the battlements might hold off the horsemen long enough to force them to abandon their quarry and be compelled to return to far pastures to tend to families and herds. But the Song elites cared little for military service, and many of their cities had outgrown their crumbling old walls. The populations were more inclined to feasts and festivals than to enduring battles.

So when the Song could not impose a peace, they had to purchase it from the encroaching tribes to the north. But these arrangements didn't last long. The Song paid no increased attention to matters military, and they struggled to show the various horse confederacies any respect. The Song also proved treacherous patrons, trying to play clients against each other. When the

Song capital, Kaifeng, finally fell to the Jurchens, erstwhile vassals who'd finally had enough of Song machinations and mounted a bold attack on the empire, the sack of the city was brutal.

The Jurchens chose to cleanse Kaifeng of its ruling classes. In their wrath, they must have felt the Song to be soft and corrupt and decided that they should be marched deep into the Jurchen homelands, where they would be shown the Jurchen way. Noblemen, scholars, concubines and their children were driven north from the capital on foot, carrying their treasures and finery. Those that survived were welcomed to the Jurchen court in the fashion of the hunter: naked except for pelts.

The remainder of the Song elite fled south across the Yangtze. They set up court with a Song relative as emperor in Hangzhou, at the southern end of the Grand Canal. Diminished but still immensely prosperous, the Southern Song dynasty proved an ebullient period for art and ideas for another century and half. Throughout this time, however, there was constant menace.

Mongol tribes were experiencing an age of unification and expansion, and exerting themselves more and more effectively across the Eurasian continent on the great steppe that nearly connected the Amur to the Danube, a veritable highway of conquest. It wasn't long until the Mongol hordes began descending upon the northern frontier. Their terms were simple: complete submission or total annihilation. The great armies would not stop in the north—the lucrative Song centres of the Yangtze basin were too tempting to ignore. Here too the endless surge of hordes proved irresistible, and the Song fell to the Mongols in 1279.

Like previous mounted harassers of China, the Mongols were deemed uncouth outsiders by the Chinese. But there was no escaping their armies: they subjugated all of China, took the centre and interrupted the ancient cycle of Han rule over China.

The Mongols first established their capital in the north at Yanjing, which they called Dadu—that familiar outpost on the northern fringe of traditional China that is now the Middle Kingdom's great capital, Beijing. But like the horse princes before and after them, the conquering Mongol chiefs, once exposed to Chinese culture, quickly came under the influence of Chinese ways. They relied increasingly on Chinese labour and grain for nourishment and came to prefer living in the centre at Hangzhou, the Song capital, close to the food source and far from the fringe.

By the third generation of residence, the great khans spoke and wrote primarily in Chinese. As the Yuan dynasty, they sponsored Chinese institutions and became preachers of Chinese cultural superiority—a discourse that undermined their authority among both the Chinese and their Mongol cousins of the great steppes. Although the Mongol holdings were larger than any empire the world had ever seen, the Mongols remained a people of the horse. The dry pastures of central Eurasia were ill-suited to Chinese customs and came increasingly under the influence of Islam.

Neither quite Chinese nor Mongol, the descendants of Genghis and Kublai Khan—the emperors of the Yuan dynasty—became more and more detached from worldly affairs. Their governments became increasingly incapable of guaranteeing harmony and prosperity. When the prosperous central regions began to suffer calamities, the Chinese people everywhere became hardened and angry. And so it was that a Han peasant leader from middle China, Zhu Yuanzhang, led a revolt against the Yuan and brought an end to Mongol rule in China.

The Ming dynasty that Zhu founded marked the beginning of a new expansion of Chinese culture; the traditions of the centre once more blossomed out into a vast empire. To mark this expansion, the first Ming seat of power in Nanjing, on the banks of the Yangtze, was eventually moved to Beijing. It stood on top of the old Mongol capital, Dadu, where the Jurchen capital of Zhongdu had once replaced the Tang fortress of Yanjing. By building this new north capital, the Ming erased much evidence of foreign command in China. Although relics of Ming-era China can still be witnessed all over the land, to get a sense of Yuan glories—or those of the Song before them—one has to return to the centre.

Viv and I are still hours away from Shanghai. The mountains of the central Yangtze region give way to the coastal plain, a territory made rich by forty-five million years of minerals that have slowly been deposited here. The land is wet and fertile. The climate is also conducive to agriculture: hot, humid summers and mild winters.

The last days of September, I remind myself as I scan the horizon. But nothing indicates that it's autumn already. Now the great city is making itself felt. We're on a major highway, passing excessively cultivated areas, flat, rich plains. Village life has perhaps not disappeared but been transformed. Concrete is everywhere, and more and more factories and housing complexes are repeated along the edges of the highway. The traffic is thick and fast. We're in the pull of something big and strong.

In terms of Chinese history, Shanghai is still an infant, born of an insignificant village on the muddy banks of a tributary of the Yangtze a mere two centuries ago. It was nonetheless a town that had to be. The maritime age had begun, to the great advantage of

133

Western powers, which needed a place like Shanghai to access the Chinese economy.

Beyond its position on the Huangpu River, an offshoot of the Yangtze's main current, Shanghai has no natural elements of geography. It's flat. It's also huge, a sprawl of concrete-and-glass towers. Cutting through the city, the river now seems more of a canal than a water flow.

When I first visited Shanghai in 1990, the east bank of the Huangpu, called Pudong, was still hardly developed. The huge television tower had not yet been erected on the swampy ground. There were only ramshackle tenements. My father had told me that when he first went to Shanghai, in the late 1940s, the Communists threatened the city and the exodus of westerners and industrialists had begun. Emptied of their usual patrons, the grand Western hotels on the Bund, the riverside boulevard, were as such within the reach of the young independent traveller. The view from his luxurious room, he recounted, was unforgettable: he could gaze out across the river at rural China—rice paddies, huts and earthy peasants. The waterlogged ground on the eastern banks forced the city to sprawl westward, away from the Bund, on more solid soil. Spurred on by the real estate boom of the Deng era, the authorities dredged and drained the east bank and built the emblematic television tower in 1991. No symbol speaks more to new China's prosperity: where there once was mud and squalor in Pudong, there is now glittering wealth. The tower is hardly beautiful: a huge shiny ball mounted high on three slender concrete pillars. The ball is topped by a giant antenna that stabs at the clouds.

Night is falling when Viv and I arrive in Shanghai. We proceed through the immense city on elevated highways and huge crowded boulevards. Prosperous Asian cities put on fantastic displays of light at night. The Shanghai skyline is not quite so luminous as Tokyo's Shinjuku or New York's Times Square, but on this thick-aired evening, the powerful logos of enterprise emblazoned high on dark towers cast a commanding presence. The lurking hulks of concrete are like stone Cyclops standing in every direction. Shanghai is a hugely powerful and complex urban behemoth, with a big and heavy pulse.

Shanghai's giant streets are chaotic. Everything is pressed into service. Whatever was once meant to be beautiful is now crowded by the city. At its best, Shanghai is magnificently tree-lined. Beneath the encroaching vertical sprawl, some streets and neighbourhoods have been preserved as they were when Shanghai was a colonial city. There, the stone walls and low-storeyed mansions are unaltered. Plane trees and dim lighting almost make the massive city withdraw, almost give the illusion of silence and serenity. But the heavy vibration of countless ventilators and motors echoes through the thick air and seems even louder when, deep in the night, the horns, sirens, and screeching of tires and of people dies out. The sky is not black but purplish-pink as the coloured lights reflect off the dense, humid air. In Shanghai, there's really no escape from the action; it's always present.

We're staying at a cheap hotel. Anywhere in China, Shanghai included, thirty dollars or less gets you a room with a private bathroom and clean sheets. Hotel lobbies may be recently retiled, brightly lit. The reception might be gilded in gold and framed by red velvet drapes. Staff is usually plentiful, neatly dressed and cheerful.

The elevators are modern and swift. Our rooms are on the fifth floor of this modest concrete tower. My room's window is high on the wall and faces the next building. Unlike the lobby, the cell is perfectly drab. No bother—the chamber will fulfill its role nicely. I drop my bags, quickly shower and rush out the door. I'm expected at a supper for the groom. Viv stays behind. A bachelor party is no place for a young woman.

I join the party in a large, high-ceilinged Guizhou-style restaurant. Guizhou is one of China's southern provinces. It's heavily mountainous and covered in jungle, a place of ethnic minorities, mostly hill tribes. The people of Guizhou eat a fresh, spicy cuisine—the perfect, straightforward food to accompany serious beer drinking.

Most everyone at the party is English. A tall, fair lot on the whole. A wedding in Shanghai has some draw to it, and friends and family have come from far. People trickle in over the course of the evening, but a solid group is there from the start. The groom's inner circle is composed of residents of China. One might say they are shipwrecked in China, caught like my friend Deryk. He and the groom, James, have been happy captives of China for well over a decade. They have shared many adventures in China and have seen many of its mysteries. They are deeply in love with China. A reckless, all-consuming love, but hardly an affair without precedent, especially in Shanghai, where over the years a steady supply of westerners have come to settle for good.

The English are drinkers. The Chinese, of course, are aware of and comfortable with collective excess. If they have beer and food in front of them themselves, they're amused by the cheer of foreigners, happy perhaps to share in its warmth. They're no strangers to crude revelry. Tonight, our group is noticeably coarse. These are big boys with heavy bones. They shout at each other and knock things over. They make wild, sloppy gestures. Boisterousness is a Chinese trait. But I pause to wonder whether the boisterousness of a dozen male foreigners might bring back bad memories. Shanghai once belonged to the white devils, I tell myself. Foreign soldiers, sailors, merchants or bankers who on occasion caused all sorts of suffering to the Chinese, usually with great impunity.

Luckily, jet lag begins to take its toll on this bunch. And the shipwrecked have already given themselves over to China too many times to lose themselves to the barbarities of their hearts. Plus the groom's two best Chinese buddies make an appearance. Allen is a suave young businessman from a village near Ningbo, a prosperous city south of Shanghai. James taught English there on arriving in China a decade ago; Allen was one of his brightest students, and James had stayed with Allen's family on numerous occasions. Allen is something of a prince. He's athletic and good-looking, courteous and patient with all, his manners impeccable. He's always ready to help, to serve when needed. As a class leader and star pupil, he was noticed by the Communist Party and accepted the honour of joining its ranks. This has helped his rise to a position among the young business elite of Shanghai. Still, Allen's ascent has been fast, even for those who know and admire him.

His financial success seems to follow the city's fortunes. He drives a sleek new car and sports the latest smartphone. He wears fine clothes and travels frequently. He's unwaveringly smooth and good-humoured. He has just flown in from Sichuan, he explains, and apologizes for his late arrival. He is cheered by all.

The groom, from Middle England, is a football aficionado. Many of his mates are football buddies. In fact, a soccer game is to be conducted the next day. Allen has been designated captain of the Chinese team and has the odious duty of assembling the necessary Chinese players for a game fought along racial lines. If this weighs on Allen, it doesn't show. A few revellers even do provocative boasting of the Anglo-Saxons' clear superiority. To this, Allen smiles enthusiastically.

Then a second man arrives, known simply by the nickname Lito. He comes in with a swagger and gives off a nervous intensity. Perhaps he has already been drinking. He has the features of an intellectual, wears his hair long and pulls off a somewhat dishevelled look.

For a few years after their first stint as English teachers, Deryk and James had been active in the Shanghai film scene. A Shanghai-area native, Lito had gone to the capital for his studies and was fresh from the prestigious Beijing Film Academy. His final short film had made its mark on the community, and it had generally been decided that Lito was bound for glory.

In those days, Lito was a dashing figure in Shanghai. He was brilliant, poetic and charismatic. The underground was new then. And the first vanguard of artists had the run of the night. Lito was a man to follow deep into Shanghai after dark. For Deryk and James, who got by in Chinese, Lito was above all else a conversationalist. Deep in the night, Lito was insightful and frank. His sense of truth was razor-sharp. And he loved Shanghai.

"But he always had a reckless side," says Deryk, who is there from Beijing for the wedding. He tells me of a time when Lito and his policeman half-brother, both of them heavily inebriated, began to berate a foreigner whom they believed was insulting the Chinese people with his lecherous behaviour. "It was not like the white man was doing anything unusual," Deryk says. "He was just drinking, leering at women and taking up a lot of room. Something white guys are doing all of the time in Shanghai. But before I knew what was happening, Lito sends a bottle flying through the air at this guy. I grab Lito just as he's pouncing on the hapless Dutchman. Then I feel myself being pulled to the ground by Lito's brother and I'm protecting myself as best I can from an onslaught of flying fists. It was not a happy evening."

Looking back on the incident, Deryk confesses to being amused by the barroom drama. It highlighted both his friend's qualities and his shortcomings: a feisty idealism and a poetic sense of chivalry combined with a tendency to recklessness and excess.

Despite the tremendous promise that everyone felt for Lito at the time of his graduation, destiny has not been kind to him. Early on, he turned down a few serious jobs he thought beneath him, yet none of his own ideas found sympathetic ears. He did not direct another film for five years. He watched younger directors freshly graduated from the big schools earn the successes that he had hoped for. And recently he began to accept any directing work he could find, mostly low and crude commercial work.

"Those of us who dreamt of making it as artists couldn't help but feel sympathetic," says Deryk, "but he became even more reckless. Now that we have women in our lives and more sedentary jobs, this causes problems. I'm quite frankly surprised that he was invited to the wedding. But I'm not unhappy about it—I miss the guy."

I'm curious about Lito. There's a problem, however: his English is poor. It was never particularly good, I'm told, but these past years it has further deteriorated. Lito is seated on the other side of our big round table. I attempt conversation. "See any good movies recently?" I ask.

He shoots me an interested smile, urging me to repeat through the noise. I do. He offers up the name of a famous Italian director from the 1970s.

"Oh yeah! What about new movies?" I ask.

He can't decipher my question. I repeat, but to no avail. Someone between us intervenes to help.

Lito finally responds. Our Samaritan interlocutor translates for me. It's a recent Hollywood title that I've heard of but dismissed as drivel—a juvenile romantic comedy, I think.

"So you like pop art? POP ART?" I ask, sounding him for an angle.

"Yes, pop art," he says, nodding sympathetically.

I'm intrigued, and perhaps puzzled, since he cuts such a bohemian figure. By then, we have both decided that communication under the present circumstances is hopeless. With a disappointed nod, Lito agrees to postpone our conversation. He goes home when we leave the restaurant.

No matter. The weekend is to be one of festivities. It's the eve of the Mid-Autumn Festival and National Day holiday, a time for friendship and family. From the restaurant, we proceed to old haunts of the shipwrecked.

As we emerge from the fleet of taxis, there's immediate disappointment, as if an error had been made, a bad decision. Deryk and James are reminded once again how fast things change in China. But it's too late to intervene; drunken boys are already engaging with the scene.

"I knew our old outdoor cafés had turned grimy," James laments.

"No matter," Deryk says, chuckling. "The experience might rattle a few cages."

It's a brightly lit, treed street, lined with a series of single-floored businesses. Each one is a bar at some stage of metamorphosis into a nightclub. The front windows or terraces are mostly closed up. Scarred and devious-looking doormen guard the entrances.

Clearly, this street is meant to answer the foreigner's appetite for sin. Here are wandering westerners not descended as old from the ships but nonetheless in Shanghai with a thirst formed of long and hard journeying. Here, the lone businessman who hinted to the taxi driver back at the hotel that he was in search of company.

The newly arrived foreigners mix with those long marooned in Shanghai, the club's regulars never numerous but always present. They come searching perhaps for the company of fellow foreigners of any sort. They're men with tanned and grim faces, old boys with airs of repressed desperation, with a need to remember—or to forget.

Here, the Chinese serve: the petty thieves who man the door and whose job it is to extinguish any violence that might erupt; the drinking staff whose balanced countenance carefully ensures that product is exchanged for money as smoothly and easily as possible; the bartender, the waitresses, the almost invisible young men and women who keep the tables clear of clutter; and, of course, the companions of fortune. Some are free agents, maybe offering more than just sexual gratification. Most, however, are urban labourers, indentured to a guild and meagrely maintained. Among them, older women, battered veterans forever caught in the trade, supervise the younger women, who are mostly from the fringes of China or beyond. Mountain people or people of the western wastes. Minorities or Mongolians.

This too is an economy and functions like a production process. Labour is combined with primary resources, and tender extracted. But it's a dirty business, relegated to dark powers. A world of human smuggling and contraband and violence.

In these kinds of places, one might be tempted to conclude that after a period of puritanical repression, vice has returned to the new China. But it's absurd to think that vice can be altogether extinguished anywhere. Human passions are managed. Balances are sought. In its early days Communist China may well have been rather puritanical about sex, but it still embraced other more vicious and fanatical aspects of human nature.

Once more, the place is hardly suited for conversation. The boys are already half-pickled and take their drinking even further. I stick close to Allen, who barely drinks, and to Deryk, who drinks alcohol like it were water.

"Where do young Shanghainese go out at night?" I ask Allen.

"Oh, I don't know."

Deryk will have none of it. "What about that big place past Julu Lu?" he prods.

"It changed its name. It's now called Armani," Allen says.

"And?"

"I haven't been yet, but I hear it's very popular," he admits.

"Well, I suggest you two go there," Deryk says. "I'll help the groom home and meet you there in a bit."

It suits me. I would like to get a less sordid impression of Shanghai nightlife, and Allen is always ready to oblige.

The taxi speeds us through the Shanghai night. Lights, colours, people roll by. After a while, we come to a stop beneath a huge yellow neon sign: Armani.

By its facade, it appears to be some sort of super-club. Heavy bass rumbles from within. After a doorman looks us over, we enter the antechamber, where we quickly pay cover, then move toward the music. The first room is a huge and crowded dance-hall. A strobe light matches the fast beat, catching momentary poses of the figures on the dance floor. People are committed to the rhythm. Everyone's young and Chinese. Along the edge of the room are booths where people lounge around low tables. Many have their eyes turned on the action. The crowd has a fresh and honest look, as if people aren't abusing themselves.

There is a second level to the club. Passageways can be seen above the dancehall. Allen seems to think we're more suited to this exclusive section, so we head to a staircase and follow it up. We pass a more intimate bar and head down a long hallway. A series of small rooms give onto it. Some of the doors are open and I can see that the rooms have windows overlooking the dance floor. These, I understand, are the VIP rooms, for private parties.

We settle in a room on the opposite side, a luxuriously appointed windowless cell. The upper walls are mostly mirrors. Three sides of the room are occupied by a red wraparound couch and coffee table. On the other side is the console: the LCD television and the karaoke machine.

Maggie, our hostess, introduces herself. She's unusually tall and quite extroverted. She declares in English that she struggles with the language and doesn't enjoy speaking it. So she continues in Mandarin and wishes us a happy evening, urging us to let her know if we need anything. A couple of waitresses soon bring bottles of juice, water and canned foreign beers. They also bring up a karaoke playlist on the television.

Then the party girls arrive. Giggling, they politely sit beside us and serve us beer. One of them stands to dance to the music. She is awkward, like a private-school debutante. She is soon joined by her friend and together they try hard to sing their way through an American pop song. We are not in a critical mood and heartedly applaud their efforts. We are soon engaged in a conga line, stumbling about in the confines of our party chamber. For a moment, there is much glee and laughter.

But I soon return to the main dance floor to embrace the anonymity of the electronic music. Here, dance replaces the questionable innuendo of the VIP treatment. In their exhibitions and exchanges, dancers revel in the potential of contact, not its actuality. I'm more a creature of these fleeting, unrealized fantasies, happy to dance alone in the crowd, full of ideas that will never happen.

Around me, I sense a growing commitment to similar ideals. These dancers are not the attendants from the red chambers above. They are not working for the pleasure of paying customers. They are here escaping from work or even avoiding it altogether and living off their parents. But one cannot reduce the revelry to economic irresponsibility. These are people propelling their bodies into the void, tentatively suggesting that their bodies and the individuals within them are each unique, that they have broken away from their surroundings and are momentarily free of all demands on them.

A few give themselves completely to the ritual. With closed eyes, they search for the rhythm like monks in search of enlightenment. Others have come to commune. Two girls next to me are clearly close friends; their smiles to each other reinforce their excitement. They launch into ever more daring poses, thrilled to be openly exposing the potential of their bodies.

But many of the young people seem more cautious about the experience; they huddle together, giggling frequently. Dancing is something they are learning in small, sporadic increments. Some might become adept; others may return to more responsible and conformist practices.

Although there is little puritanism toward sex in China, even in a trendy Shanghai nightclub, the individualistic abandon required to dance is still in short supply, though clearly it is growing.

Travelling alone and too shy to reach out in any other way, for me, the dance floor has often been a way to commune if not communicate with the locals. A kind of complicity is established among dancers without a need for words. For a moment, dazzled by the rhythm, I might feel myself a part of the place. I might feel myself known and loved by the beautiful strangers around me. Invariably, however, my nights would end like this one: alone. A little tired, a little happy, a little wiser maybe, riding through the night toward my cell.

In the balmy twilight, the taxi is a comforting vessel. Busy cities are momentarily empty of people and cars. The vehicle moves swiftly. The driver is quiet yet somehow full of solicitude, carefully offering passage to a lone soul on his way.

Friday morning, I need to buy sneakers for the soccer game. I should also pick up some DVDs to refresh my supply. I'll cast a glance at the consumer economy exploding in Shanghai.

After our trying trip down the river, Viv surely needs a break. She's meeting up with a school friend at a central landmark. We'll travel to this spot together, then go our separate ways. We head out on foot northbound toward the new city centre.

Our own neighbourhood is fairly modern, residential and Chinese. And downright ugly. Yet somehow it speaks to me. No building in sight has been erected with art in mind. Almost everywhere I look are concrete towers. At their base is a hodgepodge of structures: older buildings of stone or brick, stained black with years of exposure. Occasionally, a new tower clad in glass and pale plastic stands out. Or a new superstore, all white and shiny in its cloak of carefully aimed lights, appears like a beacon, radiating materialistic optimism through the grey manifold, as if to say that all problems can be solved by consumption.

Still, the neighbourhood interests me because it's pure Shanghai. It's a place where the people live, where by the hundreds of thousands they return to sleep and eat, huddled close in tiny apartments stacked high. Their surroundings are devoid of history yet already aged and worn. I cannot guess who these people are, what they do, why they live. In their number and density they are anonymous, going about their lives unnoticed, each a master of a miniature microcosm.

Sure, recognizable forms are present: the retired pensioners, the young working couples. But among them, the different, the dissident or the deviant can dwell beyond the cares or interests of others. People go to work in every possible direction and at every hour, passing in the streets and elevators without the faintest recognition of each other.

The neighbourhood is also short on services. There are but a few restaurants and shops. For five hundred metres in either direction from the hotel, there's only a primitive laundromat and an electronics mall. The latter is a five-storey beehive of cluttered booths all selling computer accessories and cameras. Further on is a newer strip with real estate offices and a Carrefour superstore selling mass-produced foodstuffs and appliances; the latter is popular, displaying almost the same frenzied consumption visible in similar stores in the West.

As far as prepared food goes, the offerings—usually so plentiful in China—are truly sparse and inadequate here: a coffee shop, a couple of low-end Western fast-food joints and generic Chinese noodle chains. The lack of commerce emphasizes the area's deeply residential character but makes the inhabitants that much more disengaged. People are not to be seen doing anything. Rather, they're stowed away in their dwellings or coming to and going from them. Their needs must be filled behind closed doors or elsewhere.

After ten minutes of walking, we begin to transition into a different neighbourhood. This new area has two faces: the old and decrepit, and the splendidly refurbished. As we walk through it, it reveals itself to be an old commercial district. Brick warehouses abound. The first ones are still occupied by petty merchants and tenements. In a cramped space along a particularly dirty strip, I locate a DVD shop. As usual, it's manned by a youngster.

By now, I know the routine: you position yourself at one of the bins and quickly flip through the titles, withdrawing anything that's remotely interesting. Within a few minutes, you end up with a dozen or so titles at a dollar apiece. The only caveat is that films that are too recent have usually been recorded with a camera pointed at a movie screen; the image and sound are pitiful. They are to be avoided. One could lament the copyright infringements involved in the sale and purchase of such pirated DVDs. But what strikes me is just how rich a media diet it provides. People are exposed to far more stories than they ever would otherwise have been.

These films and TV shows are a means of communication; at higher prices, the communication simply wouldn't happen. The financiers derive no profits from these sales. This may be unfair, but still the dreams and ideas of those who made these films find through this distribution ever more distant resonance.

Viv laughs at my quick selection of more than fifteen titles. "The Chinese government only officially imports ten foreign movies each year," she says, "and heavily censors them. No surprise our appetite for entertainment needs to be satisfied through these unofficial means."

After a few more grimy blocks of petty merchants like my DVD privateer, the neighbourhood undergoes a transformation. A strip of old brick warehouses has been remodelled into a luxury pedestrian mall. Once cleaned and fitted with slick windows and fancy lighting, these old buildings become elegant.

The past actually has to be eradicated for nostalgia to take effect. Here is the Shanghai we westerners want to see—the East-meets-West theme, an image implanted in our heads by Hollywood movies and magazine articles. A dignified charcoal austerity—the forms of industry and stability—upon which a sensual brush has left its strokes of red, black, yellow and purple.

We picture the lady in red silk approaching on the cobbled street as we duck into the familiar coffee shop for an overpriced soy latte. It's a marriage of familiarity and fantasy that we cannot resist. Here are brands we find at home, yet in these surroundings, we feel that we can afford them, or that we need them—and with our plastic cards we incur debts we know not when we will reimburse.

As I walk through the mall, I see another Shanghai above and beyond. Viv and I are nearing the centre, and glass towers loom large above the brick warehouses. The morning is grey and overcast. But several skyscrapers are lit so as to glow bright in the daylight. In the business core, the city becomes much bigger and even more depersonalized. People don't ramble about in the streets; their businesses don't clutter the sidewalks. Everything is indoors. The outside is an increasingly hostile territory of smog and overpasses, traffic and noise. Luckily, most of the buildings are heavily armoured against this atmosphere; they wear plates of metal and glass. The remaining older buildings have gradually been fitted with armours of aluminum and plastics. With their beacons of light, they all promise safety within.

I may be no sucker for luxury goods but I too need my brands. I too can confuse a branded product with a quality product. If I can't recognize a brand, I'm suspicious about the product's manufacture; I sense shoddy workmanship and cost-cutting measures. Of course, the shoes are quite probably made in the same place with the same process. But I cannot conceive of wearing a sneaker simply made to function at a soccer match; I need a sneaker that speaks to the world, that says that I'm talented and cool. So I want to buy it in clean and well-lit surroundings. Yet I entertain the thought that in China I'll pay less for the same glitter.

The shopping centre occupies the bottom floors of a massive new tower. It's a labyrinth of levels and escalators. The athletic brands have their own floor. Viv has a few minutes to spare before meeting her friend, so she tags along. The shop is clean and well-lit. The selection is impressive, and employees outnumber the clientele.

Followed by a young attendant, I quickly choose a brand and settle on a pair of retro-looking blue-and-gold sneakers. They are machine-signed in memory of a Brazilian soccer player whose holy support I will need to play a game I haven't played since I was twelve. If the price is better here than back home, the difference is negligible. But with my single purchase, perhaps I paid the equivalent of the store clerk's weekly wage or two weeks for the worker who sewed and glued the shoe.

We rise to the surface to meet Viv's friend. She's even more petite than Viv and clearly has made concessions to the Shanghai predilection for brand names. I show her my new shoes, then take my leave of the young women.

I'm curious to check out a shopping-centre food court. My choice turns out to be poor, and I am faced with a generic selection of restaurant chains. I enter a popular joint selling a Sinofied version of the Japanese classic, ramen, itself an early-twentieth-century adaptation of Chinese egg noodles in broth.

The park where the soccer game is to be held is on the other side of town. I study my map to see how to get there. The subway will take me close, but I have to change trains twice and then still walk a ways. I never bother with buses—when you get on one in a strange city, only God knows where it will take you. A taxi would be the right option, but I don't know how to say where I'm going. Even if I did, more often than not, the drivers act as if they have no idea what I am saying. And Shanghai drivers will scarcely look at a map. So I take a moment and trace out the Chinese characters I read on the map. Even this is tricky; drawing a character is meticulous work. And in copying names off a map, you can never be quite sure whether you are drawing the characters for Friendship Park or for public washrooms.

When I emerge from the mall, the city core is frenzied; people are everywhere, moving fast. The streets, clogged with cars and trucks, are hazy with fumes. For the millions of working people in the city centre, it's time to get out. The beginning of the National Day holiday and Mid-Autumn Festival is hours away, and already people are vying for the exit.

I'm one of many competing for a taxi, in order to return to my hotel before heading over to the soccer match, so I decide to walk toward a less congested area. Along the way, I manage to flag down a cab, but the driver scoffs when I show him the business card of my hotel. I suppose my hotel is too close to be considered a worthy fare at a time of such high demand. A little further on,

I catch a cab that has just dropped off its passenger. I show the hotel business card again and don't wait for an answer before offering three times the going rate. He accepts but seems unhappy and antsy. I don't dare ask him to wait for me while I change into sports clothing.

When I emerge from my hotel but a few moments later, the city has undergone yet another transformation. The streets in the hotel's neighbourhood have grown surprisingly quiet. Occasionally, a taxi passes but not one is available. The concierge is also unhelpful. He tells me that over the past hour he has called for cabs twice and neither has shown up.

With only twenty minutes remaining before the game starts and knowing that the wait at the hotel would drive me crazy, I decide to begin the long journey toward the park on foot, hoping to hail a cab along the way. As I move westward, it dawns on me that I might well have erred by setting out on foot. I suddenly realize how big the city is—and I need to get from the southeast corner of it to a southwesterly point. I cross a large swath of residential neighbourhood, then walk beneath a couple of elevated highways. A few times I raise my hand upon seeing a taxi only to have it pass me by, already occupied.

Eventually, I enter an area that has recently been flattened. Billboards and plastic fencing enclose an unlit and inactive construction site. Although the traffic flow beside me is steady and thick, I know my prospects for a taxi have plummeted. No driver will be circulating here looking for a fare. A glance at my map and cell phone reveal that I have covered but a third of the distance in twenty-five minutes. My comrades will start without me.

I grow anxious and frustrated. I try to laugh at the thought that Deryk, ever competitive and trying to foment energy and enthusiasm, has already made jokes about people wimping out of the match. All would conclude that I was among those unwilling to accept a challenge and test my skills. Meanwhile, here I am crossing a Shanghai wasteland on foot in my new Pelé sneakers.

The sky is getting darker. I am faced with the choice of diverting north toward an area with a couple of major hotels or staying the course toward brighter lights on the horizon. As I ponder my options, a slick new city bus pulls up beside me and opens its doors. Inside, a driver sits without expression. The bus is bright and clean. Outside, the air is thick and gloomy. Clearly, I must board this bus.

As I fumble with my money to pay the fare, the driver curtly ushers me on with an impatient wave of the hand. He doesn't want my money. The bus is full but not overly so. I even spot an empty seat. As I walk toward it, people barely lift their heads to notice me. The bus travels westward. I begin to chart its course on my map. Like a missile, the bus burns through the wasteland and emerges into a neighbourhood more suited to it and its passengers, a well-lit and modern area. The bus begins to drop off its passengers and pick up new ones. My impatience has vanished; I'm enjoying the ride.

As they come and go, people barely look at each other. They all carry themselves with a quiet and humble dignity. Even the elderly wear their clothes well; the items fit and were obviously chosen for their gracious properties. When in pairs, the elderly share in muffled conversations full of smiles and pauses. The young people are fresh-faced and energetic. They carry trendy shopping bags and sport white earbuds. Most tap away at their smartphones, likely texting their friends about holiday plans.

I'm now forty minutes late, but at least the bus has travelled in precisely the right direction. As it arrives at the park, I prepare myself to run the kilometre or so north to the playing field.

Soon, the field comes into sight. I see people embracing, some sportsmanlike handshakes and high-fives. I've missed the match. With my new shoes pointless, silly even, I march onto the field to greet my friends. A young Chinese player comes forth to shake my hand in congratulation. He must think that I played. Or perhaps he's applauding me for my support.

I pass a clique of English players whose celebrations have resoundingly aggressive undertones. One particular gent, ruddy, balding and full of posture, scowls. "If they'd played that way in England, they'd have been fouled off the pitch!" he says.

Confused, I find Deryk and ask how the match went.

"We won," he says, "but some people were taking the game more seriously than others." He turns to James, the groom, and with a lowered voice asks, "What do you say, they let us win?"

"I think so," James admits, "but you never know."

Just then, Allen appears, looking fresh and happy. He exchanges a friendly nod with Deryk, who thanks him for making the match happen. The other Chinese players whom Allen assembled have by now collected their belongings on the sidelines and are heading toward their vehicles or being picked up by friends or girlfriends. Allen refers to them as young business associates. They, like Allen, drive shiny new white sedans and have slick cell phones and fancy watches. They radiate optimism, health and confidence.

The humidity and haze brought the night early upon Shanghai. But the dying sun breaks through on the horizon and momentarily paints the grass and trees with gold. On all sides, the city rises above the park. Its buildings cut a jagged contour against the ashen sky. The soccer field's lights come on, creating a luminous halo in the thick air that envelops the city. I watch one of the white cars leave the park and merge into a stream of vehicles. The city is still humming and spinning, people moving in all directions. The purpose in the air is overwhelming.

Saturday is wedding day. But first Viv and I meet an acquaintance of mine, Min, for lunch. Min is an intellectual that I had met once before through friends. We talked only briefly through a translator, but he had a perspective on history and Mao that was unique. He suggested we meet at a restaurant near his work. Viv is curious why he's near his office, in the old centre by the river, on the first day of the autumn holiday.

We head down there early to visit the Bund first. The Bund was the premier boulevard of old Shanghai. Like the Malecón, the seawall that connects all Havana, the Bund has been a defining feature of development in Shanghai. The word *bund* comes from India by way of English seamen; it means embankment. Old Shanghai lined up against it. All things and all people showed up on the Bund at some point.

It was on the Bund that Sassoon and Kadoorie set up shop. They were both of Middle Eastern extraction, from Jewish merchant families who had built clever alliances with British imperial traders throughout Mesopotamia and up and down the Arabian and Indian shores. They were men who could get you what you wanted. Moving east with Britain as it expanded its empire and interests, these men gravitated toward Shanghai, which was fast becoming the most important trade city of the Orient.

From their stone fortresses on the Bund, Shanghai's merchant houses commanded trade networks connecting London and San Francisco to every port between Basra and Bali. The world's greatest banks also opened branches in Shanghai, to bankroll increasingly ambitious enterprises in the East. These too stood on the Bund.

Shanghai of the Bund era was a central node of a global community of capitalists. An original special economic zone, Shanghai was in China, yet Chinese law did not apply to foreigners here. Excepting the brief Japanese reign during the Second World War, no single power could claim absolute authority over Shanghai. It belonged to everyone and to no one. It was the kind of place great entrepreneurs loved: booming and loosely regulated.

A few old buildings of the Bund still stand, and some of the old hotels continue to operate. What was once grand now seems cramped and crummy. But the Bund is undergoing a facelift, with prestigious new buildings arising to replace what has grown soiled and inefficient. The new Bund has nothing to do with the area's jazz-era glitz. New China has set up shop here now. Those who walk the Bund or glance at the buildings and the river are not the free operators once essential to Shanghai. Those who come here now do so at the pleasure of the people of China as represented by the Chinese Communist Party. The Chinese have also dwarfed the Bund with a city built all around it that commands attention far more than this old strip.

When we arrive on the Bund, it's overrun with peoples from the north and west of China. They come as families or groups of old men or women. They wear the utilitarian clothing not worn by the cosmopolitan Shanghainese, a robust or even military accoutrement, clothing meant to survive the dust and wind. They merrily emerge from tour buses and subway stations, cross the

Bund at a hurried pace to the river and stand there with their backs to the gloomy stone palaces. They're not here for the emblems of a foreign past. They gaze at the Pudong skyline across the oil slick. Filled with wonder, they look upward toward the ball and spire, and at the massive new towers of metal and glass that touch the skies. There, it is bright and clean, powerful and promising, unlike the quarter of the city's heyday.

Off the Bund, old Shanghai is even less captivating. Many of the quarter's old buildings now seem prosaic and small-time. There's little glory left in addresses in the old quarter. Min's work in the old quarter is not at the cutting edge of anything either. His trade is old, stiff, conservative and reliable. And no one gets rich in his field. We arrive at the restaurant of his choosing. It's upstairs, huge and empty. We take seats and wait for Min to arrive.

He's medium tall and skinny. His almond-shaped eyes and receding, wavy hair give him a slightly foreign appearance. He comes in carrying a light raincoat and umbrella. He wears the attire of the middle manager: dark slacks and a pale polyester button-down. The burgundy sweater-vest must be his concession to the weekend. He immediately asks what I have been up to in China. I tell him that I have been going to different kinds of places and meeting different sorts of people in an effort to understand China. I can't help but smile bashfully at my vague yet pretentious answer. Min, however, is generous-natured and urges me on.

He wants to know precisely where I've been and where I'm going. I list off my itinerary quickly. I admit that it is but a small picture of China and a short window for observation. I tell him that I'm investigating a few key themes: China's relationship with its past and its relationship with the West, Chinese values—family, urban, rural, traditional and modern—the economy, the environment, food, religion and sex. Again, we share a laugh at the scope of my ambitions.

I remind Min that when we last met he had talked about modern China's attempts to grapple with its recent past—how for many years under Mao, China tried to escape its past. And how now it's again reshaping it. I ask him to continue his thoughts, to explain what the shape of this past might be.

Min's reflections, translated by Vivien, are nuanced. Viv must work hard, and I pay close attention to Min's expressions and gestures to track when he is switching from exposition to synthesis.

Min deals in historical perceptions. He starts by explaining that the initial enthusiasm for Communism in China was not well-thought-out; it was first and foremost a visceral reaction to the constant instability existing in China. He admits that it was also widely thought that China had become bankrupt and morally corrupt, that the class system was broken and oppressive.

In any case, fear of violence is a powerful motivator, he explains, and China was full of violence a hundred years ago: the ghastly Taiping Rebellion, the Boxer Uprising, foreign aggressions, warlordism and tyranny big and small. The people were suffering and confused. They had a growing desire to see things change fundamentally.

Two new elements also combined to enhance revolutionary sentiment: the arrival of the outside world in China and the liberalized media. The former brought in powerful new ideas, both political and economic, but also brought violence and helped the Chinese focus their frustrations on clear culprits as bad things happened to them. The free media gave acute suffering a broad and even intellectual resonance—something not missed by anyone who could read.

Perhaps these circumstances gave the people a stronger than usual willingness to embrace chaos and risk, to make great sacrifices, to bring about some kind of deep change, Min says with a smile as he waits for Vivien to convey his argument.

"Rage is a tool," he then says, "something to be used." He goes on to tell us that the only thing that gave the movement any unity was the collective desire for change. Among early revolutionary leaders, the ideas for change ranged across a broad spectrum: all the types of socialism—Leninist, Stalinist, Trotskyist—industrial worker–based or peasant-based movements; a handful of anarchist sects; various liberal reform ideologies; neo-traditionalists; cultish spiritualist movements like the Taiping; and many more.

Necessarily, the first task of the revolution was to order and harmonize this cacophony of ideals. This was Mao Zedong's speciality, Min says. By 1949, Mao commanded the national narrative. He had made himself seem to be at the centre of change, the galvanizing element.

Min takes an aside to mention the Korean War. He describes how, in his opinion, many people miss just how much the war helped Mao. The war came at just the right moment to help the chairman solidify his command, despite the heavy losses incurred by China. Once more a great power was threatening invasion. It was widely perceived that only a terrific show of unity, with Mao at the helm, could break this foreign advance.

So the chairman's authority became sacrosanct. But it's critical to understand, Min emphasizes, that Mao himself wavered between contradictory ideals about the magnitude of change necessary. He swung between seeing change as a reorganization of material forces and seeing change as something far more radical—a fundamental reshaping of the human being, the New Man theory. It's in this tension that one has to understand the official relationship with the past, Min explains. For the past really is the shape of all material forces. If one endeavours to go beyond these forces, one has to set new terms for the past or, sometimes, erase it altogether. This is the background of the Cultural Revolution, his own historical specialty, Min concludes.

We take a moment. Min is happy to be going on the record about his intellectual pursuits. I'm similarly happy. This is rare stuff that he's explaining. I am also perpetually curious about the Cultural Revolution. For her part, Viv tries to share our enthusiasm for the conversation, but she's too busy translating to share in our giddy excitement.

At one point, I interrupt her to ask her to ask Min if he considers himself a radical. He shies away from the qualification, explaining that he's merely describing a history that is precisely moved by radical ideas. And that perhaps the Chinese have a different threshold for radicalism than westerners, who have known great comfort and stability in recent years. But, he adds, of course this too is changing as material conditions in China are greatly improving. As recent and dramatic as the Cultural Revolution was—or even the Tiananmen Square events, for that matter—they are quickly being erased from memory by comfort.

He then returns to Mao and explains that at times, the chairman was a rigid proponent of traditional practices. At other times, he called for the toppling of all monuments. Over the years, Mao shifted toward a more and more radical position. He began to feel that abusive patterns of behaviour were so ingrained in the popular ethos, all beliefs had to be dismantled, that a reorganization of material conditions might temporarily correct social ills. But the traditional ills of China were like a cancer that would soon re-emerge if not constantly contained. This is why he came to believe in the need for an entirely new type of human.

Throughout the 1950s and 1960s, Mao began to fear that the revolutionary structure itself might be infected and might serve as the locus for the perpetuation of old evils. Deep down, Min says, Mao was also fighting to keep his personal narrative central to the People's Republic. Again and again, Mao came up with radical new initiatives. But his schemes mostly failed. Each time, he blamed the failures on the influence of the pragmatists, whom he thought were vehicles for perpetuating the wrongs of the past. The implementation of his bold schemes was never brave enough, the chairman concluded. This is why he began to believe that the party bureaucracy could not be relied on to bring about the necessary and fundamental change. It had to be fomented directly among the people, especially the young, with the chairman at the helm, of course, leading the nation's children toward a world that was shiny and new.

This in a nutshell is the logic behind the Cultural Revolution, Min explains. But even during the revolution, the pendulum would sometimes swing toward the pragmatists. And ultimately, the pragmatists came out of this period on top. Passions were consumed and the people were exhausted. The people had probably lost their capacity for belief in Mao's vision.

Min goes on to say that he remains fascinated by this period and the ideas that led to it; it really has no parallel in history—a leader using the people to destroy the very government he created.

Then Min describes his work of compiling stories about the Cultural Revolution. "You and I are sitting here and we suddenly decide that our boss is a self-centred profiteer unworthy of authority. With that, we march down into the street toward our place of work, along the way convincing others of the need to act. By the time we get there, we're a small mob. We climb up to the boss's office and remove him on the spot and designate one of us to take his place." He pauses for effect, then adds, "Can you imagine this? This kind of drama happening all over the place?"

"It almost sounds as if you like this period," I say with a smile.

He explains that he likes to study it. "For an intellectual, it's fascinating," he says.

He tells us that for years now he has been compiling and collecting street-level dramas of the Cultural Revolution, similar to the scenario he just described. The passion and audacity of the exchanges are unlike anything else, he says. The human character is on display in all its fury and splendour. "I guess I am moved by these moments of pure possibility," he confesses, "the willingness to transform everything."

Min tells us that he has conducted interviews with people but prefers the written records. Apparently, descriptions of innumerable events were written down at the time—semi-official transcripts or even private accounts.

"That's ironic," I say. "The period advocated rejecting the past and you're recording it."

"I'm a believer in balance," he counters, "and now China is creating the most facile and easily packaged past. People can't live without the past, so it's manufactured for them. Simple, mass produced and ready to use. You're well aware of these forms, I'm sure. But I have made myself a scribe of the dream of pastlessness. As a reminder of what we're capable of, both good and bad."

"You're a believer in extremes?" I venture.

"Without extremes there's no middle."

"Yet you seem a mild-mannered intellectual."

"That's because all of my pursuits are intellectual. But the Cultural Revolution attempted to blur the distinction between action and intellect." Min then comments how the cult of outside ideas is growing more and more prevalent in China. Still, for all but a minority, it's a materialistic, superficial pursuit.

He turns back to the chairman. In Mao's early years within the party, Min explains, he was struggling for influence with people who had been educated in Japan and the West. People who were often in close communication with Moscow. From the beginning, at an almost instinctive level, Mao felt change had to start where the Chinese past was in many ways still present and unaltered by outside influence: the countryside. Here was a realm beyond the intellect, a realm of action. The presence of the past was authentic and brutal. People clung to repetition and superstition like a drowning man to a log in a river. In the face of great suffering, the past gave them their only assurance that somehow life goes on.

But the past is also a tool of manipulation; it can be used to control and oppress. The indolent and rich can tailor the past to be comfortable and flattering. The corrupt can use it to dominate. The liberation of the peasants from the past is a kind of explosion. As the people lift their heads from the ruts and the muck, an immense amount of raw power is unleashed. Mao saw this.

"But when we look around," I say, "sure we see Mao on the currency and Mao on the buildings, but is this really Mao's China? I see Deng's China."

Min admits that Mao's destructiveness set forth among the Chinese an idea of freedom. All had to be questioned. Maybe this was necessary, Min says, then adds, "I'm an optimist. It remains to be seen where China is headed. All agree that something big is happening to China. Some say it started with Mao; others, before him. Some think it's for the better; some, for the worse. Some see possibility opening, some see it closing. Some might worry that we are losing our way. I do not. Things are changing."

The wedding is to be held in a distinguished and fancy old hotel. It occupies a sizable area of the French Quarter. The location is spectacular. Upon passing the tall walls of the complex, one enters into a green sanctuary of perfectly manicured lawns and showy trees. The hotel is a series of grandiose but low-storeyed stone buildings. It's like a film set: the feel of luxury harks back to the 1920s and 1930s. A few details, however, hint at our current era— ultra-slick lighting and roomy elevators lead to exquisite rooms, the rooms of fancy hotels the world over.

Our event is held away from the main hotel in a separate garden pavilion. The guests are seated at two rows of tables on either side of a central walkway; at the front is an area for the ceremony. Viv and I are seated with Chinese-based westerners and their local wives, along with Allen and Lito, accompanied by their girlfriends. The ceremony interweaves moments of English mirth with Chinese customs. The humour of the Western components falls flat—there is many an expressionless Chinese face. The best man's speech, full of friendly mockery, makes for some especially tense moments. In China, weddings are about survival in this world and beyond; through them, families are strengthened and lineages are secured. So there's not much room for jest in a wedding ceremony.

It's clear that the bride and groom love each other. I can see she watches him carefully. She cherishes his subtlety and wit, his awkward outbursts of passion and his deep-seated belief in singular pursuits of heart and mind. She gently smiles as she watches him. This is a man whose core she admires and who brings out tender feelings in her. She wants to help him thrive and prosper and wants to be there when it happens. She sees so much potential in him.

He looks forward and focuses on the ceremony. From early on, I know, she enraptured him. Although she's soft and feminine, he's awed by her steely determination. He concentrates hard on the tasks at hand, trying hard not to screw up; he wants everything to be flawless. He so very much wants her approval and admiration. He feels that for her he'll become stronger and better.

Allen rises to read a poem to the audience. How much Chinese have I heard by now? A lot. All the sounds, really—so many notes drifting through my head, often leaving no trace. Perhaps I've grown to know and love some of the more familiar ones. Maybe I'm now thrilled to bounce along with the right tones applied to the simplest words.

The sounds of the words of this old poem, carefully spoken by diligent Allen, are more intoxicating than anything I've yet heard. It's the Chinese language that one rarely hears, the one required by classical poetry, full of curves and shimmies, accelerations, drop-offs, sharp pauses and surprises.

"It's an old poem from the Han dynasty times," Viv quietly tells me. "It's very beautiful. It says something like: 'Even if the snows come in summer, / the mountains sink away, / the birds stop singing, / my love for you will not falter.'"

The banquet is sumptuous. Shanghai cuisine is a luxury cuisine, replete with tasty and rare morsels in delicate and sweet sauces: Cold braised honeycomb tripe in sweet gravy. Live shrimp drowned and poached in wine. Sweet pickled radishes masquerading as chrysanthemums. Duck's tongue off which one sucks the meat from a minuscule wishbone. The little cold dishes pile up in front of us, soon followed by a series of main dishes: Crab with egg and red roe. Braised fatty pork. Fried whole fish with sweet-and-sour sauce. It's impossible to imagine finishing it all. At the Chinese banquet, one picks slowly at the many dishes and inter-sperses bites of food with much alcohol. This way, huge amounts can eventually be whittled down. But no sooner is one dish cleared than another appears in its place.

Allen and Lito's girlfriends are very pretty. Clearly, both men have game. Allen's companion is from Sichuan, a place celebrated for its beautiful and vibrant women. She's tall and extroverted. She tells me in passable English that she's a junior executive at a successful cosmetics company that's in the process of going national. With her unmistakable confidence, she seems the right match for Allen.

Lito's girlfriend also seems unusually suited to him. She exudes a kind of wounded grace. She, like her man, is pure Shanghai. She speaks no English and says little. She watches everything unfold with a kindly torpor, yet behind her foggy and benign demeanour she gives off glimmers of depth. I observe her attending quickly to the people around her and particularly solicitously toward her man, who's festive this evening and has been drinking with aban-don. Her laughing, squinted eyes and gentle smile seem to hide some great sadness that has stunned her to the world and made her ready to accept anything. I imagine her as an opium smoker—unlikely in today's Shanghai, but a fanciful way to account for her odd and intriguing countenance.

Next to me sits the red-faced Englishman who was so indignant on the football pitch. He's accompanied by his wife, a slight Chinese woman, and their daughter, a cute and well-behaved toddler. No sooner has the girl carefully picked her way through some choice morsels than she and her attentive mother quietly take their leave for the night.

The Englishman engages me.

I learn he teaches business at a professional college. He had been a middle manager for a company in northern England. He looks the part: short, stout, pink-fleshed and balding. He's a team player, but one who likes the game to have clear and identifiable rules. A pleasant and straightforward bloke at first, he's soon off on an angry tangent. China's clearly getting to him.

When the topic of what I'm up to here—conducting some kind of research—is raised, he launches into an exposé of his views. China doesn't impress him one bit, he says, admonishingly. It has a long way to go as a society before it'll be up to his standards. His students, he tells me, are supposed to be educated and promising young people, but they're absolutely without imagination. Get them to learn something that they can memorize and they'll apply it unfailingly, he explains, then firmly concludes: "But ask them to express themselves about a novel subject, to analyze something in a personal way, and all you get is complete rubbish."

He'll not have me chalk it up to poor English skills either. Or even to a different view of the educational experience: school as a place where one goes to listen and not to talk, where one should not speak one's mind but rearticulate the teachings of the master. No, these may be factors, he says, but the flaw is not superficial or even escapable. It's who they are.

He blames it on Confucius: "Not a day goes by that I don't wish the codger never existed," he tells me.

I can't help but laugh. This really gets him going.

"Just look what Confucius gets the Chinese to do," he says, scowling. "It has made them the world's greatest hypocrites. Everything is a lie. A front for what it's supposed to be. You can't always behave as you're told to behave. It means there's no real responsibility!"

I try to help him go somewhere different by referring to his beautiful family. But unwittingly I've stepped on the heart of the matter.

"That's where it's the worst," he begins, "that clawing filial piety! It's not just that my daughter's grandparents are present in our lives; it's that they attempt to command everything and set the law. How do you think it makes me feel to be told calmly that I can't have a say over my own household? Well done, Confucius! It's madness!"

He recounts how a few months previous, his in-laws sat him down and told him that it only made sense that, since their son has no children and never will, their daughter's daughter should carry their family name: "They assumed that I couldn't possibly care whether my own family name would be carried by my daughter. It's like they're trying to erase anything outside the tradition. Including me."

"I'm sorry, man," I say. But I guess I don't seem totally sincere. I can't be, really. Right then the drink gets a hold of him. His eyes cross. Crestfallen, he turns his head to his plate and hangs it there in his own puddle.

Lito has been observing us from across the table. He has tuned in to the Englishman's anger. He's in a good mood and wants to make sure the man's black bile hasn't soured my ideas or spoiled my spirit. He heads my way.

Again we struggle a bit to communicate, but perhaps the

alcohol and the poetry of the occasion have had an impact on Lito's command of English; we somehow manage to make it work.

"You've been travelling?" he asks.

"Yup."

"Liking your trip?"

"I love travelling. And I love China," I say benignly, then add, "Travelling has always been my way to know myself. China's showing me a lot about myself and much, much more."

"You've been to many places?" Lito asks.

"Yes. I've seen a few wonders. But China really fascinates me."

"You make documentaries, right?"

"Yes."

"They're travel documentaries?"

"In a way," I admit. "I guess I don't try to hide that they were filmed on the fly as part of a journey."

"How do you make films about places that you don't know well?" he asks gently but pointedly.

"You just go and throw yourself in, giving all that you are and everything you have. You try to let the place tell you what to do."

But I grow impatient to hear from him and abruptly ask, "Anyhow, what are you up? Deryk and James speak highly of you."

Suddenly, I feel that somehow this passing compliment has hurt Lito. Or perhaps it's the question itself. In any case, Lito answers aggressively. He tells me he's up to nothing worth talking about. I attempt to sympathize with a comment about the tribulations of the artist, but he'll have none of my formulas, true though they may be.

"I used to think a lot about art," Lito tells me. "This was before I really started making it. At the beginning, I studied art and thought a lot about what it is I wanted or should want from it. But then I began to find that this approach would not lead me toward art. I decided not to think about art, just to do it. Then I couldn't do it. Now I do whatever I can; it certainly isn't art, and I have no time or energy left over to really create anymore."

At this moment, Lito's girlfriend comes to his side. I welcome the opening and make awkward attempts at lighter conversation. Deryk also joins the group and manages to bring some smiles back.

In a break in the conversation, Deryk tells me, "There's someone you should probably meet. Unlike the present gang, this person won't be staying late. He taught Chinese to me and James."

I'm directed to a trellised foyer just outside the pavilion. The night is warm. The scent of flower blossoms is in the air, and the climbing vines that envelop the patio offer some protection from the hum of the gargantuan city.

A man who uses the English name John is waiting with his wife for me. They're both slight. They also have a style that I remember well but am still surprised to see here in the Shanghai night. He wears a white polyester button-down, no tie, with synthetic charcoal dress pants, no blazer. She wears a light dress with a floral print. It has bouffant shoulders and red needlework. It's buttoned to the throat in Chinese fashion. Her hair is long and straight, parted dead centre and brought up and back in the simplest of manners. His hair is shaggy around the ears and back, thick but limp. He wears a pair of robust plastic glasses with an old-fashioned rectangular shape to them. Together they look like a studious young couple of twenty-five years ago. Which is exactly what they were, and remain.

"Deryk tells me you are a filmmaker and an observer of China," John says.

"Yes, but I haven't done any filming in China yet. I've written a little about China, that's all."

"About what?"

"About Beijing and the changing shape of Chinese politics."

"Politics? That's what interests you?"

"No, not really," I'm forced to admit, "but it's work, and perhaps politics come easy to me and seemed a good place to start."

"So how do you feel about Chinese politics?"

"At bottom, I think that political structures are an easy way to access the Chinese past. For one, I argue that the dynastic cycle is still very much alive. That the Communists are just another dynasty. A bit different, but the logic's the same." I'm treading carefully, but John seems to accept what I'm saying.

"Yes, they're the same, but the times are different. So they're different. And the dynasties are all different among themselves. Have you been to Hangzhou?"

"A long time ago, in 1990, with my family."

"A peculiar time to be in China," John muses.

"It was. But I liked Hangzhou. I remember visiting the stone boats on its lake. I also remember a traditional medicine shop in the old city. Quite impressive, a beautiful merchant home made of wood, with a stunning assortment of natural medicines in jars and drawers. You're from Hangzhou, I take it?"

"Yes," John says.

"So tell me about Hangzhou."

"It's a great city, especially if you're interested in the dynastic cycle."

"Yet it was a centre of the Song dynasty," I say. "When China was at its smallest."

John tells me that the Song era was the most beautiful and

important period in Chinese history, a beautiful time in the shadows, an epoch of doubt and laughter in the warm night, of despair and creation in the final hours.

He goes on to explain that the Song period was unique. In its poems and in its paintings, he argues, the people of that time were reflecting deeply on the human condition and on the mysteries that envelop humankind. It was an existential period for China. So, sure, it was an era of slow contraction, but the sense of doom was cause for philosophical contemplation. "Wisdom," he adds, "doesn't come from triumph or success, but from defeat and a broken heart."

"I confess to having thought that existential doubt was something Western and recent. And that the malaise required modern individualism and its comforts."

"No. You would probably be surprised by how many ideas occurred here long before they were known in the West."

"Maybe not. I try to have a nuanced view of the West," I counter.

"The Song had the printing press and many books," John explains. "The empire was small but wealthy. People spent their time in craft and in studies. They had an active fleet. But power was limited, and the world was dangerous, so to protect against ruin, the merchants would buy shares in each other's commercial expeditions. There was paper money as well. The notions of value and community were already complex. There was material comfort, and the idea of the individual was taking shape.

"There was doubt as well," he says, arguing that doubt is perhaps the cause of individualism. He speaks of how doubts creep into the world around us and isolate us, making us feel alone, then says, "Art capitalizes on this doubt and creates a bond among people that restores community. A community of free men, perhaps?" he asks, toying with me. "Individuals who have hurt, lost and come to know themselves in solitude, who see the hurt in others and can empathize, then choose the rules of society for mutual protection and benefit?"

"So what happened to the Song? Where are they now?" I ask, prodding.

"The Mongols happened," he says with a grin. "The Song were a fleeting shadow. The empire prospered but was not capable of repelling such a big force. The days of the Song were good but couldn't last." He pauses wistfully, then says with a shrug, "While on the other side of the globe, the West triumphed and went on to claim free society as its own. But we who love and know the Song caught glimpses of it long ago. In those shadows."

I learn that this intriguing man is a teacher of literature. He has taught Western literature, for which he has long had a passion. His favourite period in the West is also one of shadows: from the late 1800s until the Second World War. He sees it as a period of great doubt and despair but also one of incredibly personal insight and great art. We talk about Dostoevsky and Proust and T.S. Eliot, about the celebration of the oh-so-unique and perishable human being. About our songs and beautiful illusions of truth.

I'm surprised to learn that John knows many of the young men here tonight. Deryk and James, the groom, were his students. Lito had also studied at his university. He introduced Lito to Deryk and James.

John thinks highly of Lito. His bravery is to be admired, he professes, then explains that he knew him a long time ago during the Tiananmen incident. He tells me that the teenaged Lito—he was but a young man of fifteen or sixteen at the time—protested a lot. He was often out in the streets alone, criticizing the government loudly. Coming from such a bold young man, the words were strong and people listened.

John excuses himself; he and his wife must take their leave, he says. All through our conversation she has stood quietly by his side, smiling in support of her husband, impressing upon me a sense of her complicity in his every word, as though he had spoken for the both of them. Our farewells are warm and rich. Deryk was right: John is a great teacher.

When I return to the party, people are moving to another pavilion, to what was once perhaps a clubhouse or mess hall, now transformed into a sumptuous nightclub. The stone patio at the front where people once came to drink lemonade or gin and tonics after tennis or croquet has been glassed in. Instead of tables and chairs, the area is laid out with huge low beds, each looking out through the windows at the dark lawn and the city lights beyond, each separated from the next bed by thick red curtains, each offering luxurious cushions and tiny tables—to rest the stem of one's opium pipe on, it would seem. The club ranges through various rooms over two storeys. The walls are painted scarlet. The lighting is veiled and strategic. The several bars all offer fancy cocktails.

The guests fill the chambers. We're a smaller, younger group. The ceremony and banquet are now over. This is a cash bar and an open club. A few elders—some very elderly—remain in the corners. An old woman takes a discreet perch off to the side, where she wears an expression of mild reproach, as if she were a chaperone. Yet she watches the youth intently. Almost a little too curiously, a little too interested in the revelry of youth. Secretly dreaming, perhaps, of her own youth, now so distant.

The night grows progressively looser and vaguer. A DJ beckons to us, first with easy and familiar rhythms, then gradually increases his forays into beat. The bride and groom lead the way. Their love is playful and infectious. We smile and cheer and laugh, and lose ourselves in the twilight.

A group of us take position in a nook off the dance floor. We lounge around a big sofa. I barely notice the waiter who keeps the drinks coming and am remotely aware when a bill for our many drinks arrives. Lito, seated beside me, takes one look and becomes agitated. He shouts quick hard syllables at the waiter from across the coffee table. Then he jumps to his feet and grabs the terrified young man with both hands and violently pulls him forward across the table. The slender chap sweeps the drinks off the tabletop with his kicking legs as he flies toward us. Lito winds up to clobber the man, now pinned to the sofa. But Allen and I grab Lito and pry away the young waiter, who quickly clambers to safety.

I'm not sure what is happening or why. Did Lito object to the tally? In any case, no part of me accepts that this waiter should be beaten here in front us. Luckily, I have no untangling to do. Allen helps Lito regain his balance and is talking to him calmly. I don't understand what is being said, but I can tell that Allen is simultaneously allowing the man to vent and figuring out what happened—and trying to turn Lito's mind away from the occurrence and the emotions it has brought. Allen is calm; he's acting as if nothing has happened and nothing about it will be said. Before long, he has succeeded in dispelling the tension and everything's back to normal.

But Lito's seat is empty; he has moved to the back of the room and now stands against a wall with his head low. A moment later, he has disappeared, not perhaps from the party but from our vicinity. Once more we are joyous and make merry.

I find my old friend Deryk leaning against another wall. We laugh heartedly at the drama that just unfolded. We both feel that Lito, the poor soul, will probably never be seen again after tonight. Deryk shakes his head for a while, then lifts it once more, to smile at his own adventure in this crazy world; at fate, which has brought him to be marooned on Chinese shores; at how people come and go from his horizons bringing knowledge, yes, but mysteries too. "So let's raise a glass to present company," he muses.

I join him in raising our glasses, then pass Viv on the way to the dance floor. She's sipping a glass of water. She has been dancing; her cheeks are rosy and her dark eyes are sparkling. "Are you going to dance?" she asks. "I wasn't sure you were the type."

"Really? What type am I, Viv?" I say teasingly, then say before she can respond, "No, please don't answer that."

Soon the dance has got a hold of us. There's Viv, so independent and intelligent, with a bashful and giddy smile, giving herself to the music. And Lito's girlfriend, her downcast eyes still locking away all her secrets but her smile coy and her hips decisively accustomed to the rhythm. Allen and his vivacious girlfriend perform a masterful swing routine. The bride is glorious in her white gown. Barefoot, with her black hair breaking loose of its restraints, her hands held high, she turns and turns on the floor. For a moment, we without a past are all brothers and sisters in dance.

Then the old woman makes her exit, walking slowly through our midst, led by a younger relative. Age is heavy, her hunched frame seems to say to us as she carefully chooses her every step.

I don't avert my gaze, though, and her scanning eyes land momentarily on mine: a flash of anger, shame and laughter.

"How dare you look at me!" her eyes mean to say. "I would stop here on the dance floor if I could. I too once believed in my freedom. I would join the night if there were a way. But there isn't, of course. So I move as slowly as possible and secretly drink up all the moments that my old eyes can still pick out of the shadows."

CHAPTER 7

Three Kingdoms

At dawn, the sun rises by climbing the mulberry tree.
—*The Classic of Mountains and Seas*, fourth century BC

In 1990, I visited Suzhou, one of the great cities of central China, famed for luxurious gardens, a sign of refinement and prosperity. My father, brother and I toured at least half a dozen of them. They are maintained as public parks, but all were originally privately owned. Some were immense walled grounds, the former domains of mandarins and generals. Others occupied little alcoves and courtyards in merchant homes on canals.

The genius of these gardens was their management of space. They were heavily partitioned and organized in such a way that as one walked through them one's gaze was controlled so as to always fall on a perfect picture of beauty. This was achieved by a play of contrasts expressed through wood, water and stone: the small was made big; the near, far; the young, old.

Suzhou also holds for me my first memory of bombast in China. We were in the company of a man who must have been the city's mayor or the local Communist Party leader. Whatever he was, he made it clear to us that he was the decision maker in Suzhou. He was in his early forties, tall, thin and well dressed in tailored dark blue twill. We met him for lunch at the city's newest and most luxurious hotel, which he treated as his private domain. The lunch was exquisite, and he asked us if we had yet tasted such refined food in China. As he gestured, I could see flashes of a fancy watch under his suit sleeve. He laid out his plans for the city as we toured a few important sites. Beauty would be restored to the city beyond the gardens, he promised. Careful action, he boasted through a pedantic translator, would enhance the intense real estate development that he was encouraging in the central core.

He also brought us to the outskirts of the old city and had us look out over a barren and muddy plain pockmarked with shacks and crude utility buildings. Something big was going to be built there. Although it was still an empty canvas, our host was already clearly proud of it and gazed at it with eyes filled with visions. I understand now what he saw: industry. He had visions of Suzhou making stuff for the whole world to consume.

We also visited a factory not far from Suzhou, nothing too modern: a silk factory inhabiting what looked like a 1950s workers' commune in a series of brick apartment buildings. The factory building was virtually indistinguishable from the residential buildings around it. The place had been slapped with some kind of official label—The People's Silk Institute, or some such. We were told that silk's many uses were being studied there, though the only proof of that was a silk-based hand cream that we were given as a parting gift.

I will never forget walking into one of the production rooms where the silk filament was unwound from the cocoons. The vast hall was brightly lit with fluorescent lighting. Despite the high ceilings, the room was hot and humid. There was also an unforgettable odour—sour and nutty. The process of extracting the filament involves cooking the cocoon and the worm within. At each of the fifty or so workstations, a uniformed woman sat in front of a metal basin of boiling water. In each vat, a dozen or so thumb-sized white cocoons were dancing in the rolling water. Once poached, the gluey mucus that holds the strands together is softened. The women plucked out the cocoons with bamboo tongs and examined them under powerful light until they located the filament end. With tweezers, they each carefully unrolled the single thread of silk that formed the cocoon until all that was left was the miserable and stinky worm within, boiled and bloated, to be discarded.

As is so often the case, the manufacturing experience is very different from our experience of the final product. An elegant silk garment leaves no trace of the heat and funk and energy that went into its manufacture. One scarcely remembers the little slug that dreamt of flying. Perhaps these veiled and difficult origins help give silk its tremendous value. There was early incentive to manufacture silk on a large scale: It offers many of the best qualities of wool, linen and cotton. It's light and supple, yet strong and warm. It is also marvellously pleasing to the touch.

Silk manufacturing is complex and delicate, combining elements of horticulture, husbandry, cooking and precision work. The old historians of China write that it was discovered alongside writing, agriculture and the domestication of animals by the Xia emperors. Agriculture appeared independently in many places. Earlier than the Chinese, the Sumerians and ancient Egyptians kept careful written records. Civilization, history, and property rights were established the world over. But the early silk industry was uniquely Chinese and remained mysterious to outsiders through long centuries.

The silkworms feed selectively on the leaves of certain trees, chief among them the white mulberry. Plantations of these trees need to be kept to size by pruning. Then the trees must be attacked by a specific pest, *Bombyx mori*. The population of these creatures is kept stable while a great percentage of their offspring is harvested in cocoon form. Then, as I witnessed in that smelly factory so long ago, the cocoons are cooked and unwound before being spun into thread that is then woven together. The pruning, the collecting and the processing take much time, much organization, much energy and many able hands.

Wearing silk was long a sign of status and sophistication. When lords met, the one in silk looked down on the others. For cold, silk; for heat, silk. If one wants to learn to move like the tiger or the snake, it should be done in silk. Beneath one's layers of felt, leather and metal armour, silk is also preferable. And if one must spend one's days like kings or high priests, studying and divining, or making love, try silk.

Much of what we wear and eat has been thoroughly processed. Some processes, such as grinding grain into hot meal, are as old as history. Others are much newer, such as using hydrocarbons to make small explosions in metal pistons, or fashioning silicon microresistors to transport and encode electrical impulses. Manufacture remains a defining feature of the human experience, and it ranges deep in time.

In the strictest sense, manufacture is handicraft, things made with the hands. In the beginning, it involved simple chains of processes, often conducted by the same person. For the manufacture of bread: growing the seed; cutting, thrashing and drying the wheat in the sun; grinding the grain; and cooking the flour. For silk: growing the white mulberry tree and waiting for the moth to lay its eggs; allowing the larva to emerge from its egg, eat to its satisfaction and spin itself a chamber to begin its metamorphosis; plucking the cocoons from the tree; poaching them; unwinding and drying the filament; and weaving it into cloth.

One can imagine the spinning of silk to be the work of cooperative communities, as so many have done since and before Marx—free and happy families of farmers who together generate a bounty for all, teenage maidens spinning silk beneath flowery pergolas, knowledge being taught to them in song as they worked.

More likely, silk followed the model of other elite industries in ancient China. Each was the exclusive prize of great landlords or imperial power. Ceramics and military smithwork, for instance, were tightly controlled industries and cornerstones of wealth and power. Silk might even exemplify the sophistications of such ancient hierarchies. We can imagine it as a kind of currency, available to those who could press others into service. A lord might wall off a compound and plant it with mulberry trees, then levy the village girls to spin silk with which he might cloak his court. He might pay tribute in silk to those more powerful than him, to win their patronage and protection.

Compared with working the mud or manning the front line in battle, there was value in rising to the ranks of elite industrial labourer. Silk was often a court industry; close and worthy families would provide a lord with the service of their sons and daughters. The junior courtiers would be foremen and officers. The best of them might become family members and might receive the blessings of court, titles and education.

Courtiers might themselves rise to wield considerable power as generals or masters of coin. As concubines, they might entangle themselves in the master lineage. The classic tales are full of stories of silk-spinning maidens who accede to power through the master's bed and close control of their own royal offspring.

Confucian ethics might even be deemed silk-era ethics, aimed at restoring honour to decayed and corrupt courts. This was not done by doing away with servitude but by deepening it among sons and fathers, wives and husbands, and subjects and sovereigns. Servitude, the great sage argued, is noble when it is conducted in a society as it occurs within a healthy family; respect, the only way to harmony.

Twenty-five hundred years ago, Confucius was already looking back upon an era five hundred years previous to his own and longing for the harmony he imagined there. As if he had concluded that the world was already changing for the worse.

Perhaps the sage was reacting to a gradual evolution of the workforce toward ever more alienation from the sacred intimacies of feudal obedience and the very tangible and personal bonds of court life. As a population grows, the relationship between foreman and worker, lord and subject, loses its intimate qualities. The bonds grow more abstract and oppressive as they take on the form of taxes and conscript labour.

The irony of all this is that the erosion of this ancient work ethic that caused Master Kong to wax nostalgic two and a half thousand years ago had only just begun in his age and would grow far more extreme in the many years that followed. All production eventually leaves court and family. Perhaps Master Kong would gaze disparagingly upon the present world, where our relationship with production, whether agricultural or industrial, grows ever more impersonal. We really have no idea who has toiled for our benefit. Our labours are more abstract and without spiritual value. Our loyalties ever more fickle if not altogether absent. The observance of portents is subsiding, the meaning of things muted.

The new world sits on many older worlds, still filled with ancient servitudes and superstitions. But the trend is toward a depersonalized world of individual solitudes, bound together by a globalized economy of industrial production. Perhaps the decay of the complex and subtle morality praised by Confucius is simply a consequence of increased production capacity. Modern humans are lords of their own small but comfortable domains, where starvation, injustice and servitude are mostly unthinkable.

The new humans Master Kong might encounter in the new China or elsewhere in the world are nothing like the gentlefolk of the ancient dukedom of Zhou, for which he had so much praise. Lacking perhaps in high moral qualities, modern humans live longer, eat better, own more and are less likely to be embroiled in mortal combat. More importantly, we are legion, unlike the precious few gentlemen and dowagers of old.

Mass industrialization has put great distance between our societies and the ancient ones. Scarcely two hundred years separate the modern world from the vastly different material, demographic, cultural and spiritual conditions of the preindustrial age. In China, the explosion of industry is even more recent but has occurred at record-breaking speed.

Of all the myriad products from China that are now invading the world's homes and workplaces—electronics, appliances, tools, clothing and furniture—there is one supremely important manufactured product that we don't yet associate with China: the automobile. The personal automobile is arguably the most economically significant industrial product. For the consumer, the car is a transformative tool. And in many ways, automobile possession is the true benchmark of the middle class.

Cars are significant for the producers as well. Wherever they are put, automobile plants are like small kingdoms. The employment they provide to thousands of people has a huge impact on the stability and health of local economies. They also require large resource inputs, a developed transportation infrastructure and a sophisticated collection of intellectual property. And even in free-market economies, the automobile industry is always deeply entangled with government and political structures.

In Beijing, I'd asked a family friend long established in China to help connect me with automobile factories in central China. Through his contacts, he'd arranged for me to visit a couple of plants: JAC in Hefei and Chery Automobile in Wuhu. To make it a trifecta, Viv talked us into a corporate tour of the swanky new General Motors factory down the river in Shanghai.

The JAC automobile and tractor factory is in Hefei, the capital city of Anhui Province. Viv and I take a bus there from Nanjing. As we leave the Yangtze shores and head inland, the countryside and villages become poorer. The whole area looks as if it is subject to soil erosion. In the past, Anhui was notorious for its hardships. Even now, the windswept plains, uneven roads and battered brick and earth structures conjure a return to rougher times.

The approach to Hefei is long and slow. The landscape becomes progressively more industrial, but these factories and warehouses are either terribly moribund or, more frequently, long deceased. The picture is one of decay, of a world slowly succumbing to the wastes.

Then more and more tallish residential buildings clutter the highway, which slowly morphs into a boulevard, and a city finally emerges. But it too is battered and dusty. The buildings are of worn red brick. Shops line the boulevard, but there are no bright lights or showy windows. Big metal doors open onto the street and wares spill out: tools, piping, bags of cement mix, rubber gadgets and plastic junk. The city dwellers, in the heavy canvases or crude synthetics of earlier times, seem a hardened lot.

As we advance, however, the road surface becomes cleaner and smoother. Parks and trees appear. The bricks are replaced by concrete, steel and aluminum. And above us, the skyline increasingly draws the contours of a wide and modern cityscape. Anhui Province may yet be on the move.

Our contact, a company man, is to meet us outside the bus station. I pray that he's late or that we are early, so that we can stretch our legs for a moment and have a bite and a sip of tea. But when we descend from the bus, I see him keenly waiting for us beside a company minivan. Mr. Xu, a junior public relations officer, is in his early forties and is of medium build. He wears dark slacks and the company golf shirt. We dutifully exchange business cards. He then vaguely offers help for food and lodging, but Viv politely urges him on.

"Sir, we are grateful but shall not abuse your precious time and would very much like to visit your company's factories," she courteously tells him. Viv knows that if we want to see the manufacturing processes in action, we should go now, not later in the afternoon, when things might be winding down. She also guesses that it might be awkward for our host to drive us to a hotel or a restaurant where he has no budget to help with the bill.

So Xu invites us to board the minivan. We meet a second man, the driver, who also functions as an assistant. The men offer us bottled water and packaged sweet tea that they have chilled in a cooler.

In the vehicle, there's an air of happiness. The men enjoy their job. They are proud of their company. Hosting curious foreigners seems pleasant to them. We engage in light banter and cover the basics of the corporation. I learn that JAC is not a recently established enterprise. The factories have been producing tractors and trucks since the Maoist era. But over the past decade, the company has undergone a transformation. It still makes tractors and trucks but has significantly upgraded its models. It has also shifted part of the labour force to new factories where automobiles are assembled. This new development is a natural step for a company that manufactures service vehicles. JAC makes tools: vehicles meant to do a job—from tractors to big trucks, little trucks, and now minivans.

We leave the city core and enter a sprawling area of new construction. We ride along a ten-lane boulevard. It's so new that it still shows patches of sand and gravel, and its margins, not yet landscaped, are coarse and bare. The road is flanked by supermalls and residential high-rise developments. Everything is in the final stages of construction and an early stage of operation. In fact, cranes line the corridor as far as the eye can see.

After about ten minutes, we veer right onto another broad boulevard. This one is somewhat older and quieter. It's lined with technology outfits and government offices. To the left, a fence and wall mark the edge of a huge industrial territory. Beyond the fence is an immense compound, like an airport or some kind of base. Numerous giant buildings can be seen in the distance. We ride along the perimeter for five minutes, then turn left to follow the fence south along a rough, unfinished boulevard. We turn left once more and enter the compound through huge gates. We are surrounded by immense, brightly coloured hangars: the new factory at JAC.

We are led to a single, nondescript door. As we enter, Xu tells us that it's forbidden to take photos of the manufacturing process. We then find ourselves in a vast open chamber. Shaped plates of metal are piled high along aisles. Massive presses are being operated by uniformed workers. They carry sheets of metal into the jaws, then move to control stations to close the presses. They wear royal-blue jumpsuits and hard hats, and are mostly men in their twenties, some with long hair. They're amused to see us watching them. When the piles of pressed aluminum and steel get big, forklifts move them to another chamber.

We exit this building and drive to another—the minivan assembly line. We commence the journey not on the line itself but on an offshoot somewhere near the beginning of assembly. We enter a gymnasium-sized hall with huge, high windows that catch the afternoon sun; the chamber basks in warm light. It's also filled with chunky metal parts in neatly arranged piles, all destined for an area at the edge of this chamber where the assembly line passes. The sunlight gives an unusual feel to this room. The workers here are men and women in their early twenties. Their job seems to be to get all of these parts from the piles to the assembly line.

The shift is about to end. Of the dozen or so young workers in the room, only three or four appear to be doing much of anything. Although they're sorting and rearranging piles of parts, they're doing it at half-speed, partaking in the joking and flirting that has got a hold of the rest of the group. They all seem healthy and happy young people. Some of the young men even have their coveralls rakishly unbuttoned from collar to belly.

Through careful prodding, Viv learns that these workers earn 1,600 yuan per month, which is roughly equivalent to $230. Not much from our perspective, but nothing to be balked at in Anhui Province at the time.

The production line is in a long, brightly lit chamber, but it's more intimate than the first room, since the assembly mostly happens beneath an elaborate track from which the skeletal car hangs. Technicians are building up the car piece by piece. It's moving along a series of stations worked by teams of people. At one station, two men weld a component to the build. At another, a team with compression ratchets speedily bolt widgets.

As we walk alongside the stations, we engage the workers with smiles and nods. Some never lift their heads, but many are more sociable. The workers seem to enjoy and take pride in their work. There also seems to be camaraderie among them. As they work, they joke around and provide each other assistance. At some stations, we observe dedicated transportation systems: tracks to sling parts up and carry them through the air to the car, where they're fixed; pneumatic trolleys and carts that slide along the floor; and even a robot platform that carries the motor to the build and delicately lifts it into the engine cavity without being controlled. It is a source of amazement for its new masters and their visitors alike.

As we pause in wonder, I ask questions about the car's engine. It's manufactured elsewhere, perhaps assembled somewhere on the premises—or maybe the whole thing is purchased from another company. It's a Chinese motor manufactured according to a Korean technology licence. Our hosts also admit that many of the more sophisticated instruments and devices are manufactured outside China, in Japan, Korea and Germany. But this will decrease in time, I'm told.

With more and more of the shell complete, the minivan becomes visible. Windows and interior elements are now fitted into the vehicle. It's then painted and given some rubber on which to roll off the line. The asking price is between five thousand and ten thousand dollars, a competitive price when one considers the heavy use the minivan is meant to endure, but a price well beyond the means of any of these workers, who make but a fraction of that in a year.

The product is fresh to the market and thus has not really been put to the test yet, but JAC planners and consumers alike are banking on the idea that the maker of service vehicles, of tractors and trucks that haul and endure, can probably offer a reliable minivan, ready for active service. The vehicle is likely underpowered and not terrifically comfortable, especially after heavy use and tough conditions wear down its suspension. But the minivan will endure long hours, overstuffing of both goods and passengers, and will be easy and cheap to repair and service.

This particular minivan is emerging at a time when the Chinese consumer class is rapidly expanding. But something tells me that the buyers of the JAC minivan will not soon be found packing the vehicle with children, pets, clothes and groceries for a weekend at the cottage. For now, JAC's aims are much more modest.

When we exit the factory, we see that another shift is ending. The workers in their identical colourful uniforms assemble at collection points to be picked up by minibuses. I'm told that many of these young workers live in factory housing in the compound. The young workers have a playful air to them, as if this experience were a kind of summer camp, highly rigid perhaps, but a life less oppressive than that with their families in the villages. Here, they have a clearly identified job that they're expected to accomplish with crystalline precision, but as they wait for transportation after a shift or when they retire to their dormitories at night, they can be without worries. They can indulge in laughter and flirtation, while in their villages, the expectations and concerns weighing upon their shoulders are incessant.

Our tour is over and a driver is designated to take us where we please in Hefei. We had chosen online a new hotel with stunningly low prices, but its location is something of a mystery to our driver. It's in a new part of town. We venture out of the gates in a different direction from that from which we came.

Hefei is truly surprising. Coming into town on the old Nanjing road, it seemed a dusty, post-industrial wasteland, a Chinese Detroit. Then it revealed itself as a business-oriented place with glass-clad skyscrapers, and, on the way to the factory, it morphed into vast housing and shopping complexes. Now as we leave the industrial area of the factory, apartment buildings and malls-in-the-making again spread out around us, lined up along the boulevard. But behind the rows of buildings, I can only make out empty space. After a few kilometres, we come upon something of a new city centre replete with ultra-modern buildings fitted with posh outdoor lighting. But it too is all core. To complete the picture, rush-hour traffic is heavy at this single great intersection. This afternoon, the city is also cloaked in a sooty fog that makes the empty spaces behind everything seem laden with unearthly mystery.

We turn onto another main thoroughfare and after a few blocks and some searching find the street where the hotel is located. It has been erected among a bunch of new multi-storey textile buildings. This again is typical of the way the new China works: with largesse. Surplus capacity is built into everything. A shopping mall will be topped with the hull of an office tower. A series of textile factories will be built in one go. Some will be used at once, others will remain empty for some time. While the factories are being built, the planners might also decide to throw a hotel into the construction mix.

Government entities make for strange industrialists in China. As anywhere else, they control zoning and therefore land use. As they let the market in, they continue to have broad and sometimes obscure priorities. They exert significant control over the procurement of labour and can extract and redirect resources and capital in all sorts of creative and discretionary ways. It seems that government planners at various levels were convinced that a small textile industry was called for in the new part of Hefei, and to market the product, a hotel to host buyers was bankrolled. Still, the planners hope for the free market to take hold. They wish to lure to these rooms hordes of foreign wholesalers intent on buying product from Hefei. If not, they expect corporate buyers and planners from elsewhere in China. And even if the hotel is empty, as it is when Viv and I arrive, it's not there to turn a profit but to serve other needs. Its operations will continue as long as its owning entity says it will.

The lobby is grandiose, its ceiling some seven and a half metres high. A huge granite-topped reception desk lines the back of the lobby under the massive glittering fresco of a dragon. The place is full of attendants, fresh and eager youngsters in crisp and fanciful uniforms. Our rooms are on the top floor of the garden wing. Extravagantly dressed porters carry our scuffed-up rucksacks with delicate application. My room is clean, spartan and spacious. It gazes out over a green space between more buildings.

Viv and I convene in the lobby to go find an interesting place to eat. We walk back toward the core. On our way to the hotel, I'd noticed a fancy-looking place in its own artful two-storey building. Food in China is so cheap that I don't hesitate to walk into the most ridiculously showy establishments. In the West, I usually do the opposite—I search for the most down and dirty, hole-in-the-wall restaurants, where the food's full of soul.

But in Chinese cities, what you want is a restaurant that attracts throngs of people, that has a wide selection and fresh ingredients. A place that has done itself up. These restaurants will have elaborate picture menus, an absolute must for food explorers. In these restaurants, which are all over China, you can often treat a group of friends to a spectacular banquet including drinks for a hundred dollars.

This one is a little different, though. It's understated; there's a muted and earthy character to its decor, with nice gardens out front, a staccato roofline, an elegant, polished, coarse timber entrance and a flowing floor plan creating private alcoves. Although still bright, the lighting is also more discreetly handled than usual. The place is full of respectable diners. They see few foreigners here, and we are seated at the front window looking out on a small garden and the parking lot beyond.

Viv and I explore the menu items with curiosity. I'm always looking for new dishes, though I definitely have my limits: no hair, no feathers, no veins, no raw blood, no gastrointestinal-tract contents. No legged insects except ants and grasshoppers. And no bottom-feeding freshwater fish.

Reading the menu, Viv suddenly yelps in her high-pitched girlish manner, "Oh! Stinky tofu!"

After witnessing such emotion for something stinky, I insist on ordering the dish. She warns me that it is like a very strong old cheese, and many people find it overpowering. When it arrives, it proves nothing like cheese in either flavour or texture, having the sponginess of a scouring pad and a bitter and burnt flavour, with hints of metal. Not soon a contender for my good books.

I also have my favourites. At this moment: spiced pig kidneys, mouth-water chicken and garlic-sautéed dragon beans. When I get Viv to ask the nice, young waitress if they have any of these, she points us to similar dishes and tells us they are even better.

"You are always eating dishes that fire us up," Viv grumbles.

"Yes, I want to bring my fire higher and higher," I joke.

Too much fire wears you out, she cautions, causes turbulence in the body and mind. Periodically we must eat motherly foods to restore, to soothe and to rebuild. Eating is a kind of balancing act, she explains.

The Chinese believe that the forces of yin and yang exist in all things, including us humans. Imbalances can exist in the world, in the body or in the soul; they are causes of misfortune and ailment. So one is constantly seeking to manage these forces in one's behaviour and surroundings. The old sayings give much guidance in these pursuits. And nowhere are these pieces of information more pronounced than where food is concerned. Foods have numerous meanings and auspicious uses, depending on how they are prepared and eaten. They're medicine for body and soul.

In prepared dishes, the various permutations of the yin and yang pair are many. It's perhaps easiest to understand these two prime forces in their sensual dichotomy: yang, the male element, is in strong-flavoured and spicy foods; yin, the female element, is in soft and mild foods but also in the bitter and cold. Yang gives; yin receives.

"If we keep eating all this spicy food, I'm going to burn out," Viv complains.

"I seek fire at all times unless I am sick," I tell her.

"Sounds exhausting," she says.

"Maybe. I long thought that a great bonfire is what was needed inside. Until there was nothing left to burn and all passions were extinguished."

"You believe this?" she asks with worry.

"Maybe not anymore. Maybe the bonfire might just burn my whole life, and I'd be forever without peace."

"Then you might be coming around to the Chinese way. Balance your passions and you will be able to enjoy them until the end."

"Yes, Vivien, but don't think this will stop me from ordering pickled-pepper pork flank."

Early the next morning, we take a bus to Wuhu. The town sits on the Yangtze plain. Everything downstream and east of Wuhu is part of the heartland of central China: Nanjing, Suzhou, Hangzhou and Shanghai. As an element of this important trade and manufacturing region, Wuhu has prospered.

The bus station area is new. Our hotel is part of the commercial development that has blossomed around the busy terminal. The establishment touts itself as a business hotel and is modern and incredibly inexpensive. The rooms are cramped but clean and well appointed. Many hotels throughout China sell small wares in the rooms—shower caps, toothbrushes and condoms—all labelled with a price. This hotel has pushed the concept further and offers up a variety of perfumes, condom styles and even packages of racy underwear. Clearly, all sorts of business goes down at this hotel.

Viv has called our contact at Chery Automobile and arranged a meeting at the hotel just after lunch. The hotel has no restaurant but it's connected to a mini-mall with a food court. The new food courts in China function efficiently: customers pay at a kiosk for a plastic card charged with credit, then wander among the stations offering various dishes, samples of which are on display. For little money, a customer can quickly amass a wide selection of dishes. Each station has its speciality: hot or cold dishes, say, or types of foods, like barbecued meats or noodles. Sometimes they focus on regional cuisines: a counter specializing in southwestern cuisine, another in dim sum, for instance. In one food court in north China, a particularly memorable kiosk had a large colourful sign featuring a banner-sized photo of a friendly-looking ass, forever transfixed with its wide, toothy donkey grin. The braised meat proved succulent if somewhat stringy.

After an enjoyable lunch, we head out to meet our contact from Chery Automobile. Unlike JAC in Hefei, only recently moved from heavy trucks to cars, Chery has a well-established line of automobiles. It's one of a small group of nationally recognized automobile brands. The brand name is pronounced "cherry" in English. The different spelling projects a Lenovo-like aura, something familiar combined with something strange. Toyota and Kia were once strange names to us as well, and like them, Chery products are meant to compete. In recent years, Chery has been turning out automobiles emulating the Japanese, Korean, European or American cars we drive. The Chery machines are also increasingly fitted with all the sensors and filters that make our cars legal, and all the lights and gadgets that make them appealing to mass consumers. The retail price of Chery vehicles at the current yuan rate is significantly less than even the most affordable vehicles on the North American markets. Chery's planners have realized that automobile manufacturing is more than merely churning out product. A product is not just an object but a way of life. And Chery wants to be a part of the new Chinese way of life.

As with JAC, our contact with Chery is again a junior public relations officer. He's alone and drives a Chery car as if it were his personal vehicle and we, his guests. It makes him seem somewhat more powerful than were he driven around by a colleague. A man alone with his car projects an image of personal freedom, and to North Americans, this image seems more potent and appealing than rigid hierarchies.

The Chery industrial complex is at the edge of town among immense rice plots; the people who work at Chery may well be descendants of the disciplined workforces that have laboured in these fields for millennia. The compound is fairly new. We pass a long barbed-wire fence beyond which a giant parking lot is filled with row upon row of new cars still partially cloaked in plastic. I can make out several huge white hangars where production must occur.

Mr. Wu, our host, engages us in light banter. There's a muted confidence to him. He's a little unsure of who we are but can see that we're clearly not corporate big shots. Still, his instincts tell him to be candid only to a certain point in his answers to our questions. Yet Viv and I try to turn questions in such a way as to not demand difficult answers that might potentially embarrass our host. Although requiring more patience, the soft approach often rewards us with spirited candour in appreciation for our courtesy. Wu takes us for intellectuals and shares with us his mostly unsatisfied desire for a more intellectual life. But he confesses that climbing the corporate ladder brings him satisfaction, even if it's mostly materialistic.

Our visit to the Chery assembly lines repeats many of the experiences of JAC. There are also notable differences. At each step of the way, we are joined by a production engineer with expertise about the vehicle and its assembly. Our technical questions are answered frankly and in detail. Chery is far more geared toward corporate relations than is JAC. Tours like ours are more routine. The workers here are more urbane, and pay us no attention.

We visit a production room high above on a gangway. It's the engine assembly, something we did not see in Hefei. Big red boxes house hermetic forging and welding processes. Engine machining is far too precise a task to be left to humans and is completely automated. These great machines that make the engines are not made in China but have been purchased from Japan and Germany. The Chery engine aims to be as detailed and computerized as its counterparts in the developed world, but the technical precision to produce the metamachines that make sophisticated car motors still eludes the Chinese. They seem to have accepted that this niche capacity is one they cannot reach for the moment.

Everything is more organized at Chery than it was at JAC: the way we are kept at a distance from the production and hosted by specialists, the way the assembly lines are articulated. There are no chambers where car parts are piled up haphazardly. No frolicking of the workers as they wait for an item or get ahead of the chain. The process unfolds with a minimum of excess and looseness. The branches of production flow together and form a single movement forward.

We forgo visiting the body presses. Viv explains that we visited this part of assembly at JAC, and our Chery hosts confirm that the process is both extremely boring and scarcely visible, since, like the machining of the engine, much of the manufacture happens within big machines.

Chery produces a line of sedans from the economical to the mid-size. They have small engines. They are low on metal and high on plastic. They are highly functional yet inexpensive. They compare to the starter cars many westerners purchase when they first buy a new car, and in many ways, this is exactly what Chery offers: the first-car experience.

As we witnessed in the Hefei restaurant the night before, there's a growing class of consumers who will own the car as they own a television set, a rice cooker or an air conditioner. These consumers can now be spotted on any road or highway. At least ten million Chinese must join the middle class every year. But to whom, then, do we refer when we talk about a Chinese middle class? I picture people who buy cars and apartments and who frequent big restaurants. People who make choices: what to do, what to wear, what to eat, what to buy. Whom to marry. Who to be.

Beneath them are those who have few choices and almost no mobility. Circumstances force their hand, and they accept whatever work they can, usually for very small amounts of money. They can afford only what is cheapest—and very little of it. These people are several hundred million strong in China, but their numbers are declining.

Above the middle class is the group whose notion of choice is again blurred as possibilities multiply. Plus the management of wealth for its own sake brings on a whole gamut of expectations and responsibilities—a sparse group to be sure but one whose numbers are also growing.

Of course, manufacture for the middle class is where the big money is. Selling to hundreds of millions is far better business than selling luxury items to the chosen few. So Chery squarely targets the so-called middle class. Its brand speaks to the modest yet honest success of the gainfully employed. It's a car built for the quiet pride of new beginnings, not for the exuberant pretention of established standing.

Outside brands have been courting the Chinese for several decades. A walk through any shopping mall in new China makes clear the exposure to foreign fashion brands. Although I often suspect that, outside the biggest cities, the luxury clothing stores are only marginally profitable, these shops are prestige stores aimed at raising a shopping centre's profile. The Chinese love to shop in the vicinity of these stores, without actually buying the expensive products.

Still, the majority of Chinese industry exists for the export market, not the domestic one. With automobiles it's different, though. They are for the Chinese. The export market was initially not even an option. But increasingly, Chinese-made cars are being sold into countries throughout the developing world.

If a free global market truly existed, a large proportion of automobiles on earth might soon be manufactured in China. But automobile manufacture is a long way from a free-market affair, remaining a sacred cow for developed economies. Essential in government labour schemes, automobile plants are mostly spared the merciless mechanics of free trade. Although parallel products like generic tractors or mechanized farm implements are exported from China for sale by Western retailers under various brands, Chinese cars still have little to no access to Western markets. Instead, Western car makers that have been lured into China aim to produce their brands for the massive Chinese market.

Viv has secured for us a private tour of the General Motors factory in Shanghai. A massive and advanced production facility, it's a piece of an empire. China now accounts for a third of GM's global sales.

To get to the plant, Viv and I take a long taxi ride through the sprawling new industrial districts, far from the city's historical core. The GM lot, near the coast on the way to the city's new airport, is huge and efficiently organized. We meet our contact in a showy front pavilion. With its glass facade and atrium, it feels like a dealership, except it houses only a single glittery demo car, a Buick. Our contact is a tall thirty-something woman with a business-like attitude. She has the cold politeness you'd expect. GM is all about public relations in China; as much as it is selling a car here, it's also selling a brand, and an efficient style of industrial production.

The GM production facility in Shanghai is state-of-the-art. Everything about it is high-tech. We follow the assembly lines from gangways, looking down on a process that is meticulously organized. The diverse streams of assembly are calculated from the start. The smallest gadget is produced in synchronicity with all the other constituents of an individual automobile, the elements carried along production lines to merge at precisely the right moment. There's no surplus production and no wasted time. Exactly the right elements are produced at the right moment.

We're told that the large majority of vehicle components are produced on site: body, frame, motors, instruments, and so on. We briefly check out earlier phases of production, but there isn't much to see. The components are produced in closed and automated circuits that originate all over the immense compound and flow toward the assembly proper in a huge chamber; the multiple circuits converge upon a single line along which cars slowly materialize. Depending on which components are fed to the assembly, slightly different models are produced by the same line.

The workers, with whom we have no contact, are older than the workers at the other factories we visited. They're not the happy youngsters we observed in Hefei but grave forty-year-olds. They go about their work with unflinching seriousness. They earn a fair bit more as well—based in Shanghai, this GM factory has access to a skilled and mature workforce but must pay much higher wages than its counterparts.

Along the assembly line, the workers are organized into teams, each responsible for a specific phase of production. A team's work is gauged by a traffic-light system. A green light means the team is on or ahead of schedule. A yellow light means the team is falling behind in the assembly process. A red light means the team has caused a delay in the production, forcing the downstream production to wait. A female voice chimes over a public address system to encourage a team that has been accumulating green lights or to chide the one that is causing a delay.

The automobiles produced at this plant are brands from the GM family, Chevrolet and Buick, but the models are unique to China. The Volkswagen or GM factories in China bring with them a wide range of proprietary technology. They have established new corporate entities specific to China, which purchase expensive licences with GM in America or VW in Germany and agree to stringent production requirements.

With GM and other such partners, Chinese domestic capacity has taken huge leaps. In the plants, workers become habituated to the most advanced forms of labour organization, engineers witness how high efficiency is achieved, and complex industrial models and intellectual property are leached into Chinese soil.

Deeper still, China grows powerful in this alliance. Foreign multinationals operating and profiting greatly in China do so at the pleasure of the Chinese state. As such, these global companies make for potent allies in foreign capitals. Once combined in a concerted manner by the Chinese state, this network of globalized industry can be leveraged into a mighty tool to extract strategic concessions, possibly subservience even, from Washington, London and Paris.

After our visit to GM, Viv returns downtown while I am picked up by Allen, who has offered to give me a tour of Shanghai and help me purchase a bolt of raw silk to replace some curtains back home. He takes me to the silk broker's market.

"Nobody cares too much about silk anymore," he admits. "It's only worn by women for special occasions, and even then less and less. The industry's still alive, but it must be shrinking fast."

The silk market is on the outskirts of town, somewhat close to the GM plant, in a nondescript multi-storey building like so many other commercial bazaars I have seen in China. Most of the shops display prototypes of manufactured silk products for wholesale orders. But I want the raw stuff from which everything is made and have a swatch of the decaying silk curtains I hope to replace. After inquiries about where I might buy a bolt of silk, Allen and I are directed to the interior-decoration section of the market. We choose a shop with an exuberant presentation and are met by an attendant who clearly knows his wares. After examining my fabric, he brings out several big folders of textile samples. It's quickly clear that my fabric is of a higher quality than anything I'm shown, its silvery sheen made more ethereal by a more natural grain of filament.

Our helper readily admits defeat: he doesn't have this quality of silk on hand. But unwilling to give up, he pledges to find me a supplier that might be able to satisfy my needs. I explain that I'm passing through town and won't be able to come back soon, but I take his business card anyway. Allen offers to help, but unwilling to burden him with such a personal task, I decline it.

While on the topic of home decor, Allen offers to show me a house that he's contemplating buying in a neighbourhood nearby. Along the way, he explains the nature of his business to me. His company brokers industrial tools for Western distributors. His particular niche is cable-pulling tools that he sources from various suppliers.

"My company has been successful at supplying a particular American company in this niche but can organize production in any number of niches. Recently, we have moved into supplying pool-maintenance equipment to foreign wholesalers," he tells me.

"Can't the foreign companies go straight to the Chinese producers themselves?" I ask.

"They can, but we mostly deal in new production. My clients come to me with prototypes, and I get them made for them. Even if they could find the appropriate production facilities, I'm sure they couldn't negotiate unit costs as well as we can for them."

Allen explains something important: "There is a side to production in China that is not well known, especially around here. Many of the producers see actual production as a chore. Production and sales are thus not their main revenue stream; it's real estate development. Some even sell their production at a loss. Over the past years, there has been more and more indifference toward selling product; what matters is selling value-added land."

"I don't understand. They produce goods without caring about revenues from their sale?" I ask incredulously.

"Some do, yes. Here's how it works: An industrial entity will turn to the government to ask for a good price on a plot of land to build a new factory. The government is usually ready to rezone some piece of farmland for industrial use and hands it over. Then the company builds and operates the factory for a short time, documents some sales, then finds a reason to go back to the government for a new, larger facility, so that more land can be rezoned. The original factory land is then developed for commercial or residential use and sold off at a huge profit. And on and on it goes."

"How long can this be sustained?"

"You'd be surprised. But yes, real estate always has limits. You can't make more land."

"Could the bubble burst?" I wonder aloud.

"I'm an optimist. It could burst. And probably will. Speculators and investors will lose out. We'll maybe see a slowdown and increased unemployment. But still there's simply no going back to the old ways. Whatever happens, China moves forward. But not quite as fast as before."

CHAPTER 8

Down South

A good traveller means never to arrive.
—Lao-tzu, fifth century BC

The door stands before us in the shadows. Sue, the young Cantonese beat reporter, has done what I asked her to do. She led us through the maze of the undercity to the entrance of a brothel.

A gloomy staircase leads upward. The building is a four-storey cement block structure. Its facade is narrower than the others. Its sign is but a couple of characters in black mounted on a red light panel. Red lights are common in China and not necessarily a reference to flesh. This sign is alone in the alleyway; it reads, *Massage*.

Massage parlours and brothels are plentiful in China—ubiquitous but discreet. The country has seen massive population movements and newly disposable income among the people. Crowded together and bent to purpose, their appetites don't go unanswered. Like there are places to eat, drink and laugh, there are also places for love, or if you prefer, lust. With so many people far from home, intimacy and human touch—and satisfaction and release—become precious and tradable.

We're in Guangzhou, deep in a living quarter as densely inhabited as anything I've seen. A massive, rambling labyrinth of concrete-block apartment buildings. Not quite skyscrapers, only six or seven storeys, but they hug each other so closely as to leave between them only the narrowest of passages.

The great casbahs of old Morocco are dense and full of strange passages and wondrous sights. The old city of Jerusalem is a knotty mess. The shantytowns of India, Africa and South America take one's breath away. There are even walled quarters across Europe that give some sense of human compression, absent the filth of old. But urban density is different in pockets like this, grown vertically on precious little real estate. Steel and concrete compartmentalize human lives like nothing else. Planned utilities—piped water, sewage and electricity—however rudimentary, bring some harmony to life in the colony. Overseers are also necessarily involved. They'll profit in the enterprise, or be blamed if disaster strikes and people find themselves mired in excrement and disease.

It feels like a shantytown, though, abruptly populated by hordes of people packed into close proximity by scarcity of land. There's an unmistakable energy, as if anything could happen and everything could be found. Chinatown, baby.

Guangzhou, once known as Canton, is on the shores of the Pearl River. For centuries, the south coast of China has been a staging ground for human migrations. With its islands, bays and protected river outlets facing the welcoming currents of warm seas, the coast has long been an orifice through which people and things go in and out of China. By the late eighteenth century, Canton was at the epicentre of a vast commercial network that linked up with Southeast Asia and beyond. Through these networks, Cantonese language, culture and food came to shape the world's notion of China. Canton also became a worldwide hub for Chinese labour. Cramped masses huddled here, expecting long sea passages toward foreign lands, destined to build railroads or monuments in the West. Chinatowns grew out of this trade in human bodies. Now more archetype than reality, they conjure up alien energies, strange odours and feelings of wonder and unease.

Tonight I am back in Chinatown. The archetype comes alive as we venture into the maze and seek out this brothel. The human body trade is all too real.

Sue explains that the neighbourhood is relatively new. But constantly trod by recent arrivals from the countryside, the streets are so thoroughly used that it doesn't feel new at all. The grime's heavy on the concrete walls of the buildings, yet the quarter is clearly maintained. Garbage has been removed, and storefronts tidied, the streets mopped. But God forbid an earthquake. Here, human activity is compressed and relentless. It's already night and the arteries of the quarter are full of noise and light. The air's warm and thick with smells.

The occasional glance at the white man and the two young women walking through the quarter is justified. Foreigners might occasionally enter during the day, and it's perhaps not unheard of for a white man to be seen walking the streets at night. But wouldn't he be led by someone from the neighbourhood? Wouldn't he have come for some shady reason?

But I am here with Viv, from the north, and Sue. She's short and dark skinned; she has cropped, spiky hair like a teenaged boy. Her clothes are contemporary and loose fitting. Her face is round and holds an even and happy countenance. She has a fast, decisive manner, and a confidence and purpose in her gait that say "I belong." Viv pointed out to me earlier that Sue is from a place up the coast famous for its gangsters. Though not from this neighbourhood, she's still plenty local.

Sue smooths our passage through the quarter and somehow allows it to make sense, but only just. With her dainty ways, Viv is clearly an outsider. Beside me, is it not obvious that we are observers, not participants? How suspicious the strangers who witness without involvement or those who pass without sacrifice, leaving nothing. I urge us to move swiftly, as if we are heading to an engagement, as if there will be participation and purchase.

We plan to climb the stairs and enter the establishment, and Sue will engage the management—with any luck, it'll be a woman. We have money and we want to meet a masseuse. Once in private, we'll ask questions.

The story of Chinatown is one of the flesh, the consequence of the body factory China has been through the ages. Spikes in population growth led to sporadic demographic crises and mass migration. Locally, these movements have been a part of Chinese history for over two millennia. But it took the age of discovery and maritime trade and powerful ports along the south shore to make Chinese migration a worldwide phenomenon.

Chinese labour was a fascinating part of the growing maritime trade. For newly industrialized economies, slave or conscript labour grew less and less feasible through the nineteenth century. Empire builders needed an alternative. A Chinese workforce could be quickly and cheaply applied to massive construction projects like building railroads or digging canals. Unlike slaves, Chinese coolies could be acquired without any great violence, and the liability involved in feeding and lodging them would be short term. Builders could purchase labour in bulk for limited contract use. Plus the workforce generally came with its own support structure of Chinese foremen, paymasters and cooks, a veritable turnkey solution for Western entrepreneurs.

Just as they had to be fed and washed, all the moving bodies occasionally had to be nurtured as well. So around the cadre of cooks and washer folk there grew a community of specialists: agents of ports and providers of medicine and sexual gratification. These elements combined to shape all Chinatowns, from the sprawling quarters of San Francisco and Vancouver to the single alleyways of the frontier posts.

Of all the things that made Chinatown seem strange and different to outsiders, I imagine the gap between growing Western puritanism and Chinese practicality was one of the more potent. Among the rich and powerful, polygamy was widely practised in nineteenth-century China and, indeed, admired. Women's bodies in general were a commodity. It was expected that sex be traded for money and protection. If the trade led to long-term advantage for an individual and her family, the business might even be deemed honourable. Fathers traded their daughters away in such a way—although not prostitution in the narrow sense, it did nonetheless involve the implicit notion that the daughter's body would be served up for enjoyment and procreation, and that this use of her body would be rewarded.

As I stand before the staircase my own puritanism comes crashing down upon me. I'm suddenly uncomfortable to be thinking all this sexuality through, or at least saddened by the thought of intimately engaging a young woman about her sexual existence. I shudder to think of an embattled soul subjected to scrutiny in her place of work and conclude that our approach is all wrong.

I picture the bashful young girl having to explain herself while sitting on a bed, as if confessing her wanton behaviour to her parents. It's too cold and hard for me. I can't imagine happy events conspiring to have her work here.

The brothel's also not a private place. Her young colleagues fill the rooms off the halls, and her employers are at the front and back, all surely aware of her confessions. Not to mention the clientele. These girls know all sorts of things that must remain private. We were wrong to seek to interview a prostitute in her place of work. I'm now ashamed and want to leave.

"That's it," I say.

"What?" Viv says, scratching her head. "We're not going in?"

"Our plan's no good."

"Well, let's at least go up and see, now that we're here," she says.

"No, let's go back," I insist.

Standing in the red light, I claim I already know everything I need to about the girl up in the room. I don't actually need to go there. The real lesson here is about privacy. Privacy in the body factory, not communion. Respect, not exposure.

Viv and Sue don't quite understand, but there's nothing more to say. We walk back through the quarter to the strangely quiet main road. On the other side of the street, one open shop: a medicinal tea shop, my two companions explain. The specialty: a bitter concoction brewed to bring one's fire down. I sarcastically quip that I'm indeed a good candidate for having my fire lowered.

The hot liquid is held in a large brass vat mounted on a table directly in the open storefront. It's served in a paper cup. In addition to being bitter, the dark liquid is earthy and a little funky. This is not a romantic drink, and I drink alone. Where is Qingdao's Fat Sister when you need her?

A brothel is not hard to find, but there isn't a single bar in sight. In fact, the notion of a place exclusively for the consumption of alcohol is not terribly germane to the Chinese. Convenience stores might serve it by the glass. Restaurants all serve alcohol with food. Patrons might linger long after their meal to drink beer and spirits. But there's nowhere selling alcohol to be found here.

On this main artery of Guangzhou, the only drink offered tonight is a bitter tea, not to dull one's senses and allow forgetting, not to give one courage or make one merry. Its remedy is metaphysical. For those bound to their own selfish passions, for those hardened into action by purpose and obsession, this balm promises acceptance and contemplation, a retreat from the ego and its battles. It has no noticeable effect on me.

A taxi takes us to the hotel, a nondescript tower in the centre of the business district. As we ride, we draw up a plan for the coming day and I give Sue taxi money to get home. Sue works for one of the major newspapers in town. She covers accidents and crime. Young journalists are not well paid, so a quick contract as a helper to a foreign journalist is welcome. She'll work for me for three full days and at the end be paid for her time.

Sue accompanies us into the hotel and up in the elevator to our rooms. Viv's floor is first and she takes her leave. Then Sue follows me one more floor up, out of the elevator and to my room. She stands there as I open the door, leaving me puzzled.

If she wants something, money perhaps for her day's work, she doesn't say. She says nothing at all. Seeing me safely to my room, is she? After a moment's pause, I smile and say, "See you tomorrow" and softly shut the door.

In my mind, she remains on the other side of the door, challenging me: "You call yourself a traveller? A journalist? A witness?"

In the morning, we emerge to a blaring sun. Sue awaits on the sidewalk, with few words to say. What's our business, she implies.

My request is simple: factories. Places where things are made. This is one of China's great manufacturing centres and I want to see some industry.

We head out by taxi across several bridges. One rises quite high as it spans the water, allowing us to see over a large area. The hot white haze in the air blurs the details, but I can see that the Pearl River at Guangzhou is more properly a wide inlet. The protected coast might once have been broken into lagoons, marshes and waterways, but now every bit of shore seems secured for inhabitation and use.

We pass a few industrial parks but are not headed to this kind of manufacture. The big, new complexes are gated and not interested in drop-ins from journalists and foreigners. Instead, we're heading toward small industry, textile manufacture to be precise.

The taxi drops us in a dense but orderly low-rise quarter. The buildings are not new but they are recent. They're clad in cheap sheet metal. The ground floors house shops. The three or four floors above seem like industrial space. But the neighbourhood is strangely inactive. There's no bustle in the streets. Few shops are open, and the upper floors seem quiet. We seem off-target. Sue is perplexed.

Just then I spot another shop with a brass vat out front. The previous night's medicinal tea shop was apparently part of a chain. As Sue checks with locals about the factories, I draw Viv into the shop to help me get another dose of the mysterious brew. The shop offers no food of any kind. Viv explains that it sells not just the bitter, black stuff in the front vat but a whole menu of herbal concoctions. I urge Viv to order me a different brew.

"Each tea's for a specific reason," she tells me with muted annoyance. "You are supposed to have a reason to drink these teas."

"How about something to soothe ragged nerves?"

Viv's a good sport. She knows I'm not being sincere about my nerves, but neither flippant nor smart-assed about the serious matter of medicinal teas. I'm only killing time and conducting another coarse but valuable experiment.

"Nerves, then?" she says, scanning the menu for prescriptions. Sue arrives to help. She apparently knows exactly what's needed for frayed nerves and my order is passed on. The two women order for themselves the same tea I ordered the previous evening.

My tea is a light golden colour and grassy tasting.

"The factories here have moved," Sue tells me. "No one is quite sure where they have gone."

This doesn't make a whole lot of sense to me. Some kind of self-censorship at work, I figure. I let it be.

"Then where to next?" I ask.

Sue has ideas of where to go, but she isn't quite sure how to get there. She heads back into the street to ask strangers more questions.

"Things are changing fast; it can be confusing at times," Viv comments. "In places like this, people come from all sorts of different places. They're busy; they don't get to know the city well. Even if they do, the neighbourhoods change fast."

"Do dialects make things difficult?"

"In big cities, people don't usually speak in their dialect to strangers."

Sue is back. "We need a taxi," she says.

So we walk a few blocks toward a larger boulevard. I ponder the real estate conundrum surrounding us. How could such large buildings be empty yet still serviced? Who owns them? Who is suffering from this vacancy and paying for the upkeep? Land here is expensive, and utilities as well.

Maybe they're not actually empty. But evidence would say otherwise. As I peer up at the buildings, I see few lights. The neighbourhood is clearly running at a very low capacity. State ownership or big business lurks behind the situation, I conclude. These were textile factories, probably built in the 1980s but recently shut down. Labour was redeployed. A number of converging factors explain this, I figure. Multi-storey production is not efficient. And capacity is reached quickly.

I conjure an image of the neighbourhood running at full capacity, churning out product: the constant din of ventilators and air conditioners, freight elevators taxed with all the lifting, the streets choked with delivery trucks being loaded and unloaded with materials and product, the air thick with fumes, masses of labourers filling the multiple floors of the buildings, toiling away at sewing machines. Vast mobs forming when shifts start and end. Impressive. Reckless. Problematic. And now implausible.

In China, industrialists are scaling up production. Planners and market forces both seek higher efficiency. Old-school industry like this kind of textile production, which occurred here only recently, no longer has a place in Guangzhou.

The Pearl River economy possibly invented the sweatshop, but they're no longer easy to find here. Well-ventilated factories are built out of lighter materials. They produce higher-value items. Electric forklifts move pallets toward shipping containers. Humans are moved about more carefully between high-efficiency operations and better-planned settlements. Low-end, high-scale production exists, but elsewhere—inland, upcountry. In smaller cities with cheaper property and labour. Or across Southeast Asia, where labour is less expensive, industrial options more limited and risks more easily ignored.

Here, it's hard to tell what'll happen. The area can hardly be left in such a passive state. Light industry, I guess. I imagine computer widgets or packaging of some kind being manufactured here. But who knows? Perhaps the neighbourhood will be destroyed, the utilities improved and huge residential complexes built. Consumption replacing production. Perhaps.

Our next stop is on reclaimed land. We cross a swampy river. The area is suddenly grassy and the road roughly surfaced—in places, earthen. It's almost like we're heading into the countryside, but we're not; we are coming through the back door. Buildings quickly multiply around us. They are made of crude cement, at most two storeys high. Some are tiny houses; others are more commercial in feel, with high ceilings and big doors. People are everywhere. Open hangars emit the sound of machines or the bright blue flashes of welding torches. The smell of fumes but also of wet earth and fresh sawdust. We'll not be seeing sweatshops here, but raw human industry.

We instruct the taxi to take us deeper. He tells us there should be a market up ahead. But it's slow moving now; we share the rough and narrow road with trucks, carts, pedestrians and even animals. We see that we would move faster on foot, so we settle the fare and exit the car.

Narrow streets lead off the main road, each one to more activity. People are making metal implements, wooden tools and furniture. They're packing things into crates. One shop is quiet and filled with identical appliances in their boxes. Perhaps a local speculator got an inside deal on a whole pile of locally made air conditioners and is hoping to sell them off en masse to a retailer.

Another street is geared toward recycling. Piles of old televisions fill a yard. Clusters of computer keyboards are laid out unceremoniously on bare earth. The smell of melting plastic and burnt metal permeates the air. Inside, small walls of desktop units stand behind a group of workers who are opening them up and stripping them down. They unscrew the fans, amass the wiring, then go at the circuitry, prying off condensers and chips.

Elsewhere, carpenters are assembling bathtubs out of planks of wood. They are fitted around a central plate and banded together —a luxury item for new Asian wealth. Such a tub is a finicky affair to keep in good working order but affords a luxurious soak to which your average Chinese workaholic is ill-accustomed.

"How much?" Viv inquires.

The bathtub builder takes a moment to think about it, then tells Viv that he'll accept the equivalent of forty dollars. He's grinning with the thought of a guaranteed sale to us fine people. Alas, we move on.

Here, there's no indolence and little waste. What's new about this neighbourhood is not its industry. Switch out a few variables of production and decor and this neighbourhood might closely resemble the old Pearl River Canton. What's new is that the bustle is occurring in an economic boom of unrivalled proportions. Total mobilization.

In these rough dregs where everything is happening on a small scale, there's an excess of paid work. Even the toothless illiterate grandmother finds her station sorting motherboards. She's paid but a pittance, I'm sure. Or she donates her time to her family, who run the salvage business, in exchange for food and shelter. But there she is, in an earthen-floored concrete garage, toiling away for long hours, making the tiniest contribution to a gargantuan economic phenomenon. Her work too will be turned into product. Her time will be rewarded by further consumption—not the wooden bathtub, perhaps, but the air conditioner possibly will find its way through her toils to her modest home.

Sue, Viv and I ramble through the quarter, eventually stumbling upon the market. It's big and mostly covered, but without walls. The space under the roofing is packed with people and products. It's a food market with many rows of fruit, root vegetables and leafy greens. I'm more interested in the animals. Several carcasses hang in brightly lit enclosures with soiled tarps for walls. Bloodied butchers hack away at steer or pig and lay quarters and cuts of meat on the display tables alongside glistening organ meat.

Even in this heat, the market doesn't seem to make much use of refrigeration. Fish are piled up in buckets or boxes, mostly without ice, shiny and slimy.

The myth of Chinatown tells us that the Chinese eat everything—birds, reptiles, monkeys, dogs, cats and insects—all sold alive. Upcountry, this may be true. But not here. Despite its roughness and spontaneity, this place is no village and offers up no bush food. The neighbourhood is a migrant labour encampment in the middle of Guangzhou. People from all over feed off the action, however marginally, slowly trying to get ahead or at least dig in.

The Cantonese themselves have a taste for refined and rare food, much of it from the sea. Abalone or flying fish roe. A bed of congealed saliva woven together by tropical swallows living high on volcanic outcroppings over water is the famed bird's nest on the Chinatown menu. I have yet to come across it. I've enjoyed frogs' ovaries, though; they're sold as a topping over sweet creamy shakes in Hong Kong. You would never know what they are from eating them; the clear gelatine is mostly without flavour and disappears quickly into the drink. I'm always amazed that people eat amphibian egg sacs in such a casual manner.

These delicacies are not well represented in this coarse market, though. Still, there are many rows of caged chickens, ducks, geese and small birds. The flesh of domesticated birds is loved by the Chinese, rich or poor. An ancient source of animal protein for Chinese peasants and a cornerstone of the menu throughout the land but especially in the south, these birds are well suited to high-density cohabitation with humans. Compared with larger animals, birds are less polluting, an important fact when one considers the great pressures on drinking water in China. Fowl can be raised on the tiniest parcels of land, or in and around rice paddies or drainage ditches. They even function as a kind of pest control.

China has run out of land, and hundreds of millions of its citizens live in concrete cities now. The country has become a huge importer of frozen foreign meat: beef, swine and sheep from places where land is cheaper. China's also fast adopting industrial meat production methods of its own. Chickens and pigs can now be kept and fed by the thousands in warehouses from the moment that they are born to when they are ready to be eaten.

When these industrial practices combine with the traditional preference for live animals, as is clear in this food market, one senses a danger. One imagines flu viruses mutating through dense populations of animals brought to markets alive and then into people's cramped apartments. Add to this modern air travel and we begin to understand the origins of previous pandemics—old culinary habits coinciding with new food production methods, high population densities and easy air travel.

Sue wonders whether we might be interested in eating snake.

"Yes, we must eat snake at once!" I say in jest. I ate snake many, many years ago in Hong Kong. The meat was tough and brown. It had been cooked in a light broth and had a faint but peculiar aroma. Still, I'm curious.

We find another taxi and travel over a few bridges and through brush-covered hillocks toward the outskirts of town. Our destination is a stand-alone banquet hall on the side of a minor road. Its huge ornate sign depicts a variety of snakes, laid out in an encyclopaedic manner.

It's well into the afternoon and there isn't a client in the place. Young waiters jump into action to attend to us. I'm made to understand that all the snakes they serve are slaughtered on the premises. I'm asked if I would like to choose a snake for our meal. How can I refuse? I must see the snakes before eating them. Viv and Sue tell me to follow one of the waiters; they'll remain at the table.

I'm led to the back of the building and to a grimy, stinky area on the back side of the kitchen complex. In the dim light, we are met by a tougher-looking employee in dirty, dark brown uniform-like shirt and pants. The snake wrangler, I assume. He leads me to a wooden door that opens onto a windowless room. Fluorescent lights turn on and I notice a desk and filing cabinet to one side and a dozen or so tall baskets in the middle of the room. Baskets are quickly thrust in my face, each holding live snakes. There must be several hundred snakes in this little cement room. Thankfully, I detect no peculiar odours. And unlike with poultry, there is no such danger as snake flu.

What do I know about choosing snakes to eat? I turn down a couple of slender banded types and point at the bigger baskets. I'm casually shown some pretty menacing-looking creatures and settle on a thick, inky-black type; a creepy-looking beast for sure, but at least it's big and meaty, and I hope its shiny eel-like appearance might make for more tender flesh.

The man starts gesticulating for me to pick one of the dark snakes from the writhing snake salad at the bottom of the basket. I can't take him seriously and laugh out loud.

Ever more insistent, the man reaches into the basket with a metal tool to pluck a snake out for my approval. I'm already heading for the door, but I turn back to see a long black snake with a pale underbelly wiggling from the wrangler's tongs like a giant worm on a hook. I merely bark out, "Right, right, thank you!" in Mandarin and exit the room. Enough with the chamber of snakes! The way things were going, next I'd be invited to help the guy carry my chosen snake to the kitchen and asked to hold its body down while the cleaver severed its neck.

Back at the table, Viv and Sue explain that people mostly eat snake for vigour. It's food to bring the fire up. Many men think that snake will help them perform in bed or be more fertile.

"A little too obvious for my liking," I say.

The snake arrives in a series of dishes. Its organs with country herbs. Its bony tail dry-fried with salt and spice. A brothy soup with its head. Then a bigger dish: sweet fried snake sections. I reckon these my best bet. The sauce is sweet and tasty, but the meat is beyond tough. On one side of the morsels, the black skin is like stewed belt leather. On the other side are portions of the creature's bony rib cage, equally difficult to chew through. Only by pulling the skin hard away from the ribs can I nibble on the sliver of meat between the two.

I am left wondering whether this snake business is just a gimmick. Then I think of all the live animals in the back; it's no small affair to catch and assemble so many of them. Snake eating must be serious enough business to some people.

A waiter asks us how we are enjoying the meal. The snake is too tough for enjoyable eating, I say. He quickly offers to take it back to be cooked more. Pretending to be a connoisseur, I declare that snake should be cooked right the first time.

Jokes aside, I conclude that I'm going about it all wrong. The skin and bones are probably relished by avid snake eaters. I picture a lustful lover coming here to chew through a whole bunch of snake gristle, believing the meat's resilience and endurance will wear off on him and his member. Too much for me.

As we leave the restaurant, Sue unexpectedly takes her leave. Her newspaper has called and she has to report to duty for an event on the other side of town. She promises to meet up with us later. So much for seeing the sweatshops of Guangzhou, I muse to Viv.

Viv reassures me by saying that Shenzhen, where we'll soon be heading, will have more of what we are looking for. We make a plan to tour some historical sites. But we soon realize that we are in the middle of a rather strange place with no taxis for hire. We walk toward a large boulevard with newly manicured wide lawns on either side. There's no traffic, only brand-new mid-sized apartment buildings, looking barely occupied. A pleasant neighbourhood, I guess, but not yet very practical for living. Unless one's idea of a pleasant night out with the missus means an evening walk to go nibble on sweet fried snake.

We finally flag down a car. Viv persuades the driver to serve as a taxi driver and take us back to downtown Guangzhou. I want to see the old docks. A tiny section still exists on the shore. It's no longer a functional port, more of a tourist quarter. It has also been overwhelmed by the city; an inhospitable freeway cuts it off. Our citizen driver stops along the highway to drop us off. Viv and I find a pedestrian bypass to scamper over the dark canal that separates the small island from the mainland.

As we descend into the old quarter the rich canopy of mature trees soothes us with their presence. The construction also catches the eye: official and colonial. The neighbourhood is deadly quiet. I chirp up that slow dereliction offers beautiful puzzles and hides good stories.

We walk beneath grand plane trees and less familiar tropicals—tamarind or mahogany, perhaps. A few awesome specimens indicate that beneath all the masonry there's wet mud. These trees grow here as they would have long before on the flood plain, adapted both to heavy, saturated soils and compacted hardpan, something similar in effect to the compressed dark matter beneath the quarter.

Once upon a time, this quarter was China's gate to the world. The streets were filled with ship officers and customs officials. This was once the official quarter of Canton. Here, the captains of incoming ships would come ashore. Before air-conditioning, leafy giants were needed for shade. In those days, cholera and yellow fever were frequent banes of the old Pearl. Then the shiny uniforms of the foreign officers would be especially important, suits of armour against filth and corruption.

The buildings are Western in design, many of them stone monuments erected by great Western commercial houses for their agents in this rich port. A hundred years ago, when they were built, foreign governments would have had offices here alongside money changers, underwriters and the rest. There's also evidence of expatriate residency in the quarter. Maybe even the residues of tenement Chinese, discreetly mixed in for all the dirty jobs of the time.

The quarter speaks of the time when the West ruled the world. On the docks of old Canton on the Pearl, it shaped itself a door into China's great wealth, made it strong and respectable, staffed it with the stiff-shirted type who flipped deftly through a big book of rules. For a good while, the Chinese Imperial Maritime Customs Service was a kind of foreign entity, run and staffed by a large cohort of Englishmen, supplemented with Germans, French, Americans, Russians and eventually a few Japanese nationals for good effect. Clearly, it was thought that China could no longer function properly, that the Qing court was no longer fit to oversee international trade and properly collect customs duties. The responsibility had to be outsourced to a power that could. China was on its knees.

This period of Chinese subjugation started in earnest in this harbour in the 1830s when foreign ships blasted Qing officials into submission. The cannons were English and their demand was simple: trade with us or we'll continue to fire on the city. Beyond the warships were merchant ships that carried in their holds something China craved: opium from British India. With their battery of guns, the British officers were insisting that this merchandise be sold into China.

I can imagine the Qing officials of the day distraught over accepting the terms of these violent foreigners. From the Imperial Court far to the north, there could be no understanding for bending to such seaborne rogues. The business made also no economic sense. The trade being demanded of the Chinese meant seeing large amounts of valuable Chinese production, such as porcelain and silk, traded for a substance that despite its great popularity brought little to China except sloth and misery. The officials probably also felt that the imperial treasury and their own pockets were not benefiting enough from this trade. In the end, their homes and city were burning and not much could be done to silence the English cannons. So, in defiance of Beijing, the Cantonese officials ultimately surrendered to the foreign fleet and the limey came ashore to unload his drug.

Viv tells me the story of the high official Liu who stood up for the Qing in Canton and initially held firm against the foreign bully. At the emperor's court in Beijing, some twenty-two hundred kilometres to the north, he was initially praised for his honourable actions, then sacked and punished when they failed and Canton was burning. The war on drugs had failed.

Britain had another demand as well: land. Victoria needed a place to park her gunboats and cargo ships, somewhere she wouldn't have to deal with the nuisance of Chinese laws. Hong Kong island, at the mouth of the Pearl, would do nicely, thank you.

After the docks, we head uptown in search of the city's biggest shopping mall. Failing a glimpse at manufacturing, we want to at least see how and what the Cantonese are consuming. We pass nothing too telling or impressive, only a glitzy new car dealership geared toward the middle class. Amid a general low buzz of shopping activity, Viv and I quickly walk several floors of a fancy department store. In the bathroom section, we are amused to run across the same wooden bathtubs we had seen assembled earlier that morning selling for around three hundred dollars.

The afternoon traffic is picking up and we head down the

street to a large park for peace and fresh air. We stumble upon the Sun Yat-sen Memorial Hall, buy refreshments from a vendor and take a seat across from the doctor's statue. Dr. Sun—Sun Zhongshan—is the father of modern China and set his country on the path to healing. A good follow-up to the old docks and foreign-controlled China, we agree.

A glimpse at Sun's biography or even his likeness reveals the archetypical Cantonese gentleman bridging decaying imperial China with modern China in all its tumult and glory. Sun is revered both in mainland China and in Taiwan.

Born into a privileged and worldly Pearl River family in 1866, young Sun was exposed to the wide possibilities of the Pacific Rim. A much older brother was a landowner in Hawaii, and by his early teens, Sun was studying in a Christian school in Oahu alongside European and American children, mastering English.

By his late teens, he was in Hong Kong finishing his studies under proper English masters. After that, medical school in Guangzhou under American Presbyterian supervision, then back to Hong Kong where, not surprisingly considering all his Western schooling, he converted to Christianity. From the protection of the British Empire in Hong Kong, he then began to observe the continued breakdown of the Qing Empire and soon vowed to devote all his energies to saving China.

For the young Sun, already an iconoclast, saving China increasingly meant fomenting republican revolution, often with overseas Chinese support. His early efforts were unsuccessful, and they forced the doctor into long wanderings in foreign lands. In Japan, he plotted with other Asian revolutionaries also bent on freeing their countries from foreign domination. In the West, he bounced from Chinatown to Chinatown, seeking support for his republican efforts among both the Chinese and the occasional foreigner.

Eventually, he settled in Southeast Asia, from where he directed revolutionary uprisings against the Qing in the south—bloody failures each and every one. The doctor was proving himself a poor conqueror. But where Sun failed, others were succeeding. Even without his agency, uprisings continued across south and central China. One rebellious faction even managed to secure a pocket of resistance in the strategic city of Wuchang (now part of Wuhan), on the middle Yangtze and at the crossroads of China.

With faith in rebellion bolstered, Sun returned to China and parlayed his overseas connections into enough clout to rise to the forefront of the fractious movement. In December 1911, he managed to get elected as provisional president of the Republic of China, which held sway over more and more pockets south of the Yangtze. Nanjing was even chosen as the capital before it was secured by the rebels.

Prying south China away from the Qing was one thing. Manchu command in the south had been growing weaker for a long time. Sun was also adept at evoking scenarios that the poor, the republican intelligentsia, organized crime and the diaspora might all support. Gentleman traveller, doctor-poet, he embodied ancient notions of the scholar-bureaucrat and combined them with polished modern and worldly manners. Daring as he was, he was also reassuring to the Chinese people.

Unifying all of China under a single republican government, as Sun hoped, was a far more grandiose objective and well beyond Sun's reach from the south. Unification meant bringing the north under republican command. Power in the north had long been military. Beijing and its reaches could not be secured without battles. The surrounding plains and steppe lend themselves to the type of mobile warfare that had propelled the Mongols and the Manchu to domination in China. Sun had no comparable assets. He would have to acquire the north by alliance. Fortunately, the late Qing Empire was not lacking in potential usurpers, including the powerful military commander Yuan Shikai, the very man to whom the Imperial Court entrusted the mission to put down the rebellious south.

Thinking they could use each other, Yuan and Sun were soon negotiating the balance of power in post-Qing China. Provisional President Sun had the republican state apparatus and domestic and foreign credibility; he also had accessed the rich trade networks of south China. Marshal Yuan in the north had the soldiers and guns of China's professional army.

Back in Beijing, Yuan soon turned his army on the palace and forced the young Qing emperor to abdicate sovereignty in favour of the Republic of China. For his part, Sun handed the presidency over to Yuan Shikai, who became the first real president of the Republic of China. The capital was to be established in Nanjing, with Sun's united revolutionary party meant to provide the state apparatus.

Yuan was nothing of a republican and harboured far more ambitious designs on power. He also refused to govern from Nanjing. Sun and his republican ideals were sidelined as Yuan turned the presidency into a military dictatorship, based in Beijing. Sun's allies were killed or persecuted, and Sun himself went back into exile, calling once more for uprisings, this time against the imposter Yuan.

Before long, Yuan declared himself the Hongxian emperor of

a new dynasty, claiming legitimacy of rule. But he'd overplayed his hand; the people acknowledged no heavenly mandate. Yuan's closest war captains soon turned on him, and China broke into pieces. Within six months of his imperial proclamation, Yuan, widely despised and ridiculed, died of kidney failure. Warlordism descended upon the Middle Kingdom.

Sun returned from abroad and settled again in the south, where this time he fashioned himself military commander of Guangdong, making it clear that he intended to win the Chinese republic through violence, which he would start in the south. To acquire the required military power, Sun courted both American and Soviet advisers and drew ideas from nationalism, capitalism and socialism. But the doctor did not live long enough to put his ideas into practice or stare down their contradictions.

This battle would be left to his successors: on one side, Chiang Kai-shek, the nationalist, who proved a better military commander than the doctor had ever been and managed to finally seize the north and set up a unified republic; and on the other, Mao Zedong, the Communist. Each one claimed himself to be the true heir to the father of modern China, Sun Zhongshan.

Viv and I are strolling downtown when Sue returns to us. There seems to be a buzz around the city's conference hall. We go to take a look. To our amusement, it's an exhibit devoted to traditional Chinese sex toys.

Mostly young people visit the collection, including more than a few young couples, although several pensioners are also viewing it, dwelling at length before the display cases. There are dildos— wooden ones, ivory ones, stone ones, bumpy ones and smooth ones—as well as sex balls of different types, a few odd antique contraptions, a wide assortment of aphrodisiacs and excerpts from classical texts describing elaborate sexual practices.

It's very much a museum exhibit. The tone and manner of the presentation suggest that the subject could just as well be a collection of ancient cooking implements. The displays elicit giggling from the Chinese, but by and large they just take it in with a seemingly dispassionate curiosity. But I suspect they wouldn't be lining up for antique kitchen tools. The exhibit is also clearly a business venture.

In the West, it wouldn't play out this way. Sex toys are naughty business. An exhibit like this would not be held in a minor state hall as if there were nothing risqué about it. A for-profit show about sex toys would not be welcome at city hall, for instance. It would be serious business, with warnings and restrictions, for public edification. I struggle to imagine whether a collection of antique sex toys could even be assembled in my country.

With the Chinese, with my female guides, all I discern is a resounding nonchalance about the inference of erotic massages, bondage, masturbation or other rather lurid ideas. Like us standing at the bottom of the staircase to the massage parlour, poised to go up and have a look without shame.

The evening is balmy and there's a buzz in the air. I want to see more of the extremely dense neighbourhoods. Before long, my companions and I are walking deep into another maze.

It's still early and people are out. The narrow alleys feel more like the rows at that morning's market, with people bumping into each other, merchandise on all sides. Looking up past the bright lights, I see the buildings rise up six or seven storeys. Way above, a narrow slot opens to the darkening sky beyond. Wires and clotheslines bridge the gap. Windows are open and people talk to each other across the way.

Food and clothing are laid out on tables in the streets. Basic nourishment but splendidly varied. There are meats, noodles, dumplings and kebabs. Bright colours, strong smells. We turn into a passage not two and half metres across. The buildings above us overhang the street and leave barely half a metre between them.

"Imagine living up there somewhere," Viv says, looking up at the apartment windows in the slot above.

"Just the kind of place where I could sit down and finally write my novel about the human condition," I joke.

Sue tells us that the city has been trying to tear this neighbourhood down for safety reasons, but people have been mobilizing to resist. They'll likely fail in the end. This place will surely be destroyed soon enough; in the meantime, it's amazing that someone would come to the defence of such a place. More amazing still, Sue recounts how many of the defenders were not property owners but renters.

We make a right turn into a passage that slowly ascends. Just then a troop of teenage boys flies past us, jumping up onto a ledge to clear us without slowing. Up ahead a smaller group is calling out to them, playfully promising retribution. They're in the middle of a game. These alleyways, these buildings and all the rooms they contain are a kind of run for these boys, an ecosystem of their own.

Beyond their cramped apartments, the whole neighbourhood—the dense tangle of private and public spaces—is home to this moving, changing yet somehow constant mass of people. The noise, the action, the smells, the compressed existence of so many dwellers are surely not just hardships they need tolerate. These dwellers might even miss these things if, now that they're accustomed to them, they all suddenly disappear.

Everyone here is in a good mood tonight. This is no dead end. People living here are not unemployed, not squatters like in most shantytowns. They're not at the margins but at the base. There's a spot for them in the new China. So they pay their rent, pay their dues, raise their families, look forward and keep smiling.

"Does this place seem unhappy to you, Viv?" I ask, with no expectation of an answer.

When we finally find our way back to a main artery, I'm surprised to come across used booksellers. I can't picture a whole lot of reading being done in this anthill. I stop to inspect the titles. There are a great many books on how to do things, on how to get somewhere: how to master computer programs, how to cook, how to learn English, how to help oneself. I quickly choose some well-illustrated books on Cantonese banquet-style cooking. Viv then points me to a large section on Chinese astrology. Instead, a bin filled with foreign paperbacks entices me. I scan the titles: mostly just a collection of pulp novels in English, read quickly and abandoned by travelling westerners. Not much to learn here, I'm about to conclude, when a slightly larger, well-used and floppy softcover in English catches my eye: Shirley MacLaine's *Out on a Limb*. Not my type of book, but I'm amused to find it here and decide to buy it for Viv.

"This woman was a friend of my father's. Quite smart and entertaining, but quirky. I guarantee there are some highly debatable things in here. But look for the mad cult of the free spirit so important in the West, especially remarkable among independent women like the author," I tell her.

"Thank you. I'm touched." Viv blushes. "I'll be sure to read it."

Why do I keep forgetting how powerful even insignificant gifts can be?

Shenzhen lies two hours away by fast train. On the north side of the gulf formed by the widening Pearl River, Shenzhen is the last bit of mainland China before the Hong Kong peninsula and archipelago and the seas beyond. Here, the People's Republic set up its own shops to imitate and complement the Hong Kong manufacturing economy. Free of the real estate concerns of Hong Kong and able to access vast amounts of labour from throughout China, the student has surpassed the master. Shenzhen's port is now the world's third biggest, after only Shanghai and Singapore.

Having failed in Guangzhou, Viv and I are keen to visit factories in Shenzhen. Viv has been dialling contacts. She's playing connect the dots, looking for people who might know people connected to Shenzhen industry. I'm always amazed how well this game works in China. I suppose that the density of people and their extreme mobility greatly facilitates the transmission of information. Everyone in China is but a few steps removed from a huge number of people, theoretically assuring access to virtually any information about anything. Someone always knows someone who knows something.

Connecting the dots works even better among young journalists. What comes around goes around, they say, as they constantly exchange contacts with each other. They're also always ready to cold-call people. I listen with fascination as Viv dials up a succession of complete strangers who are somehow connected to manufacturing corporations. Viv obtains these names from people who know people she worked with years earlier.

With the landscape flying by outside, she takes on her daintiest voice and politely yet obliquely tries to arrange for us to visit a factory, while giving out few details about who we are and why we would possibly want to see widgets being made. She finally secures an appointment. Tomorrow afternoon, we're to visit a facility for the fabrication of micro-condensers in a newly erected technopark. As codified a society as it may sometimes seem, there's remarkable spontaneity in China.

Shenzhen has been called a city with neither class nor soul, hastily thrown together and bent to base purposes. Forget trying to stay somewhere interesting here; you'll find a concrete-and-glass tower with a gaudy lobby leading to an elevator—and beyond, a generic room.

Viv and I head out immediately to find food and do some people-watching. We walk a large circuit through the downtown core. It has emptied out this evening and reminds me of many a North American business sector that can run at a low din after dark. The newly tree-lined boulevards seem unused. Food options are limited. We don't want to eat instant noodles or greasy fried food from the fast-food joints we pass. Looking for action of any kind, we finally enter a large, brightly lit mall. It too is new, rolling out its selection of boutiques. We pass the predictable assortment of luxury shops. Shoppers are mostly absent. Instead, giddy youngsters walk arm in arm, or linger in coffee shops, sipping bubble tea.

Upon completing the circuit, we laugh when we discover that the best food option is in fact the restaurant right next to our hotel. We eat surprisingly delectable dishes served to us under the guidance of the kindly and attentive owner of the establishment, who stands watch between our table and the restaurant's open doors.

Neither Viv nor I feel surprised by what we have seen so far in Shenzhen. Our present neighbourhood strikes us both as a serious contender for the most boring one in China.

I figure that it's a good time to take up the subject of Taiwan with Viv. During our time together, we'd already worked our way through the roster of subjects important to Chinese geopolitics: relations with the West, relations with Russia, relations with Japan, Korean unification, the Tibetan and Uighur independence movements.

Viv often surprises me with her liberal and even pacifist views. I find myself marching Chinese nationalist arguments at her progressive ideas, to test them. For her, a strong China is desirable, but her idea of it does not mean that it is callous toward minority peoples or seeks conflict or even dominance over its neighbours. She laments the destructive colonization of Tibet by the Han. She accepts China's deep reach into central Asia but wishes that relations with the Turkic peoples could be more harmonious. She also resists recklessly fast development pursuits that bring undue stresses to the people and the environment.

With regard to Russia and Japan and the West, she reasons that China can no longer be bullied by foreign powers but also must avoid becoming a bully itself. The schoolyard squabbles are of no use to anyone anymore. Without any great optimism, she holds out hopes for democracy in China and believes it necessary to usher in a period of calm and prosperity in the Far East whereby old regional enemies might move toward peaceful trading relationships and become partners in meeting the great environmental and spiritual challenges facing humans on earth, especially the three billion-odd souls of the Pacific Rim. Her views are balanced, humanist and quietly proud of both China's great heritage and the awesome future she envisages for it. She remains, however, an acerbic critic of most present-day Chinese leaders and the system they stand for.

Among all these brave and dissident positions, I could feel that Taiwan stands out in her discourse. With Taiwan, I wouldn't need to be arguing from the flanks. Viv's beliefs in democracy, in minority rights and in self-determination don't quite carry over into her thoughts about Taiwan. For her, China and Taiwan are like two pieces of a broken heart, and the whole subject is charged with emotion. Viv, who despises her Communist government, wants the reunification with Taiwan as fiercely as it does.

"There are a lot of indigenous peoples in Taiwan, people with very little to do with China," I begin to argue.

"Actually, they're all but gone," she counters. "All that is left is a few scattered populations in the mountains. The Japanese were brutal to them, you know."

"Han Chinese settlement on the island is rather recent in the grand scale of things—1700s, I believe. It's not part of dynastic China until recently, under the late Qing, and then it evolved under the Japanese," I argue.

"People who know Taiwan well say it's more Chinese than the mainland. At least, Chinese classical culture is better preserved there," she responds.

"For my part, I have always been struck by how much Taiwanese food culture borrows from the Japanese."

"Stop trying to goad me!"

"Anyhow, we are wrong to think the point is even a historical one," I continue, "even if, yes, history makes Taiwan diverge from mainland China in various different ways. What is important is that Taiwan *is* different and independent from China now and that the Taiwanese people should be able to choose the fate of their nation. If they decide through a majority vote that they want to stop calling themselves the Republic of China and opt to call their nation the Free State of Taiwan, on what grounds can we outsiders oppose them? That's the liberal position: people always get to choose."

"I can't imagine the Taiwanese choosing to reject China altogether," Viv says. "They would need serious protection, American or otherwise. But no protection would be enough. No Chinese leader would allow this to happen. An invasion would be guaranteed."

"Realpolitik may well work like that. The Americans and the rest of the world may well concede Taiwan to the PRC. That doesn't mean that it's right, that the Taiwanese aren't entitled to choose for themselves."

"Is this how you feel about Quebec's separation from Canada as well?" Viv asks pointedly.

"Absolutely. Personally, I am against Quebec's separation from Canada, of course. But not against Quebec's *right* to separate if ever that were the will of a clear majority there."

"Well, if Taiwan actually broke with China, it would be too sad. Think about all those who fled China in 1949. How sad it would be for them: the graves of their ancestors in a foreign land."

"I am not sure you would feel the same if you yourself were Taiwanese," I argue. "Why should you have to become responsible for all these things? Why would someone else's past hold precedence over your future?"

"A permanent split would mean ending the dreams of Sun Zhongshan, of Chiang, of Mao and Deng. Everyone would lose. China needs Taiwan. Without Taiwan, China cannot be whole. I fear that China needs Taiwan back for it to proceed and evolve.

Taiwan and Hong Kong, for that matter, must be part of China because their inclusion can give inspiration to end the one-party state and finally make way for a liberal-democratic republic."

"There might be violence in those ideas, Viv. You must see that."

"I sure hope not."

I leave it at that. We all have our own mythologies, beautiful and flawed like us their creators. Blending in both light and dark, everyone holds a few things sacred. Some wear their hard limits on their sleeve. Others have them buried deep inside. When it comes to Taiwan, bigger issues are clearly at work for Viv.

Perhaps because the universe is not created anew each moment, that which was started must end. Maybe the dark and light must come spiralling together and families must be made whole. Maybe the sons, Mao and Chiang, must return to the father, Sun, and his vision for China—whole, harmonious and free—must be realized. So says the Tao?

By day, Shenzhen doesn't make easy sense to the visitor. It goes on and on without form or history. It doesn't help that our day's appointments are at opposite ends of the city. In the morning, we head to the far eastern end to meet with Zhou Litai, a lawyer of some note who has made a name for himself representing injured migrant workers against huge corporations. Our connection to him is that he once represented our noble friend from Chongqing, Li Gang.

"I feel I should warn you that, from our phone conversation, he strikes me as slightly eccentric," Viv says cryptically.

"How is he eccentric?"

"He's boastful."

Zhou's office is on a big commercial boulevard that's in a state of construction, and there is dust everywhere. This hasn't stopped the bustle; as far as the eye can see, shops line the road.

Zhou greets us at the door to the building and we follow him up to the second floor. He's short and stout and incredibly energetic. From the moment we step into the large space of his office's main room, he engages in a high-speed monologue to establish his credentials. He claims his firm to be the most important one in China for the defence of worker rights. He brings us before a wall of indecipherable degrees, awards and certificates and carefully points to each one as he explains it.

It's hard to get a word in. Viv doesn't try to translate his tirade.

"Like I said to you earlier, he's eccentric," she merely says under her breath.

Zhou has us sit around an ornate conference table and returns with a stack of photo albums. He hands one to Viv and one to me and urges us to browse through them. Each album is full of classic Chinese-style portraits of groups of people standing upright in rows against a colourful backdrop. In page after page of such portraits, Zhou is often at the centre, grinning like a Buddha. He tells us that they are pictures of clients, officials and dignitaries.

Hovering over us, Zhou bounces between Viv and me, making sure we don't miss a single page. When we're through our respective albums, he intervenes to pass them between us and urges us not to forget to peruse the three other albums remaining on the table. He leaves the room to fetch something else for us. Viv and I exchange an amused look.

Zhou returns with gifts and press clippings. The gifts are ornate publicity folders for his firm, with multiple business cards for himself. Each for a specific purpose, he explains. Litigator.

Consultant. Chairman of some legal association. He hands us photocopied newspaper articles about himself, explaining and justifying each one as if he were filing evidence in a case: *Zhou Litai v. The stillness of the universe.*

Finally, Viv intervenes to get some useful answers out of him. We want to know the specifics of what he does. He starts in on a long series of case descriptions with the same energy he used to establish his credentials. He handles injuries, like Li Gang's, but also wrongful dismissals, complaints about working conditions, about wages. He also mentions lawsuits around worker suicides—families wanting compensation from abusive employers for inhumane conditions.

The abstract of these explanations would go something like this: China in general and Shenzhen more especially are filled with huge manufacturing entities. They sprout up like weeds. In all this activity, labour standards are difficult to uphold. Some entities employ tens of thousands of people. They are rarely simple structures; many subcontract out elements of production to other entities, so the line of responsibility between executives and employees is often blurred and complex. Oversight is also poorly conducted. Trade unions are absent. Production and labour structures are organized ephemerally. Whole operations are constantly being shut down while others spring up. Market forces do work for labour when it comes to wages. Salaries have been growing steadily. Profit, not any notion of welfare, is the prime driver of all this activity. In the confusion and bustle, corners are cut. Safety is sometimes compromised. When there are incidents, the process of filing grievances and making claims against so many moving targets can be difficult. Zhou explains that his first mandate is usually to untangle complex corporate

structures in order to clarify who or what might be held responsible for torts.

In simpler times, government was heavily involved in labour
issues. Party players would intervene to manage grievances and
hold elements responsible before any legal proceedings even
kicked in. Now with industry growing so fast and the heavy orientation toward foreign clientele in the export market, government
is often more interested in its cut than in labour issues, so this
work must be dealt with through the legal process and in the
courts. As it should be. But many corporations manage to hide
their responsibility. There's great impunity here, and lots of work
for Zhou.

Behind his outrageous boasting, Zhou shows real insight into
social-political realities. His work does involve intense clerical
and forensic research. He waxes into rhetoric when it comes to
the human rights dimensions of his practice: Doesn't the little guy
need a voice? How else is he ensured the dignity he deserves in
this world of giant factories and globalized economies? He needs
an advocate. He needs Zhou Litai.

One might think that human rights advocacy in China would
put him at odds with the Communist government. I lead him with
questions along these lines. He seems entirely unconcerned about
his government. Perhaps *human rights law* is also a misnomer
for his practice, a glorified term for something more mundane.
Labour and injury lawyer might be more appropriate. As such,
he's of use to the government rather than a nuisance as it slowly
and knowingly surrenders its responsibilities to society at large.
Zhou does something the government can't entirely do anymore:
hold corporations accountable for negligence toward employees.

We ask Zhou whether the continued strong links between various tiers of government and large corporations might make things difficult for him. There, he concedes, we might be on to something. The courts are not always terribly impartial. Settlements in favour of his clients are sometimes ridiculously small for substantial negligence and debilitating injuries. Still, he adds, even in the face of localized corruption, higher levels of government generally want justice to be done when it comes to corporate responsibility. The Communist Party of China—the CPC—deems the exercise important; it's part of the drive toward the ever more sophisticated economy that the CPC usually desires.

As Viv and I finally exit into the street, we quickly conclude that we like Zhou Litai. Eccentric as he is, China would be well served by more like him. For the rule of law cannot just be imposed from above but must also rise up from the trenches below.

To get to our factory, we need cross all of Shenzhen. Our taxi driver is pleased with the distance involved in the trip from the far east to the far west. We even allow him to pay tolls so that he can take the northern peripheral around the city.

Thus I get to see the outskirts. Shenzhen doesn't taper off into the countryside but ends abruptly at a solitary range of hills, all covered in jungle. As we glide along the highway beside the forest fringe, I can see that it is quickly falling to exploitation as well. Strip-mine excavations are occurring all along the hillside, making way for high-end residential complexes and golf courses. Then, as we come off the ridge heading south, a vista momentarily opens for us. In the distance, the hazy gulf of the Pearl is dotted with ships: ferries, immense cargo vessels, the tiny specks of fishing boats. The shoreline is a swath of human activity: port, shipyard, industry, inhabitation and construction. From our position on the hill to the gulf several kilometres to the south lies only city, or city in the making. When the highway drops from hill into city, people, production and distribution disappear. Our single mission shines out to us again in the abstract.

"Viv, tell me about our factory."

"I'm at a bit of a loss. I frankly don't know what it is that's made there. Something for electronic devices or computers, I think. And please don't ask me how it is that we are visiting this factory."

"Why not?"

"Trust me, my explaining how I made the contact would be too long and boring."

"At least admit that it is funny that we are travelling to this one obscure factory through what must be the world's greatest manufacturing centre. It's like looking for a single tree in a great forest."

"I hope it will be useful to you. But don't blame me if it isn't."

The highway morphs into a grand boulevard that leads to others. Suddenly, the city tapers off into a dusty wasteland, at least a square kilometre of bare earth, recently scraped clean of whatever had been there before. To its south, I can see the water again. We are working our way to the shore.

Past the wasteland, the city starts again. It's sparse and rough. The taxi halts at the side of a wide, unfinished turning circle. After the driver gets directions from pedestrians, we turn onto a final boulevard that has an almost industrial-park feel. Seven- or eight-storey industrial buildings neatly line up along the boulevard, intercut with sections of manicured lawns. We are going to building 10. The taxi driver says he'll wait for us.

Viv and I walk around the building, looking for an entrance.

We don't find much of a lobby, only a door leading to a stairwell and a couple of elevators. Viv gets on the phone with her contact, the company manager, Mr. Jiang. He tells her to come to the sixth floor.

Jiang, a relaxed man in his forties, meets us as we exit the elevator. He ushers us into his office, where we drink tea. He seems perfectly at ease with our interest in the operation. As is often the case in Shenzhen, our host is a Mandarin, not Cantonese, speaker. He passes us his company's trade catalogue. His outfit makes tiny electrical components for circuit boards, the tiniest needles in the largest haystack, a product so deeply embedded within the chains of production as to have almost no identity with the consumer, like a support column in a building, completely overlooked but necessary.

The resistors are partly for local production, partly for shipping elsewhere in China, but rarely for foreign outfits. Jiang explains that his company has expanded quite a bit in recent years and will be taking over more floors of the building in the coming months.

I ask where his employees live. He tells me that bigger companies nearby have employee housing facilities, but his company doesn't have any dedicated housing. Fifteen years ago, employers had to provide lodging because there was nowhere for people to live and local transportation was undeveloped. Now, people sort themselves out. But it has been getting more difficult to find labour, he explains, even if the wages offered are comparatively high. He hopes that the flurry of development in this part of Shenzhen will help increase the potential workforce.

Jiang invites Viv and me to don white coats before entering the production facility. *Factory* would be a strong word for the facility; it's more like a large laboratory. Thirty or so workers sit in tight formation, each performing the same tasks. They are nearly all women. A few of the supervisors are men. The women all wear white coats, hairnets, face masks and gloves. The room is windowless but brightly lit and well ventilated. Jiang explains that because the product is precision equipment, the company must carefully control the conditions of the facility.

The women work at their stations, peering through large magnifying glasses. They pick components from trays that contain an assortment of pieces, organized for assembly. They insert the minute parts into tiny white cylinders. The work reminds me of Chinese miniature painting, just as meticulous but more monotonous.

I am at a loss for questions to direct at our host. There seems so little to say. What sense can I truly make of this production? I ask about the workers. They work six days a week, I am told. The women seem mostly in their twenties. They have a pleasant if intensely focused demeanour to them, not surprising considering the precision of the handiwork. Like our grandmothers' embroidery work, Viv comments. I do wonder about what dreams might come to them at night after days spent repeating the same few actions.

In the next room, the resistors are processed through a series of machines. A handful of employees supervise these automated processes. With some effort, I manage to get Jiang to comment on what's involved: heat, pressure, then a vacuum. Another group of employees run a series of electrical tests to ensure that the resistors are up to spec. Finally, the finished product is packaged up in boxes.

We complete our tour in the company's cafeteria. Some employees are on break and are engaged in happy banter among themselves in Mandarin, scarcely aware of our presence. Many employees originate from other provinces and don't even speak Cantonese. In this way, Shenzhen now forms a strong link between the Pearl and the rest of China, a link long absent in a region that so often stood apart.

We emerge from the building into the golden light of the late afternoon sun. A group of workers coming from another facility walks past us. Cheerful young men and women, happy to have free time, no doubt. I can't quite picture them heading to night-clubs or massage parlours. More likely, for bubble tea at one of the new malls, proud to merely look at the fancy merchandise that they won't buy, just excited that they could.

I can't say what will happen to all these workers—whether they are in Shenzhen for good or they'll eventually return to their villages and towns. A bit of both, I guess. While they're here, everything's changing for them, and if they do return, they'll be different people arriving in changed places. There's no going back to the grime and isolation of before.

"It's a happy time to be Chinese," I say to Viv. "Such possibility opening up for the young people here."

"I agree, it's an exciting time. But the base needs to be built upon. Work is good. But the Chinese must work for more than wages, for more than just consumer possibilities."

"Patience, Viv. The new life's only just starting for them now."

An elevated train takes us to Hong Kong. There's a border con-trol but it seems perfunctory. Back in the free world, some might think. I've flown back and forth from China into Hong Kong a number of times before, but have never gone by land.

"Of course, we should oppose borders for what they stand for and who they really benefit," I tell Viv, "but I like the scenes at border crossings. If they ever disappear, I will miss them, masochistically perhaps."

"I remember when I first came to Hong Kong five years ago," Viv says. "It was for an internship at the *South China Morning Post*, my first time out of China. It was after reunification, and I was excited to be visiting a place that had evolved under a completely different political system than mine. I can say that I was also proud that Hong Kong had been returned to China, that an old period was over and a new had begun. I know many westerners were afraid of this happening, but for us in China, Hong Kong's return was a moment filled with much hope. It could only be good for us."

"For me, Hong Kong has always been a sanctuary," I say, "a place to enjoy some comforts after much rougher travel. I remember dreaming of this place throughout my lengthy 1990 trip to China. I couldn't wait to go shopping for electronics. And coming out of the sweaty tropics of Southeast Asia, I would find Hong Kong's balmy climate ideal and its orderly ways relaxing—I'd go to the cinema."

"I find it graceful. Or what's the word? *Genteel*?"

"*Genteel*! Difficult word. Maybe better to use *refined*. Do you mean to say that Hong Kong has better-preserved Chinese culture, like Taiwan, than China itself?"

"Yes, perhaps," Viv says. "There is also more dignity here maybe. From the freedom, I guess. When I first came here, it helped me make up my mind to pursue my studies in the West. There was also something else that struck me—another difficult word, *melancholy*, is it? A sad longing of the heart?"

"Yes! Melancholy is indeed a sad longing of the heart! You're hilarious!"

"Not a strong emotion but a pervasive one."

"And is it good or bad, this little sadness in Hong Kong?"

"Does it have to be one or the other?"

"Come on! I mean, do you like it?"

"Maybe. Ask me again when we leave."

We are heading toward Causeway Bay, a favourite neighbourhood of ours. We have reserved rooms in one of the many tenement hotels in the district. They're perfectly suitable—clean and safe—but tiny and without private bathrooms. Our establishment is a converted apartment nestled into the upper floors of a commercial building. The tiniest reception area has been set up in the apartment's entrance to manage half a dozen or so rooms. The advantage of this simple accommodation is its proximity to the action. We descend from our modest rooms into incredible bustle. Causeway Bay's streets are largely overrun by pedestrian traffic. The buildings are high and tightly packed together.

Hong Kong surely rivals New York for its urban jungle. The skyscrapers are like behemoths in a giant forest. Crawling between them, humans, even cars, are like tiny insects. The sky is distant and abstract. The streets are not laid out according to a grid but forced to wind around Hong Kong island's shoreline and rugged terrain. This breaks the lines of sight and gives one a boxed-in feeling between all the buildings.

The buildings are in the process of being upgraded. When they're all finally gone, I'll miss the old ones, those built quickly some sixty years ago. These lesser towers speak of the time when Hong Kong was not the glitzy powerhouse it has become. The

British Empire was crumbling, its protectorate, Hong Kong, a battered redoubt in a Far East swept up in momentous change.

Real estate has long been a problem in Hong Kong. To the islands initially acquired from China at the close of the First Opium War, the protectorate added first the Kowloon Peninsula and then an even bigger mainland tract called the New Territories. By the 1950s, China was unified under Mao and could not be made to cough up any more land to foreigners. From then on, Hong Kong would grow in great confinement. From 1945 to the mid-1950s, Hong Kong's population at least tripled. British subjects returned here after the Japanese occupation, followed by a constant trickle of people from the collapsing colonies of the East. A powerful presence but minute compared with the droves of mainlanders who fled the revolution in China.

To accommodate this expanding population on limited real estate, the city could grow only vertically. Both industry and habitation were soon packed into cheaply built concrete towers, nowhere so densely as in Causeway Bay, the most Chinese of neighbourhoods on the original Victoria Island.

Wartime industry had taught developed economies highly efficient new forms of production. These would be put to good use in Hong Kong, where labour was plentiful and cheap. This is the Hong Kong that still peeks through in cramped Causeway Bay. Unlike the megatowers that are replacing them, the old buildings have identifiable windows, not just metal-and-glass plate. They bear clotheslines, noisy air conditioners and visible wiring. Cheap metal signage hangs haphazardly off the facades at varying heights.

The manufacturing economy has long moved out of the neighbourhood, but intense mercantile activity remains. The buildings are filled with the administrative offices of producers, distributors and brokers. The ground floors are home to countless shops. Over the years, the shops have moved from selling low-end merchandise and cheap clothing to offering high-end luxuries. Parts of Causeway Bay are now most fashionable and expensive.

Viv and I snack on skewers of fish balls and wash them down with coconut milk–tapioca tea topped with frogs' ovaries, a perfect accompaniment for people-watching. Come rush hour, the office workers pour into the tight streets to mingle with shoppers. For a couple of hours, the urban energy rivals any other great city for the world's most impressive spectacle of noises, people and lights.

Viv and I ride the tide and wander through the flowing crowds, revelling in the sights. The faces are young and, with few exceptions, Asian. The attire is classy and understated.

"Look at how genteel these two look," I say teasingly to Viv, pointing to a dashing young couple.

"No joke. It's stylish here. When you meet him, I'm sure you will also agree that my old boss, Milton Chang, is the perfect gentleman. He's very smart but bashful and self-effacing. Not the norm for a newspaper editor, I might add."

I have every reason to think Viv was an excellent student. Out of university, she was selected among her peers as a "cadet" at surely one of the most desirable newspapers for an aspiring Chinese journalist, the *South China Morning Post*. The internship was especially coveted because it involved a stint at the *Post*'s headquarters in Hong Kong. The cadets perfected their English-language skills and were schooled in the great tradition of Anglo-Saxon journalism, arguably the finest in the world. The best of the cadets might even be offered permanent jobs at the daily. Another sign of her competence: after the internship, Viv was given a job as a junior reporter for the newspaper's important Beijing desk. Milton was her supervisor and editor in Hong Kong.

"The *South China Morning Post* is not perhaps what it used to be," Viv explains. "But it's still perceived as a seminal liberal institution in the Far East. Milton will have a lot to say about it. I'm not sure that he's terribly happy there. Or maybe it's just that he's naturally melancholy. You'll see."

"All newspapers are in decline. They're not happy places in general."

"Yes, but it's not just a readership issue with the *Post* but one of changing orientation. From the start, the *Post* was not just a British colonial newspaper. It had a strong Chinese republican element to it. One of its founders was a Chinese dissident against the Qing and a colleague of Sun Zhongshan."

We meet Milton in a neighbourhood a few subway stops away. He's slight, bookish and, as expected, courteous and poised. It's fun to hear Viv adopt in English the same deferential if somewhat playful tone that I'd so often heard in Chinese.

It's very early evening and no one is hungry, but we agree that a busy restaurant would suit us best for a good conversation.

"This one is maybe too trendy. Shall we continue walking to find a café or something?" Milton says.

"It really doesn't matter," I say. "Let's just go here."

"Good. It at least seems relatively full. It's never any fun to be the only people in a restaurant."

We order soft drinks and a few small dishes. After an exchange of pleasantries with her beloved ex-boss, Viv deflects all attention toward me, and Milton obliges her. He and I pass the ball around and work through the basics of our respective biographies.

With such a proper English opening, Milton reminds me of one of my old philosophy professors, a mild but terrifically thoughtful Englishman who taught analytical epistemology. We were always on eggshells in conversations full of deflection and retreat. As if the world of thought were unstable and delicate, requiring both careful hesitations and tender solicitudes between interlocutors, especially when it comes to affairs of the ego. I'm exaggerating, of course. Still, this kind of banter—serious but neutral talk—comes naturally to Canadians. The country's colonial heritage, I suppose. Beyond a token stretch to show that I know how to converse in this manner, I usually can't sustain it for very long, or at least don't want to. Not when strong intellect is also present. Then I definitely prefer the bare ego. For me, there is more complicity, more respect, in sharing the ego than attempting to conceal it.

Milton is not long to pick up on my roguish ways and soon has me talking about war, the United States, the Middle East, Africa, Canadian politics, the usual. As always, I give out my strong opinions without hesitation.

"So why China?" he finally asks about my work here.

"It's a story for the ages," I tell him. "And we're entering one of its best parts."

"How do you plan to deal with this story?"

"As a travel writer. An extension of the travel filmmaking that I've been doing. My mission is to track glimpses, chosen moments that might reveal the grand affairs that lie beneath. Then to sew them all together into something that's fun and easy to read."

"You're not ambitious at all," he says, laughing. "So what are you looking for in Hong Kong?"

"Identity politics. Cultural hybridization. That kind of thing."

"I understand."

"Might I ask you, a native Hong Konger, to what extent you consider yourself Chinese?"

"Me? I'm ethnically Chinese. I speak Cantonese, though I live and work mostly in English. But I hesitate to consider myself a proper Chinese national. I consider myself a Hong Konger. That's enough. I grew up in a place quite distinct from the mainland, and I believe in this distinction. For me, for now at least, embracing China would mean giving up on a few things that I hold dear."

"Like what?"

"Freedom of speech. Freedom of assembly. The rule of law. To mention a few."

"Aren't you happy that the prodigal son has returned to the family home?"

"Yeah, right," he says after an initial laugh.

"Don't you feel pride in your Chinese heritage?"

"Pride in my heritage? That's amusing. Do I need mainland China for my heritage? Anyhow, shouldn't I choose what I take from my heritage? Get to decide what I respect and what I need? And frankly, have the right to do this wherever I choose to live?"

"So no good is coming out of China for you?"

"That's a harsh way to put it. I'm excited by what is happening to China. You understand that for my work I need to follow the events there religiously. Nothing is more important for my newspaper. But I enjoy it. Following the changes in China, I mean. I love travelling there. I'm thrilled for the mainlanders, that life is getting better for them. You know—more opportunities, more fun. How could I not? I'm married to a mainlander. Viv's friend, actually."

"I didn't tell him," Viv notes. "We were housemates as journalist cadets at the *Post*. I'm surprised you're mentioning it, Milton, dating among co-workers being sensitive and all."

"He's surely not a gossip journalist. Look," he says, turning back to me, "I don't trust the Communist Party of China. I don't see it relinquishing any political power. So don't be surprised that I'm not inclined to surrender any of my freedom to the idea of a unified China. I want China to move forward, but I don't want Hong Kong to move backwards."

"How do you feel about the 'one country, two systems' motto?"

"Like I said, I don't really trust the CPC. It's not sincere, not when it comes to politics. How could it be? The Hong Kong system is anathema to the party. Toxic, even. Hong Kong people want a functioning democratic system. This is pretty clear. It's a natural evolution for us. Something a long time in the making. But I'm not sure Beijing will tolerate Hong Kong ever truly becoming democratic. It makes concessions that are mere window dressing, always ensuring that it keeps control. Let's not forget the People's Liberation Army Hong Kong Garrison that is now posted here, the ultimate guarantor of control for Beijing."

"Before, Hong Kong was a colonial protectorate with a governor named in London and a large British naval base. Do you remember when those guys bombed Canton?"

"Yes, to push their drugs," Milton quips. "But that system was gone long ago. And frankly, I feel safer under the British Foreign Office's supervision than under that of the National People's Congress Standing Committee."

"Do you consider yourself British?"

"No. There is much I admire about the British system and values. I'm proud of their influence in Hong Kong. But I consider myself a Chinese Hong Konger. Or let's just say a Hong Konger. This is also not a unique position. Might even be a majority here, who knows."

"Tell me about your newspaper."

"You mean its politics, I suppose?"

"Sure."

"They are unstable. You have to first understand how Beijing pressures Hong Kong. Through carrot much more than stick—money, business, that is; that's what drives this place anyhow. And China now has the clout to buy into this place in a big way. If one could consider it a foreign investor, it would be by far the biggest on the scene. Here is an even easier way to convince Hong Kong tycoons to become pro-Beijing: China merely opens exclusive access to a part of the mainland economy to them."

"Sounds like fair play to me," I counter. "Good for Hong Kong development. A strong link to the 7 percent growth of the mainland."

"Okay, even if we accept your idea—which, believe me, has many problematic aspects to it—the CPC is not like any other corporate entity that might invest here. Even if we accepted that it was, it uses its economic control in a coercive manner in the political arena. It uses it to manipulate the 'democratic' system. Groups, not individuals, vote for our chief executive. We don't have universal suffrage."

"Have you ever?"

"No, but it's guaranteed to us in our Basic Law, our constitution signed by the Brits and the Chinese before the handover. The problem is that it was set out with no timetable. So before any real election of candidates, Beijing can use its influence over the nominating committee that approves candidatures to block anyone it doesn't like."

"I'm sorry to refer back to history, but given that Hong Kong was obtained through foreign aggression, and considering China's obsession with unity, is it so surprising that China would want to keep close tabs on this place?"

"That's easy for you to say, Sacha. I know Canada well. I admire it. But could you truly say that we here in Hong Kong would be less suited, less deserving of the freedoms that you have? Forget democracy; consider only the rule of law. Why would you ask me to give up on this?"

"Perhaps it's only a matter of patience. China's still healing. Keep bandages secure over wounds that are healing."

"Or leave them on so long and so tight that they hide rot underneath. But I wasn't finished with the newspaper. Would you like me to continue about the *Post*?"

"Absolutely."

"Since its founding, the *Post* has rightly had a reputation as a reputable newspaper—balanced and thorough. A paper one can be proud to work for. It still is. But something has been worrying me about a loosening of standards around the subject of China: management no longer has the same appetite for good reporting about the mainland. Not just for the stuff critical of the party but also for just about anything of substance concerning the mainland. We publish plenty of stories about the mainland, sure, but more and more fluff. Celebrity culture, bland announcements, disaster reporting, you know."

"Sounds like media in general. Keep people entertained and distracted."

"Come on!" Milton says. "I'm sure that you agree that newspapers have a vital role in sustaining healthy political debate. A responsibility, even. People should have access to the broadest amount of information possible, without filters."

"Who owns the *Post*?"

"Rupert Murdoch used to own it, but he sold a large share to a powerful Malaysian Chinese family in the mid-1990s. They are business-oriented. You can see how this might lead to a softer approach toward the mainland."

"It all seems unavoidable to me," I argue. "The *Post* likely makes its money through advertising, and Hong Kong corporations are more and more linked to the mainland markets and production facilities."

"Still, it's unnatural for the *Post*. It also makes for a newspaper that is growing more boring to read. And a less interesting place to work. I might have to leave. This saddens me. I'm a newspaper man, and I want to live in Hong Kong. I love it here."

The three of us emerge into the buzz of the balmy evening. We part ways fraternally. Milton returns to his gentle self to take his leave. True to ritual, I too put on some mantle of humility, only slightly tainted by my sly intentions.

I had vowed not to take my own conceits with me into China. To fight them off with every breath, as I did with Milton. But how long can I resist China bringing those conceits to me? I vowed not to carry my own republicanism into China, to be open to whatever unique constellations might guide the country. But again and again, my respected Chinese interlocutors challenge me with the same hopes for China. The Chinese, they fiercely argue, deserve every right a Canadian has. Everyone does, in fact.

Of course they do. But how do we get there?

CHAPTER 9

The Return

In a serenade of reedpipes and song, I drunkenly return.
—Ouyang Xiu, *After the Lotus Flowers Have Opened,*
eleventh century

"Long-time resident here? Or just passing through?" the famous artist Ai Weiwei asks as he receives me in Beijing.

I cobble together some sort of a reply to try to avoid his quick judgment. But even I'm unconvinced by my awkward answer. He shows no emotion. He looks tired. Or weary, is it?

I'm not Ai's first foreign interview of the day, nor perhaps the last. The man is a performer and a campaigner, as well as an artist. Whoever I might be, rube or sophisticate, he would humour me, find out what I wanted, try to give it to me and then send me packing.

It's the summer of 2008 and the Olympic Games will soon be held in the north capital. I'm starting a new assignment covering culture in China to complement the sports coverage.

Vivien is back in Beijing for the summer after an initial year in grad school in the United States, but she is staying out of the sweltering city action. She's introduced me to former colleagues who agreed to do research and translations for me. We've approached some of the city's artists for interviews about the new China.

I'm joined now by Richard, cameraman extraordinaire of the CBC, a Dakota from south Saskatchewan and a most impressive figure, tall and broad as a sumo wrestler. He consistently wears Bermuda shorts, golf shirts and hiking shoes, as if it were a uniform. He keeps his long, dark hair in a ponytail. Richard never fails to impress the Chinese, who sometimes even recognize him as Aboriginal Canadian. This awes them a little and puts them in a good mood. "Just like in the movies: a cowboy and an Indian," one artist joked as the two of us walked into the studio with our gear.

Leading up to the Games, news editors everywhere are looking for balance and trying to present the other side of all the splendour. Hordes of journalists, me included, are streaming to Ai Weiwei, who beyond his influential work as an artist is known as one of the Communist Party of China's most vocal critics.

He has just made waves in the foreign press by declaring his unwillingness to participate in any facet of the Games, all while being trumpeted as one of the designers of the now iconic National Stadium—the Bird's Nest.

"You're completely without interest in these Games?" I ask.

"Okay," he admits, "this is a great time for China. I won't deny that. But the government tells the people of Beijing that the best way to participate in the Games is to stay home and watch television. So I'm doing what I'm told."

Ai tells me that the Games are just a propaganda show. Participants are selected to carry a specific message. But the "same world, same dream" motto of the Games is hollow and meaningless. He wants nothing to do with the spectacle.

"So the people are unsatisfied?" I ask, prodding.

"The people are uneducated," he says, then explains that China is not a peaceful or righteous society. The harmony is an illusion.

"What do you make of the growing prosperity?" I continue.

"China has changed and made much progress. Some circumstances have not changed. For some people, prosperity is a big deal. But we have no democracy here. No protection from arbitrary power. Corruption is everywhere."

With camera, lights and microphones, Richard and I have Ai captive. I slip into documentary mode. Jaded reporter meets weary celebrity for a conversation. A performance structured around our different agendas. Campaigning for his own notoriety, Ai won't be let off the hook easily. He'll be made to defend his ideas. While I'll lead the witness, amuse or enrage him if necessary.

Documentary filmmaking is like sculpting with small segments of reality. Nobody watching the final product should see or feel the handiwork that has gone into it. We edit tedious, uncomfortable raw footage. We discard failed questions and answers. The rest is cherry-picked and then distilled. Intentions are sought behind the ambiguities of free speech and language barriers. Brilliance is discovered among the dross. Film doesn't need real men or women, but icons.

Ai Weiwei knows this. He has seen his share of players, princes and bullshitters. You don't become a famous artist in this world without knowing how to play the game and dance to a tune. He doesn't care how smart or stupid I am. How wise or foolish. He has accepted the audience that I bring. For them, his performance might endure. Ai enjoys himself well enough wired up under all the lights and on display in the hot seat.

Who wants to be a poor and obscure artist when one can be an icon?

Mostly he's unflappable.

Again and again, I suggest that Ai consider tempering his criticisms of Chinese realities and consider results instead of principles. But he will not. He is categorical: the current China is poorly structured.

I turn to history and suggest that there has likely never been democracy or individual rights in his country. Or a time without corruption.

"Anyone educated cannot but hope for the rule of law and respect for the individual," he counters, then calls the current state of things shameful, no matter how much wealth is created or how many advances are being made.

"Is the system economically flawed as well?"

"Yes. After thirty years of providing manufacturing labour to the world," Ai explains, "China has grown rich." But he argues that the future has been sacrificed and the current system cannot go on forever; change must happen. He describes problems of morality and of creativity at the foundations. He explains that the central government knows that the people now need more. So it comes up with patriotic spectacle and recognizes the need for art. But art does not just happen on command, he declares.

I'm dogged: "Aren't things getting better and better? I mean, the government seems to be tolerating the likes of you. This seems an improvement."

"Yes," he says. "I'm sitting here being interviewed by the foreign press, saying all sorts of things. Yes, I'm critical. I'm an artist: I say what I see. I have no choice. I have to be truthful. And yes, this is new and different. But we must do much better. We're ready for it."

I consider a photo that's leaning against the wall of his studio. In the background stands the White House; in the foreground there is a raised middle finger, dominant though slightly blurry. I turn to the principles Ai espouses.

"Having seen the world, have you seen a lot of justice in it?" I list off conflicts I recently covered and point at the dishonesty and imperialism behind them.

"Okay, good question," he says with a giggle before arguing that if I'm correct and we are indeed living in such a troubled world, then China has even more reason to be principled.

I finally relent in my assault on his liberal ideas and lob a loose question about the environment, to which he answers, "The Chinese people are as concerned about the environment as any other tradition in the world. It's part of our philosophy. But we have sacrificed this conscience too. Change must happen," he repeats, "or China will not go on."

I've filled a full hour of interview space without mirth or joy. As a guilty afterthought, I awkwardly query the man as to whether he's happy in China and in Beijing.

This he quickly answers with glee. "Oh yes, I'm happy. I'm happy with what I'm doing here."

Richard then whispers to me, "Let me do some stuff with him."

The cameraman follows Ai into the grand showroom. It's brightly lit from above and has painted-white brick walls and polished concrete floors like a proper gallery. On display are several of Ai's works: mostly massive, geometric wooden sculptures.

Without hesitation or direction, Ai positions himself over a dish of sunflower seeds set at the edge of the room and slowly stirs them with his fingers. Richard slides around him, capturing all the angles as Ai slowly lifts the seeds up and lets them slide through his fingers, dropping them one by one.

Unbeknown to me, they are not actual seeds but painted

porcelain sculptures. Ai will have a hundred million of them produced, to pile up a foot deep across the floor of a huge room at the Tate Modern. Spectators—participants—will wade through the seeds, lie in them and interact with them.

Once completed, the colour effect of *Sunflower Seeds* will be potent: a perfect grey made up of millions of black-and-white "seeds," the balance of dark and light. The earth, water and fire that went into their composition, the many hands, the distance and the gold that bring about their creation recede.

It's the tactility of the many seeds that will speak out most loudly. The feel of them underfoot. The gentle, mineral sound they make as they rattle together when one lies down in them. Handmade, each one is singular. It's unique, alive almost.

But all this is lost on me in Beijing right now. I blankly watch Ai move to caress one of his sculptures, a giant wooden form in the centre of the room. Finally, Richard directs Ai toward a large armoire-like affair and has him gaze through the round aperture that pierces it.

Ai is wearing a black-and-white outfit, and with his wide face, choppy hair and rotund physique, he looks rather like a panda. The two men move calmly, gracefully even. The patience and the peacefulness of their rapport are touching. While I'm all sound and fury, I grimly tell myself.

All I asked the great artist about was politics. I even stood in for his judges.

Still, the man proved himself. Under pressure, he was coherent, devoted, methodical and brave. He was also right. Respect for the individual is the first premise of the just society. No political conversation worth having can ever start without a vow to uphold each other's freedom and dignity.

This is dogma, of course. Or credo.

Still, who would not wish to be so resolute and brave as Ai? To calmly hold the line for such a cause? The only sad part is that it seems a losing battle for him. The dynasty is not yet crumbling. The Communist Party of China cannot endure forever, but for the moment, the CPC's China, failings and all, is solid. There will be no revolution. Only slow transformation.

Deep down, all states tend toward corporatism. Even democratic states tend to make the individual's political power more and more illusory, to restrict the people's choices, supposedly for their own good.

Power is stubborn. It accrues and resists reorganization. Majorities oppress minorities, and minorities abuse majorities. And won't the people trade in so much when they fear violence? The republic is not completely without recourse against the ineluctable concentrations of power. A truly independent judiciary held to order by an enduring code may offer some bulwark. But where can this ideal claim to be securely entrenched?

Economic power matters more. Wealth creation and the state distribution of wealth, however balanced together, aim to bring about possibilities for individuals. As long as bellies are full and minds stimulated, citizens will be more interested in themselves than in the affairs of state, more interested in what they can buy or do with their free time than in the active law-making that goes on in their name. The perception of freedom also makes a good stand-in for actual freedom. Although progress is felt by the masses, true critics, however right and respected, stand alone. There are too many temptations against taking a stand and too many fears for the consequences. Even advanced states periodically offer reminders that an individual's preservation is at stake, that those who take a stand, right or wrong, could be made to suffer or pay dearly. Think of the whistleblowers Bradley Manning, Edward Snowden and Julian Assange.

As if it were scripted, the regime eventually would crack down on Ai. He's made to suffer for the stand he's taken for so long. The outspoken critic isn't muzzled or his statements even contradicted; he's simply arrested, detained, roughed up and charged with tax crimes. The state's message is clear: this man who never shuts up to foreigners about public morals in China is himself unethical and corrupt.

Charging someone with economic crimes in China can be a little rich. Fiscal compliance is never perfect anywhere—far from it. But the fiscal situation in China is especially complex and fluid. Through its tight control of the currency and its continued role in a wide variety of commercial activities, Chinese state's coffers are filled and refilled, allowing much flexibility in collecting taxes in any systematic manner from small fry, though the laws permit it in numerous ways. Total compliance can be quite low.

In China, as in more developed societies, the pursuit of total compliance will butt up against a cost-benefit analysis. The administrative costs are determined to outweigh amounts that can be recouped by collection efforts. There's a solid contingent of working poor people in China, migrant and temporary labour, people unhabituated to the fiscal requirements of developed economies and too insignificant to be made to account for their revenues.

The Chinese government is also seeking to build up consumer equity. It lets a good chunk of free-earning people spend their incomes freely. Perhaps they even feel guilty about this freedom. In any case, sales taxes are increasingly collected to offset the gaps in income taxation or customs collection from small earners.

Finally, there are subtle and sinister benefits to complicated yet loosely applied regimes of law. Compliance difficulties mean that anyone rich and powerful has likely broken rules to get there. With the CPC more or less directly administering the organs of justice, it has legitimate licence to crush just about anyone successful when it might be strategic to do so.

Economic arguments also play out in the most recent power struggles within the CPC leadership structures. The purge of Bo Xilai, a powerful member of the inner circle, and the removal of a string of high officials like Zhou Yongkang from the security sector, unfold semi-publicly as a prosecution of these men for high economic crimes.

Unlike these fallen party members, Ai, the artist, wields no direct political power. But his presence is felt at court. His fame and power give him influence. He manages to fill a giant room in London with tiny made-in-China items. He amasses and arranges a roomful of rebar salvaged from shoddily built concrete schools destroyed in the 2008 Sichuan earthquake. He organizes thousands of bicycles into a massive aerial sculpture. His works are not only beautiful but clear demonstrations of power.

One can only imagine the costs of getting it all done—the labour involved, the energy requirements. Big money and international networks must be part of the equation. However he manages his grand productions, Ai's enterprise is complex and creative, leaving the artist exposed to aggressive government interpretations of complex laws. Since there is little transparency to the workings of justice in China, one might as well presume a measure of insincerity and fabrication in the government's methods when such important politics are involved.

Ai shows himself artful in dealing with the government and

its courts. His worldwide fame allows him to raise a substantial sum to pay for his legal defence, which he conducts with the same unflappable deadpan manner he shows me.

The fight goes on. For the moment, Ai's still standing, but his pulpit is now somewhat shaky. His ability to travel has been restricted. Much of his time and energy is now directed at holding off the juggernaut rather than at creating, educating or even making money.

Whatever happens, there is some solace for Ai. History in China is kind to the scholar-poets who speak truth to power and suffer ignominies—like the great historian Sima Qian, from the late Han, who gave unwelcome counsel to his king in a time of war. It was not a clement era and Sima was condemned to either death or castration, an easy choice for a young gentleman. Death was not dishonourable, whereas castration represented damnation, a kind of living death.

Sima chose the living death for a reason remembered to this day. He had started his book of history and felt strongly that he owed the nation its stories more than he valued his own honour. He would surrender his manhood, sacrificing all posterity to pursue his studies, to seek perhaps another kind of immortality, ensured by the endurance of his work, a book known over two thousand years later as the *Records of the Grand Historian*.

The emperor who took the visionary's balls is just another entry on a long list, but Sima's name lives on to this day. It speaks loudly and says, "The truth is worth it."

I'm working an area in northeastern Beijing around the fabled Factory 798. A former armaments factory, 798 was converted into a series of large exhibition spaces in the late 1990s. Art galleries and artist studios like Ai's have sprouted up throughout the surrounding area. Of late, the refurbished industrial area has also become a prime tourist destination for visitors to the capital, whether they love art or not.

The Beijing art scene has developed into a massive industry involving thousands of players and likely hundreds of millions of dollars. Art speaks to the tremendous new wealth to be found in the big cities of China. It goes with the intense property development that is occurring across the nation. The myriad new homes and apartments will not soon be furnished and decorated in modern art. This much is certain. But art will be present at the top and in the crevices throughout.

A thriving art scene reveals a society that has grown more diversified and allows its citizens more varied career options and consumer choices. But modern art cannot exist without innovation, without exploration, without danger.

In the car, I think about Van Gogh, whose powerful visions might well endure through the ages but who received nothing but torment from his life as an artist. He received little recognition, and little encouragement that he would ever be remembered—that his art, his suffering, were not in vain.

Is poor Vincent trying to make me suspicious of artistic success? Circumspect toward the demimonde of art, celebrity and gold?

No, the unease is larger. It's the light and noise of triumph and recognition that are overwhelming. I long again to see what hides in the quiet darkness, to scan the depths for the obscure middle managers and migrant workers. The place where no one goes and subjects to whom attention has never been paid. The person for whom a judge, a listener, an audience is a rare honour. For what grand performance of a master, repeated over and over again, can better the one-off performances of nobodies? What trend can beat true singularity?

We are travelling to meet an obscure artist, Li Bo, whose work I'd stumbled upon in a Beijing gallery. His studio is in an area that almost breaks orbit with the city and slips into the countryside. Access is through a dusty garage door at the end of a long line of garage doors—another industrial area freshly conquered by hopeful artists.

Li is tall and skinny. In the manner of the Taoist monks, he has let a tuft of hair grow to great lengths from a mole on his face.

"Why would he do this?" I later inquire. It's a sign of power, I'm told.

The young man works with photographs of near-nude subjects, women in an intimate setting. The photos are not printed onto canvas or paper but laid onto patterns made of coils of rope and string that softly blur the portraits and give them a mysterious, almost totemic, feel. The images show a deeply personal world. They show cramped apartments with spot lighting and messy beds. They show young women in their undergarments, getting ready for something or posing for the artist's camera.

Lingerie, tattoos, naked curves and the occasional pubic hair all make appearances in the images. They are *osé*, possibly even a tad pornographic. They would not be hung in one's home without some embarrassment. I'm amazed to see them on easy display in the capital.

Li tells me that all the women in his works are his girlfriends.

The work is not so much about sex but intimacy, proximity. Sex may be part of the story, but it's much more about discovery of self than of body. Turned heads and faces blurred by light and texture ensure that these are not identifiable individuals. Still, they are clearly independent women exploring their freedom— conquering portions of space for themselves to be themselves, then sharing their new identities. Does this voyeurism take from the freedom of these subjects and reduce their poses to mechanical gestures for the uses of others? Or is the freedom of these women not enshrined, and allowed to grow among those who witness it?

Art is about what is both given and received. It's never a zero-sum game but an opening, a widening of possibilities, guided by mysterious forces. If they speak at all, Li's works do so to a city filled with freedom. They speak of nights filled with people tucked away in private spaces. Of men and women, taking chances, being young, carnal and foolish, looking for love, the elusive force that both preserves and negates our singularity.

Art must be considered a portal to the future, a way forward. Either the channel is open, speaking, offering new choices, or art is not present.

From the northeast, we travel south to an area along the eastern side of the central axis that is fast becoming the new business core. Sleek new towers everywhere give the capital a fully modern feel. No alleyways, no dust, nor sign of organic human inhabitation or use remain. The fantastic crooked arches of glass and steel of the new national television station hint at a possible future as well, one of fully engineered human life, existing entirely indoors, setting off into space.

Chen Danqing lives in a slick development due south of this quarter but across an expanse of highways and train tracks. His studio is several floors up and faces north toward the dense agglomeration of skyscrapers. The wide windows of the studio catch the white light of the north sky and the occasional rays reflecting off the shimmering buildings. We marvel at the new city from the slight distance.

I ask Chen if there is any loss involved in the creation of this new capital.

"Yes," he says, "Beijing has already disappeared." With a gentle, easy smile, he intimates that one should not be upset and that losses are not to be mourned.

Chen's an oil painter in the classic style. He paints portraits and grand scenes. Unlike those who deal in performance, capture or construction, the artist who pushes pigment around to depict reality has little workaround for lack of technical skill; even the most adroit figurative painters will be measured against the grand masters for their ability to conjure depth, light, movement and meaning. Chen is best known for his series of portraits of Tibetans done in the 1980s. The paintings are masterful. They're in the so-called new realist style of which Chen is a prime proponent.

During Mao's time, art was mostly reduced to Communist propaganda, depictions of the chairman himself in heroic poses or of his idealized people—hardly portals to a real future, for one does not command art but obeys it. While choking art of its daemon, strict Communist dogma did at least manage to bestow technical skill and rigour upon its craftspeople. When the old regime gave way to the new China, the formal prowess of young painters like Chen was suddenly put to bold use.

Human faces appear in his paintings as conjurations, their singular gaze held alive, a sign of a free conscience within. These are rough Tibetan faces, sunbaked and caked with dust. The heads are cloaked in hides and fur; the clothing, coarse and strange. Their eyes are expressive and full of life.

The new realism of Chen does not turn toward what is familiar to the Chinese but to the margins inhabited by others. The handsome and independent Tibetans are in sharpest contrast with any dogma. Let them be considered as they are, Chen's paintings say. Let them come into our lives and homes to speak on their own terms.

His best works show his *montagnard* subjects in action. The scenes are mundane: people walking down the road to the market or gathering in the field to discuss something. The movements are bold and new, quietly defiant. The subjects are not moving toward a common identifiable goal, as was Communist custom. They move freely, unpredictably.

Chen is nearing sixty years old, but he's youthful. His close-cropped salt-and-pepper hair, the lines under eyes framed by 1920s-style round spectacles and his gravelly voice seem more the affectations of a young man playing an old one than the conditions of age. Like Ai, Chen spent decades outside China. He learnt to speak English and has mastered performing for foreigners. If Ai was largely emotionless, Chen is gentlemanly, neither forceful nor declarative, more suggestive.

In matters social and political, Chen proves himself no less a realist than he is in his paintings. Deep into the interview, he tells me that he knows of Chinese leaders who secretly think that "democracy is not fit for China," that it's something for Western countries maybe, but that it won't work here. They believe this but will "never speak it out loud," he says. He's quick to note that he himself doesn't want to believe this, then adds, "But I suffer when the facts confirm it."

He explains that his eighteen years in New York City make him see the huge distance between democracy in America and reality in China. Only a very few people in China can even imagine what that kind of democracy is. "Chinese people's real genius is for business," he continues. "They always find their way around the rules. They are flexible. They don't have a mind for laws or rulers, but a mind for dealing with immediate issues. For this, they are very smart."

I try to get him to consider tensions and problems to come, but he simply tells me that he's not afraid for the future. "The Chinese are too good at avoiding trouble," he says. "They are good at surviving and not asking meaning."

From what I see on display in his studio, Chen's more recent works are formal if a little uncanny. One painting depicts a scene of the late seventeenth century: a French nobleman's daughters in fluffy regalia sitting with their dog by the window. They're not moving. In the half-light, the faces seem real, their curious looks aimed at us are loaded. The curly haired girls, still and distant, peer toward us as if transfixed, searching for the strangers who might watch them from beyond.

Another painting depicts an illustration in a grand old book opened on a table. It shows a flat and celestial landscape in old Chinese style. Without movement or life, the work makes for a strange appearance in Chen's studio. Have faces suddenly grown oppressive to the artist? Is illusion and detachment now suggested? Can the old painter no longer carry the fiercer visions of youth?

He leads me to a big closet where he hangs some of his older works on sliding panels. He draws out a huge painting, potent and grave. Chen's a tenebrist at heart; patterns of white, yellow and gold shine on the darkened canvas. As in the best Caravaggio, the forms of light, though bright, seem frantic and fleeting, soon to be extinguished.

I inadvertently blurt out, "Now, this I love."

He registers the slight but doesn't react.

The painting depicts a group of men in uniform, faces anguished and stricken. They're soldiers. In the corner of the frame, one is fighting to get free of restraining hands that tear at his clothing. The man's look is one of animal rage. Around him, his fellow soldiers are pulling him along, pushing each other forward across the scene, forcing their way toward some action. They're shiny and pale with sweat and emotion. Some are yelling words of anxious encouragement. Others are wide-eyed and ashen, numbed to fearful purpose in the night.

"Do you know what this is?" he asks.

Impressed as I am, I do not and mumble like an idiot.

"The June 4 incident at Tiananmen Square. The soldiers are going to the square and the people are trying to stop them," Chen gently explains. "I can never show this piece in China. I've been waiting for nineteen years to show this painting," he says with a laugh as he slides it back into its hangar.

Mao is an overused theme in much Chinese art. Clearly, it's a gimmick for tourists. Westerners find it piquant to see the chairman or his bizarre universe transformed—mocked and juxtaposed with capitalist symbolism. Business-minded Chinese artists, high and low, churn out works playing on Mao and Red China. Pointing at the past rather than at the future, most of it isn't art but memento meant to be noticed and provoke conversation.

"Oh, honey, show them our painting from China," I hear at cocktail parties in distant lands. "Isn't it ironic?"

The Mao Livehouse—or Mao Bar, as it is known—is a famous music venue in a trendy part of Old Beijing. It is another empty reference to the chairman. The backdrop to the stage bears an image of his iconic head with bowl-cut hair, silhouetted against a bright horizon. But like his face on the bills that we exchange for entry to the club, Mao might as well not be there. The young people frequenting the venue couldn't give a flying fuck about him, his image or his name. They've come to rock it out and punk it up with their friends.

The music is pretty coarse. The bar seems to mostly offer near-amateur acts. In fact, it seems as if musicality itself is irrelevant; what matters is the raw noise, the provocative performance and the bop to the beat.

I take notice of a trio called Girl Kill Girl. The all-girl band plays a minimal and rough indie music: bass, drums and vocals. Together they drive a hard, steady beat and command our attention under the pulsing spotlights. The charismatic lead, who goes by the name Gia, wails through her English lyrics with flair.

Richard and I meet with Gia after the show. Surely she has something interesting to say about the pursuit of freedom in China.

When performers come off the stage, they're invariably a little mad. The attention of the masses is intoxicating; the withdrawal, stunning. It leaves one slightly shell-shocked, as if a great love affair has ended and one is suddenly left alone. Deep down, the artist feels used. Like someone or something has come and put words in mouth and made face, hands and body do things that now have to be owned and explained. The acts of art cannot be denied, for they are a source of love. But to the artist, the strange acts are like those of another, who comes and goes unexpectedly—making one suffer when present, while filling one with dread for the abandonment.

Perhaps Gia is relieved to have us shine lights on her in the loggia backstage, a last shot of the good stuff just as the party is ending. She sips water and tells us to give her a moment before asking our questions.

Richard goes hand-held for some visuals and begins moving the camera around her, almost as an invitation to dance. On cue, Gia begins to pose. She growls at the camera, then sticks her tongue out and lifts up her middle finger in defiance. Finally, she turns to me and says, "So how did you like our bad music?"

Off-balance, I shake my head in disagreement, trying to reject her question. She will have none it and declares that, as musicians, she and her bandmates have no talent and their music is not beautiful. I only manage to smile at her, to lift my clenched fist and shake it in support.

Then it's my turn. I ask her a slew of serious and sobering questions. Quickly, the rock star, the junkie princess, transforms into a poised young woman to tell her story:

"I grew up in a traditional family. Both of my parents worked in the government. They were strict with me. Even when I was in high school, I had a curfew of 6 p.m. I had an oppressive upbringing. I felt school was really stupid and life was boring. I wanted to commit suicide. Then I discovered rock 'n' roll, and it saved my life."

When I push her to elaborate on her relationship with her parents, she explains that one needs to understand that in the West, even old people grew up with pop music, but that in China, "rock is new to the older generations, and they associate it with sex and drugs. Naturally, they see it as quite dangerous." She admits that over time things have changed with her parents: "They now see that rock 'n' roll is something real and are much more understanding."

When I ask her about recent musical directions, she says, "I'm the type of person who's always changing. My music tastes, my preferences in art, my clothes. Punk was my way of entering the music scene. It was a start. But it's music from another time and place. It's quite distant from young people's lives now. So I just keep moving."

"What are you singing about these days?" I ask.

"Love," she says with a coy smile. "I keep finding it and losing it. Spiritually, I feel like a monster. I'm constantly fighting with myself."

As Richard and I tear down our camera equipment, Gia and I talk about the painters I've been visiting. She confesses that painting has been bringing her at least as much joy as music these days.

"I like the quiet of it," she admits.

As she predicted, Viv is now doing graduate studies at an Ivy League school in the United States. She's only back in Beijing for a short summer vacation after an internship in East Africa. After spending time in the tropics, she's not keen on more sweaty work in the heat of the Chinese capital in August and has resisted following Richard and me around on our gruelling documentary shoot. Nonetheless, touring China's nooks and crannies without her doesn't feel quite right. So between two shoots, she and I meet for tea in a small restaurant near Beijing's Drum Tower.

The girlish young journalist with whom I'd journeyed a few years before has since grown calmer and more assured. The transformation makes me wonder how, in her eyes, I too might have changed. When I tell her about my new family life, she asks if it has altered me.

"Fear has returned," I say after a moment's reflection. "Even with the loss of my brother and father, I had come to consider human mortality rather dispassionately, as something natural, beautiful even. But with children in my life now, I can't consider death with such serenity. It terrifies me again. As it probably should."

"It doesn't surprise me that little ones could do that. Speaking of which, I'm engaged now. My fiancé is a computer engineer. He recently got a job offer in Europe. I'm going to follow him there when I'm done my studies. Actually, we're considering starting a family as well," she says cheerfully.

"Sounds like you might be leaving China behind for good," I wonder.

"Maybe."

"How does that make you feel?"

"The things that matter stay with us wherever we are. What I need from China is already with me."

"Makes sense."

"Are you still defending the Communist Party?" she suddenly asks.

"You realize that I generally seek to disagree with people whose views I share. It forces us both to refine our ideas, to make them clearer and better."

"I know. You once explained to me that that was the Jesuit way."

"Exactly. But to answer your question, yes, I still occasionally defend the CPC. For one, I don't think China could have come so far so quickly without the unity and organizational power it has provided," I say. Then I tell her about my talk with Ai Weiwei. "As is my custom, I argued with him and made him defend his ideas, but deep down I couldn't help but agree: China may be ready for something more sophisticated than opaque authoritarian rule. It is time."

"Funny. On my side, I've softened my stance a bit, perhaps as a result of not living in China anymore. From a distance, the terrific challenges that China faces don't seem to have easy solutions. This humbles me a little. I've also been able to see up close how democracies work. They don't always serve the people. They too can be corrupted in many big or small ways. But I will never accept how the Chinese state can still trample people's rights. How, for example, it takes people's homes and ruins their lives with complete impunity. Democracy or not, China needs the rule of law, to which even the CPC must bow."

"Are you any more optimistic than you were about how quickly political transformation might come?" I ask.

"Living abroad, I can afford to take a more patient approach," she confesses. "But let's consider how China is changing now. Its development is slowing down. The huge gains of recent decades cannot be sustained anymore. They're levelling off. The need for outside resources is no longer so ferocious, as fewer and fewer huge construction projects are undertaken. The Chinese urban middle class now makes up a near majority of the country. These people have quickly grown accustomed to consumer choices, so they are now exploring deeper notions of individual choice. They are travelling and experiencing the world. This all makes China more introspective, and ready to evolve. But I realize not everyone here cares as much about politics as I do. Things might only change very slowly."

"How pragmatic grad school has made you!" I joke.

"It probably has more to do with perspective than my studies." She pauses to smile, then begins again. "Another thing has changed for me: I remember you teasing me about my anti-Japanese sentiments during our talks. I would like to take back what I might have said. My sentiments were perhaps logical for a girl from Shandong, but they were nonetheless a little misguided. Now that China is so strong, I truly hope it can avoid becoming an aggressive power in the world. I always used to reassure myself by simply thinking how China has traditionally been on the receiving end of attacks by outsiders and not an aggressor, but now I feel this conceit is not enough. It's too backwards-looking. Chinese nationalism has become a political tool for the CPC. Really, I don't love China any less, but I now feel very detached from this manipulative patriotism. A page must be turned on the past, and China has to be more careful about its nationalism. This too has to be part of its maturation process. It has been for me."

"Seems like we are growing wiser, Viv. Anyhow, we probably shouldn't waste too much time on politics. Aren't they just a whole lot of noise to distract us from the deeper things in life?"

"Spoken like a true Taoist," she teases.

"Yes, the Tao does have a way of taking over. Speaking of which, I'm headed to a Taoist temple this afternoon."

"I thought you didn't like temples. You told me you always preferred their gardens."

"That's true. But remember, I'm shooting documentary footage, and I need stuff to show people."

"There's a conundrum for you: showing the Tao!"

"Yeah, like making a film about one hand clapping."

For film crews to circulate freely in Beijing in the summer of 2008, a government-assigned driver is a must. Our driver is Li Nan, a tall young woman from north China. She wears pastel yoga clothes and loves cigarettes and pop music, but her quiet calm and assured physicality suggest an army or police background. Just as well, because documentary work can be relentless. Cameras, cars and crew are expensive. We are fisherfolk as much as hunters. We cast our nets wide and pack the days with content to get value for our operations and give ourselves options in the editing room.

Before long, Nan is enjoying the long days and proud to show off her own *guanxi*, or network of connections. She begins to offer suggestions for characters for us to film: monks, calligraphers, artisans and clothes designers.

The Taoist monk she knows is at a temple surrounded by high-rises. It borders the third ring on its western flank. It's mid-afternoon and the heat has broken just slightly, but the air's dull and white, and the traffic thick.

Against all the concrete of the city, the temple is colourful and well maintained if mostly bereft of nature. The yin-yang motif is recurrent. The monks are wearing tidy black-and-white robes. They perform various rituals throughout the day. They meditate and bang a gong.

Our contact is a former colleague of Nan's father. They worked together in a government department. The man in question joined the monastery a few years ago. As I prod I understand that, for him, being a monk is a kind of day job, and that he doesn't live at the monastery but goes home to his wife at night. Despite the robes and hat, he seems more like an unremarkable cadre than a man of religion. I deduce that he's some kind of government agent assigned to the temple as a liaison, someone who wears the robes but whose first devotion is to the CPC, not the Tao.

One might think this would make him unsympathetic and inauthentic, but in a way I find his circumstances even more interesting. Political power in China did once find its ultimate legitimacy in religion, but religion has long since been made mostly subservient to politics. Through the ages, rulers picked and chose from a wide array of religious traditions to enhance and extend their own power. Emperors regularly razed or reassigned temples to suit their purposes. Mad religious fervour set fire to China more than once. The heavy hand with which the CPC can deal with organized religion is not the exception.

Planting a government agent in the monastery to live as a monk is probably more a gesture of preservation than one of control. The temple shows little indication of widespread popular use. It's as though the place and the monks it contains are already a kind of museum exhibit, to be briefly contemplated from a distance, a repository for something antique and prestigious. Without the help of government, this valuable real estate might not be able to continue to serve such arcane purposes in the face of raw capital.

The temple agent seems to have embraced his job and become a genuine supporter of religion. "Modern life is full of noise and distractions," he explains. "People are solely concentrated on achieving material goals. These pursuits soon grow tiring. One can never find satisfaction this way. This is why it's good to turn to the Tao."

I grin to hear this costumed bureaucrat calmly describe these things to me over the din of constant traffic. I ask him how being a monk has changed his own life.

"Well, at first my wife and daughter thought it strange that I spend my days here. Then they saw that being here made me a happier and healthier person. So they began to appreciate what I'm doing." He adds: "The Tao tells us that the material world is a world of illusions. Things are always changing in it. As such, harmony must have something different at its foundation."

I watch the aging monks enter the main hall in procession for incantations. After that, they set up a calligraphy demonstration for Richard and me. A rather serious monk takes position at a large table with ink, paper and brush and begins to draw bold and powerful strokes. Suddenly all the monks become grave, almost forceful in their solicitude. They cluster around, focusing intently on the agent as if to make sure that he conveys to us the important but difficult message.

"It takes many years to be able to master the strokes," he finally tells me. "They're not just words that this monk is writing. Each stroke has a power, a balance."

I have not mastered the Chinese script and probably never will. I'm willing to grant it a power not found in our phonetic scripts. The separation between spoken word and written symbol frees each to their own realm. The conceptual nature of written meaning is preserved while the spoken language can indulge in all the profanities and imprecisions necessary. Over the ages, dialects are formed and grow unintelligible in orality, but the script remains, impervious to easy transformation and ever accessible.

The secret meaning of calligraphy harks back to the infancy of the Chinese script when incantations were etched into bone and turtle shells. The script itself is meant to be a portal through which higher powers enter the world to bring meaning to the chaos. Is the portal still open? Does this monk with his brush in the temple bring a little more balance to the mad world? Does his colleague in robes, the government agent, render a service to the people by being here?

Does the Tao even need a home? How about the corpse? The one god? Or the lord of love?

We take the subway north almost to its end. After clearing the rings, it emerges onto elevated tracks and charts a path through myriad new towers. We're going to see another kind of artist: a video-game artist. His compound is a short walk from the station but, in habitual fashion, it's gated and we must negotiate our way through a guard post to access the tall apartment tower where he lives.

The young man lives on the twenty-third floor of a forty-storey building. The elevator and hallways are already grimy and run-down for a building not ten years old. Finding his apartment, we knock hard at the door, but no one answers. Finally, he's reached on the phone and comes to let us in. He's confident and affable if unkempt.

He has the sloppy, pale demeanour of someone who plays video games all day. Long, unwashed hair hangs from the top of his head. The sides of his head are shaved. His clothes are loose and neglected like those of a teenage skater. The apartment is big and roomy, though sparsely furnished and messy.

In the living room, plastic cups and plates with half-eaten food on them are scattered across the coffee table. As we pass through the kitchen I see that it too is littered with refuse. He stops to offer us something to drink, then opens the fridge to a space devoid of anything save dubious packages and a plastic bottle with a dribble of bright orange liquid in it. We all laugh: beverages will not be necessary.

Unlike the rest of his apartment, which seems an empty wasteland, his bedroom is packed with stuff. He takes a seat at his computer desk, covered with papers. We sit on his bed. Next to his desk is a big window that gives a sweeping view of the forest of concrete towers.

He tells me that he's twenty-eight. He's from the beautiful city of Ya'an, on the fringe between the fertile Sichuan Basin and the Himalayas. He studied art and design at Chengdu's prestigious university for computer arts. As soon as he graduated, he got a job as an illustrator for a successful game studio in Beijing. A couple of years ago, he was poached by a major player in the industry and made art director of one of its big titles.

He generally starts with pencil on paper, he tells me, showing me some of his sketches. They're clean and elaborate illustrations of fantastic Chinese historical characters. "Then I get on the computer to draw the images," he says, bringing up on the monitor a series of impressive illustrated characters: demigod generals with unreal weapons, wild geomancers with fantastic beards and exotic half-humans. All ready, it would seem, to bring down the wrath.

"As you can see, my specialty is heroes, armour and weaponry," he goes on, "but I also do landscapes. Or at least, I oversee their creation. I have a team now. It takes my core drawings and does all the various 3-D permutations necessary for the animation."

I ask him who came up with the ideas for the game he's currently working on.

"My bosses, the company's creative directors. But I was recruited for my talents for drawing these kinds of things. My team and I are fleshing out the game from the original idea."

He tells me that games are hugely popular: "In fact, many people say there is a video-game addiction problem in China. That there are too many young people who do nothing but play video games."

"Is this true?" I ask.

"Yes, probably," he says nonchalantly.

"What about your parents? What do they think about video games?"

"My father doesn't take my work seriously. He's an executive at an important financial institution. He's always asking me when I'm going to get a real job. I tell him that I now supervise thirty-five people."

"What does he say to that?" I ask.

"He tells me that he's in charge of hundreds of employees and billions of yuan," the young man answers with a resigned smile.

"It looks like you like Chinese history."

He explains that he and his team do a lot of research for the drawings. "But we do what we want with history," he tells me.

"So what kind of game is it?"

"A hybrid war strategy-RPG. A popular type of game here."

"What's it called?"

"*Kill the Immortals.*"

I get back in touch with Gia and ask to see her paintings. She's not sure whether I'm serious, but I insist. She agrees to receive us in her apartment, where she paints. She lives in a building in the north of the city within the fourth ring. Her building sits next to a canal and park. It abuts a massive but underused boulevard, so is mercifully quiet. Her place is on the third floor, which we reach by foot.

The small apartment is almost completely devoid of furnishing—only a couple of rugs and cushions to sit on in the living room. Although tidy, the place seems half-inhabited, as if it were a stop along the way.

Gia has hung paintings and photos on the bare walls, edgy and urbane pieces if a little effeminate. The rooms are painted pastel pinks like a doll's house.

"I'm lucky to live here. My parents were smart. Property values have really increased in the past few years," Gia says as she leads us to the front. She paints on a glassed-in balcony overlooking the grand boulevard, which we can spot through the trees.

"I hesitate to show you my paintings because I don't consider myself a painter," she confesses to me. "I have no training. I don't paint for others; I paint for myself. It relaxes me."

As she begins focusing on her canvas I ask, "Can you imagine yourself getting married, buying a house and a car, having kids?"

"I want to imagine myself like that," she says, "but I feel it's not my destiny. Whenever good things happen to me, bad things always happen as well."

Drawing her brush across the canvas, she grows more oblivious to the world. Only after she steps back to look at what she is doing does she turn to me to say, "I really don't know where I'm going. But I don't care."

Pollution has hit hard this night in north Beijing. I'm riding a bicycle down an empty road, the streetlights forming halos through thick smog. Overtowering the lights and thus lit from beneath, the mass-planted poplars that line the way and veil the bleak plain so coarse and vulgar during the day are shadowy titans whose dappled foliage merges together overhead like some mysterious firmament cloaked in smoke.

I'm returning from a boozy banquet. Red eyes and irritated throat don't bother me at all now. The effect of bad air is pleasing, beautiful even, like a Hollywood night scene. True darkness does not make for a good show on the silver screen and is not welcome. Spotlights and smoke are used for effect to define and illuminate the darkness, just like the street tonight. In this movie, the capital's outskirts seem like a mountaintop immersed in clouds. The illusion weakens with the realization that the air's still save for my own movement and that the haze brings little moisture.

Tonight I'm staying near the airport with my old friend Deryk and his wife. They are now teachers at a fancy English school in the capital. They've started a family and have relocated to the northern edge of Beijing. Hoping to offer their two young daughters another experience, in a detached home with a yard planted with shrubs and flowers, hoping to get away from the pollution so prevalent in central Beijing—a strategy that seems to have failed if the thick dirty air of this evening is any indication.

My head is buzzing from the discussions of the banquet—an impromptu reunion of thoughtful, soulful people, both local and foreign—as I ride in the shadows, as I once more fall asleep in a strange bed in a strange land. As I board the big plane and take position at the portal, as I slowly return to my home and family, all the banquets blend into one. They're one long conversation, filled with wisdom and surprises.

We know the future cannot be predicted like a story. But it's never silent either. Even now its messengers have already arrived in our midst.

We ask, who are they and where do they hide? What message do they bring about who we are to become? We all see vastly different meanings.

Memories are built with desires and intentions. It's not what we think we saw and heard that really matters. The future is not hiding there. It hides in our memories like an unnoticed backdrop, a hidden detail or face blurred in the shadows, only to be released with time, deep reflection or art.

We live for stories, the ones that leave us uneasy and excited, the ones that are fresh and new. As we bring them forward and draw them up for friends, we know our words will not quite make them real, but real enough perhaps to share the feeling of what lies behind, should it ever be ready to step forward.

I suspect I'll always be a little lost in China. That the endless banquet and smoky firmament are a reminder that a part of me never made it out, of knowledge not yet acquired.

We are still ghosts upon the river, and Viv is telling me that we have not much longer to go. But the journey is never complete. China will surely haunt me forever. China comes for us all, wherever we are. Its cup spilleth over. Its stories and people come to mix with us and share its many conundrums. Its spinning absorbs us in its rhythm.

The need to remember and the need to forget grow clearer for us all now. The need to preserve and the need to destroy. The need for knowledge and the need for secrets. Our overwhelming power and our great fragility. The more they all dance together, seeking balance, the more they glitter in the shadows and beckon us on.

ACKNOWLEDGEMENTS

Vivien, without whom none of this would have been possible. Deryk Fournier, bridge builder. Alex and Jane Cockain, generous friends. Jacques Hébert, fellow traveller. Ling Xia, who started me on this road back in 2005. Maurice Strong, for early guidance. Alphonso Lingis, Philippe Rheault and Ron Graham, patient readers. Stephen Valentine, the man in my corner. Scott McIntyre, first supporter. Jim Gifford, faithful editor. Michael Levine, navigator and friend.